DATE DUE

9-3-06	
OCT 31 '06 ILL-9224 Due 3-15-07	

TABLOID *Love*

TABLOID *Love*

Looking for Mr. Right
in All the Wrong Places

A MEMOIR

BRIDGET HARRISON

Da Capo
∞
LIFE
LONG

A Member of the Perseus Books Group

Da Capo Lifelong Books

This is a true story. The characters are authentic, the events are real. But the names and identifying details of certain individuals have been disguised in order to protect their anonymity.

Designed by Jeff Williams
Set in 11-point Minion by the Perseus Books Group

Library of Congress Cataloging-in-Publication Data
Harrison, Bridget.
    Tabloid love : looking for Mr. Right in all the wrong places : a memoir /
Bridget Harrison.—1st Da Capo Press ed.
        p. cm.
    ISBN-13: 978-0-7382-1044-5 (hardcover : alk. paper)
    ISBN-10: 0-7382-1044-7 (hardcover : alk. paper) 1. Harrison, Bridget—Relations
with men. 2. Single women—New York (State)—New York—Biography.
3. Journalists—New York (State)—New York—Biography. 4. Dating (Social customs)—New York (State)—New York. 5. Man-woman relationships—New York
(State)—New York. I. Title.
    HQ800.4.U62N49 2006
    974.7'1044092—dc22

                                                                        2006003916

First Da Capo Press edition 2006

Published by Da Capo Press
A Member of the Perseus Books Group
www.dacapopress.com

1 2 3 4 5 6 7 8 9—09 08 07 06

For the New York Girls

CONTENTS

Prologue

·················

The taxi turned a corner, and suddenly we were on Pike Street. The Manhattan Bridge was right in front of us, bathed in orange sunset, arching across the East River to Brooklyn.

"No, no, this isn't right! What the hell are we doing here?" I shouted, shoving my head through the gap in the cabbie's bulletproof-glass partition. "I want 91 Clinton Street, it's back by Delancey. You've come way too far down."

I threw myself back on the seat, cursing for not having paid attention. Instead I had been rummaging in my bag for a phone number—a date I wanted to cancel—which I still hadn't found.

The cabbie did a U-ie. I looked at my mobile. Shit. It was 4:30 P.M., already forty minutes since I'd left the office and less than an hour before deadline.

"There, that way, go that way." I stuck my head through the partition again as we crossed East Broadway. "It's definitely north from here. In fact, give me a map. Have you even got a map?"

Infuriatingly unperturbed, the taxi driver handed me a battered Street Planner. Under my terse instruction we clanked back up Allen Street, over Delancey, turned down Stanton, and crossed five blocks, finally hitting Clinton. I saw immediately the numbers were too low, but we couldn't turn right.

"Bugger, stop. *Stop!*"

I handed back the map with a wad of dollars and slammed the taxi door. Then I slung my bag on my shoulder, and for the fourth time in a week found myself sprinting down a New York street in high-heeled boots. Fate, for some reason, made me late for everything.

I could tell immediately which block I needed by the crowd of people amassed on the pavement ahead—shopkeepers, residents, passersby, all lingering with the sheep-like curiosity that follows an accident, staring at the building across the street as if some new calamity were about to burst out of its windows.

"NY1 News" and "Channel 7 Eyewitness News" had set up camera tripods by the curb, their cameramen looking across the road and smoking cigarettes. I felt tempted to go beg for a smoke, but there was no time.

Three cops were keeping the crowd to one side of the street and number 91 was opposite—an open black door, sandwiched between a Dominican barber's shop and a Chinese toy store, that led up to a five-story walk-up apartment block that had a rusting black fire escape zigzagging down its front. A woman wearing a navy-blue windbreaker with "Medical Examiner's Office" emblazoned in yellow on the back guarded the doorway. That meant the bodies were still inside.

Panting now, I weaved my way through the gawkers, checking for other reporters. Then I spotted them, the only white guys on the block. They stood a few yards down the street, gathered around a burly, bald man in a beige detective's suit and scribbling earnestly in their notepads. Shit, the press briefing and I was missing it. I dodged a cop and sprinted across the road towards them, pulling my notepad out of my bag as I went.

". . . she was strangled, lying on the floor. He was hanging from a pipe," the detective drawled as I pushed into the group.

"We're hearing they were in the bedroom. Can you confirm that?" asked one of the reporters. His green press tags said *Newsday*.

"Yeah. They were in the bedroom. The three-year-old son found them," replied the detective.

"What did he strangle her with?"

"A nylon cord. It was around her neck."

"So . . . he came into the bedroom, strangled her with a nylon cord, then hung himself from the pipe. Then the kid came in. Was it with the same cord?"

My phone buzzed. I shoved it under my jaw while scribbling "she floor, he pipe, nylon cord, bedroom, three-year-old son" in my notebook.

"Hey, you crazy Brit. Jeff here. Hope we're still on for tonight?"

Bugger. My date. "Um, hi. Yes, of course we are."

"The nylon cords he used appeared to be different. The one he strangled her with was thinner than the other," said the detective.

"Was one from a dressing gown?" asked the *Newsday* guy.

"How about eight at Olives in the W at Union Square? They do awesome martinis. And then we can decide if we want to go on from there," said Jeff.

Union Square was a fifteen-minute dash in a cab from where I was now. "Go on from there" meant he was waiting to decide how much he liked me when he saw me again. "Awesome martinis" meant drinking on an empty stomach—a classic start to a New York date.

"No, it wasn't a dressing-gown cord, it was more like synthetic rope. You should also know there was a prior history of abuse," said the detective.

"Jeff, fine, see you there." I dropped my phone back in my bag.

"So where's the little boy now?" I asked.

"With his aunt. You're not getting near him," said the detective.

My phone rang again.

"City Desk, hold for Jack," said a copy kid at the office when I answered it. My heart did a flip.

"Hey, are you nearly through on that murder-suicide? We've got early deadlines tonight." Jack's familiar voice was terse. I adopted a similar tone.

"We're just getting the details now. I'll file as soon as I can."

The line was already dead.

Two hours later I was in another taxi, speeding back up Allen Street. I held my left eye open while trying to apply mascara. I had already pulled on a cashmere V-neck that I'd had stuffed in my bag all day. I'd interviewed (with translation from a Spanish-speaking photographer) the Dominican brother of the man who strangled his wife, on whose door the little boy had timidly knocked, saying, "I think my Mommy and Daddy are dead." Then I'd found two tearful nieces who said the husband drank and had a bad jealous streak and that they'd begged her to leave him—and now it was too late.

I'd phoned over my story, waited for the two body bags to be stretchered into an ME van, and now at 7:55 P.M. was about to be ten minutes late for Jeff. By now all I wanted was quality time with my sofa.

I had met Jeff, a gynecologist with salt-and-pepper hair and insanely blue eyes, at a singles mixer in a ritzy steak house called Houston's on the Upper East Side. The event had been like a cocktail party on a cruise ship, except you could boldly flirt with any guy without worrying that he was someone else's husband—at least not any longer. Jeff had asked me for my number—and I had always wondered if gynecologists had hidden talents.

He was thirty-nine, never married, and had climbed K2, I reminded myself as I now walked towards him through the low light of Olives. I automatically switched on my "hello, I'm your sexy date for tonight" smile.

We embraced, during which he gave me the surreptitious "small boobs? big bum?" glance which guys always think you won't notice. I hoped the V-neck-and-tweed-trousers combo had pulled off the transition from murder-suicide wear to date wear.

"Sorry, bit of a hectic day. I was on a really sad story in the Lower East Side about this three-year-old kid who—"

"Nothing a dirty martini won't cure," he interrupted, hailing the bartender with a $100 bill. Okay, so he wasn't a listener. But at least the drinks would be free.

"And how was your day? Did you tend to a lot of women?" I asked chattily as he slid a cocktail in my direction.

He shot me a look like I had just called him a snaky-fingered pervert.

"I mean, you were busy too. With your patients, your practice. Right?" Damn. Maybe it wasn't appropriate to ask a gynecologist about his line of work on a first date.

Clearly not, as Jeff swiftly changed the subject and asked me if I knew the name of the band playing on the bar stereo. Not sure if this was a test or a genuine question, I took a wild stab at "Coldplay"—which always seemed to be playing in bars.

"*Coldplay?* You're kidding, right?" He looked aghast, the bartender looked pityingly at me. "And you're a Brit. How could you not recognize Radiohead?"

"Sorry, I knew that," I mumbled.

Then Jeff asked me if I liked dogs. I told him I had recently attended a Chihuahua's second birthday party but had left when the hostess tried to make me woof "Happy Birthday."

Jeff enthusiastically told me he had a chocolate lab who had celebrated his own birthday in doggie daycare last week.

"Great, good for him," I said.

Next Jeff asked me whether I smoked pot—to which I loftily replied "only with tobacco."

He told me he grew his own weed—which he only smoked pure—that he never dated women who didn't smoke pot, who didn't like dogs, or who lived in the Tri-State area beyond Manhattan. Confused, I pointed out that he had told me he lived in Old Brookville on the North Shore, Long Island, which was definitely beyond Manhattan. He shrugged and told me these were his rules for women, not the other way around.

"I have these little mental checks. I mean, I'm a busy guy and I can't afford to waste time with women who aren't my type. But don't worry, you're the cutest of all the women I followed up with from that singles mixer, and I *love* the *Post.*"

This guy has a way with the compliments, I thought.

But it transpired that even if I was the cutest of the unspecified number of women whose numbers he had harvested that night, I wasn't quite cute enough. Or maybe it was because I said I smoked pot with tobacco. Jeff soon announced he had to meet a golfing buddy who was going through a divorce. I didn't believe him—and didn't object. We parted on the corner of 16th Street with an efficient peck on the cheek.

I walked the six long blocks along 14th Street towards my apartment, planning a sushi delivery order—two salmon sashimi, one dragon roll, edamame, miso soup—and a new topic for a column I wrote about being single in New York: "Dating Deal-Breakers"—those little things that people do and say which makes their date decide they'll never get to a second evening. I'd start with a gynecologist who will only go out with women if they like dogs, smoke pot, and don't come from Long Island—even though he does.

Arrive, connect, conclude, depart. I had discovered that the same approach worked for both dating and news reporting. I had moved to New York three years before, a total novice at both.

Part One

············

New York,
New York

Twenty-nine is still young, right?

"New Year's Day, Treasure Beach, Jamaica. Year 2000. The first day of the century!!!"

I sat on the sand in the shade of a palm tree with my diary balanced on my sunburned knees while my gang of old friends from university played soccer in the surf. Considering the hangovers we'd woken up with that morning, their energy was admirable. Angus, my boyfriend, was splashing up and down at the water's edge like he was auditioning for *Chariots of Fire*. I smiled, then went back to munching my pen.

Making lists never really worked for me. I always lost the pieces of paper before I could efficiently tick off any of the items, but desperate measures were needed. In four days I'd be back in London in my office at the *Times*, having to make what felt like the biggest decision of my life.

"Go to New York for four months?" I wrote.

Pros:

Get to be news reporter for mad New York tabloid and fulfill life-long ambition of becoming Lois Lane (cover world-changing news stories . . . investigate evil exploiters . . . Maybe meet hunky Clark Kent fellow journo).

Have life-enhancing experience in new city before turning dreaded 3-O.

If don't go now, never will, as may soon have babies—will be handcuffed to a Bugaboo?

Four months really not that long time to be away.

Cons:

Have lovely boyfriend in London already, so don't need to meet Clark Kent.

Soon turning dreaded 3-O, ovaries shriveling at accelerated rate, need to be thinking about babies v.v. soon.

Why go to strange city where I know no one and be away from man with whom I want to spend rest of life?

I looked up to see Angus running through the surf in his faded Vilebrequin surf shorts.

"Henry, mate, here, over here!" "Annabel, luv, not there, here! Pass it, make a pass!" "Oh, fucking hell, Rory, you choker." I smiled, but then a familiar feeling of uncertainty hit me again.

Do I want to spend rest of life with Angus? More to point, does he want to spend rest of life with me?

Four months long time to be away if future of relationship at all uncertain.

Lose everything and end up lonely spinster with cats???

I had been offered a work exchange to News Corporation's sister paper in New York—the *New York Post*—the city's famous daily tabloid known for its juicy crime stories, salacious gossip, and outrageous headlines (including the greatest one ever written: HEADLESS BODY IN TOPLESS BAR). If I took the exchange, I would become a news reporter for the paper—a job I had fantasized about all my life.

Since leaving university, I'd wangled work at newspapers and magazines—mainly through heaps of unpaid work experience and shameless sucking up. But my illustrious career had kept me in features departments—making photocopies, pulling clips, and coming up with story ideas for other people to write—always secretly ashamed that I didn't have what it took to be a "hard news" journalist.

So surely going to New York was the opportunity of a lifetime, I told myself for the hundredth time. I put my diary down and looked back at my cozy gang of old mates, most of whom were in couples too.

Or was I mad to start messing around with my life when it seemed so nearly sorted?

And it was, I had been going out with Angus, an up-and-coming film director, for nearly two years. I lived in a cozy terraced house "with potential" in Shepherd's Bush with Kathryn and Tilly, two rent-paying girlfriends, which took care of my mortgage. I was the grandly titled Assistant Features Editor at the London *Times*—and even if I was sometimes frustrated, who wasn't on some mornings slogging to work on the Central Line?

Yes, on the brink of my thirties I could even dare to assume I might be on target to tick all those aspirational boxes girls quietly dreamed of—a diamond on the finger (preferably a vintage family heirloom), a raucous but moving wedding (preferably in a picturesque village church with adjacent country house), and ample time to crank out three children to a great dad before one's ovaries turned into prunes.

So was I insane to jeopardize it all for some crazy tabloid newspaper in New York?

The smell of frying bacon greeted me as I opened Angus's front door in Kentish Town six weeks later. He stood waiting for me—his fair hair now cut short, his fading Jamaica tan offset by my favorite navy Paul Smith shirt. I threw my arms around his waist and breathed in the familiar scent of his Eau Savage cologne.

"Hello, gorgeous. How's the packing going?" he said as he turned back to the kitchen.

"Okay, I suppose." In less than twenty-four hours I would be in Departures at Heathrow Airport.

In the end, I had told myself to stop being such a wimp and had accepted the exchange to New York the day we arrived home from Jamaica. I had bored everyone to tears since then with my big talk of being a tabloid reporter in Manhattan—even though I had no idea what it would actually entail. But tonight my Lois Lane fantasies were fizzling back into panic about what I was leaving behind.

Angus's kitchen was its usual scene of domesticity as he deftly threw together a big salad of sliced cherry tomatoes, watercress, spinach, and bacon. I watched him as he moved around with his characteristic grace. Angus. Mr. Pretty-Nearly-Perfect. He was the only person I knew who'd be willing to get up in the middle of the night with me and drive to the country to watch a meteor shower—not that we ever had. He had great taste in clothes (and home furnishings), which was useful, as I was a style desert. He could read a wine list and wield a Le Creuset pan, whereas I fell apart at simmering a packet of frozen spinach. We were best friends, we had all our friends in common, and we definitely loved each other. But were we the loves of each other's lives? The problem was that after nearly two years, we still didn't seem to know. And my fantasies about New York only highlighted the questions.

I picked up an open bottle of Brunello di Montalcino from the sideboard, poured myself a massive glass, and refilled his. Then I fished in my bag for a new packet of ten Marlboro Lights. I had given up smoking for New Year's, sort of, but this evening I needed one.

I walked next door into Angus's sitting room to retrieve the clay ashtray that he kept on his coffee table, and I stood taking in the room's lovely familiarity.

Walls of books, two deep blue sofas facing a TV with all the flashy gizmos, big sash windows that overlooked his white-terraced North London street. We had spent a million evenings cuddled up there, him trying to stay awake for Match of the Day, me pretending to be "ideal girlfriend" enjoying it. What if my leaving now meant we never watched TV together in this room again?

I went to his cluttered mantelpiece to look at my favorite photo—one he had taken of me a year ago in Paris as I was trying on a green suede dress in Armani. I did look pretty damn sexy in it, I had to say. He'd bought the dress for me as a present, and then we'd gone for oysters in Saint Germain. A girl's holiday heaven.

Next to it was a group snap of us all in Jamaica on New Year's Eve. There were four couples in the picture, two had since become engaged—and we'd only been back a month and a half. There were already several other embossed wedding invites propped up on the mantelpiece—along with a snap of Angus's one-year-old godson.

Recently it felt like the whole world was getting engaged, getting pregnant, as if it had become a competition to prove who had their life sorted. I'd sworn that I would not be intimidated by this big rush to nest, but then even Sandra, my ever-wise editor at the *Times*, had reminded me that as a woman, I didn't have that much time. "See this as your last adventure and damn good experience for you," she had said when she wrote me the letter of recommendation that assured I'd be accepted for the exchange to the *New York Post*.

"Before you come back and marry Angus," Gill, her secretary, had added sternly. "We're all still banking on that big-hats wedding, you know."

"You're missing one small detail—that Angus might not want a big-hats wedding with me," I reminded them.

They rolled their eyes. To everyone else, that I should get married to Angus seemed to be a no-brainer. To us, well, we planned just to see how things went while I was away in New York. Angus had said he was fed up with my always looking over my shoulder in case I was missing something. But I knew it wasn't just me who secretly looked over their shoulder. I knew both of us wondered if we were really right for each other. What if there was someone else out there who would take away our doubts?

"Just don't forget, you're not twenty-five anymore. You have to think about the future at some point," Gill had said.

"But twenty-nine is still young, right?" I'd said. "It has to be."

And four months in New York was nothing. Wasn't it?

It was drizzling in a typical February way the following afternoon when I arrived at my parents' Ealing, West London, suburban house, with its crazy paving and paint-splash '70s curtains that my mum refused to change. Specks of rain carried on the wind as my dad put my suitcase in the car and my mum appeared with a Crunchy Bar and apple for my journey. I refrained from bitchily pointing out that Virgin Atlantic served meals.

Crafty Angus had left the airport honors to my parents, and as the three of us drove up the M4 towards Heathrow in their red Rover, I felt like a teenager being ferried to boarding school. We climbed the fly-over across Brentford, and I stared out at the collection of abandoned office blocks built next to the motorway, each emblazoned with forlorn banners promising "prestige office space." What an illustrious welcome they must make for visitors driving into gray old London from Heathrow for the first time. But I was leaving them behind!

As we passed the last of the rained-on suburbs—rows and crescents of red-roofed, semidetached houses adorned with spiked TV aerials and satellite dishes—I pictured Central Park surrounded by the grand, old apartment blocks I'd seen in Woody Allen films, leafy Greenwich Village streets with stoops to drink coffee on, and those chic minimalist cafes they always frequented in *Sex and the City.* Not that I actually knew anyone to sit in cafes with—or anyone in New York at all for that matter.

"You're sure you haven't forgotten anything?" asked my mum, glancing back at me tearfully.

I took my hundredth mental check of my luggage. New green Nicole Farhi overcoat for the biting winter weather, a selection of Miss Selfridge and Ghost party dresses just in case I ever got invited anywhere, sexy Dior underwear given to me by Angus in Paris—which I'd brought only to remind me of him, of course.

But the only thing I truly cared about was a photo in a chunky brown frame, which was my going-away present from him. It showed us at a pheasant shoot at his father's country house in Gloucestershire, wrapped up in old Barbour jackets and scarves, laughing. He had his arm around my shoulder, pulling me into him. I had cried when I'd opened it after supper the night before. We looked so amazingly happy in it.

I reminded myself that I had actually felt like a tacky suburbanite that weekend, because I'd made the country mega–*faux pas* of wearing my mum's yellow Wellington boots. And that moments after the picture was snapped, hundreds of half-dead, flapping pheasants had rained down around me. But then half the beauty—or problem—of looking back was remembering things as being perfect.

We arrived at Terminal Three, and I told my parents that I could check in alone to save them from having to park. My ruse fell on deaf ears. My mum rushed off to get a ticket and a trolley as my dad took my two bags from the trunk.

"This reminds me of when Mummy went to Paris to work as a secretary before we got married. It's important to experience new cities," he said. My mother had been twenty-three, and a year later my father had flown from Birmingham, where he worked for the BBC, to Paris to propose. They'd made their big move to London the following year, choosing Ealing because it was good for the tube—and thereby consigning me to a productive teenage life of standing around outside Ealing Broadway train station trying to look cool with the rest of the suburban kids.

My mum protectively clutched the handle of my trolley while I waited to check in. From the Economy Class line, we watched a girl about my age with inconceivably glossy white blonde hair, pushed back with Gucci shades, sweep up to the Upper Class desk and announce "JFK" in a loud transatlantic drawl. She was wearing an annoyingly chic sheepskin coat over a miniskirt and cowboy boots.

"That's not a very sensible outfit for traveling," said my dad.

"Well it doesn't really matter if you're in Upper Class," I said, feeling distinctly un-Manhattan in my jeans, sneakers, with fussing parents at my side. I vowed to return miraculously transformed into Sarah Jessica Parker—although perhaps with slightly less expensive shoes.

My parents walked me to the rounded glass of the Departures entrance for their reluctant good-bye.

"Do look after yourself, Bridgie," said my mum, her eyes wet again.

"It's not like I'm going to the moon," I said, holding my handbag tightly, although suddenly it felt like it. My moon was New York City: a seething metropolis of eight million people, three thousand, five hundred miles from home, where I didn't know a soul.

Girl's subway terror

"We can help you with just about anything, except if you get pregnant!" said *New York Post* publisher Ken Chandler jovially as he shook my hand.

Get pregnant? What was he on about? Here I was nervously facing my epic new career as a New York news reporter, and he was talking about sex?

"We did have that happen," said Anne Aquilina, the equally jovial *Post* administrative editor in whose office I was standing. "One of ours came back pregnant from the exchange program to Australia. Her girl Kate's nearly two now. Adorable child."

"I've already got a boyfriend in England, so I think I'll be okay," I said tersely. Would I never escape the infernal baby boom?

It was my first day at the *New York Post*, and that morning I'd walked heart-in-mouth through the clamoring, crowded Midtown streets that smelled of steam and hot dogs, to News Corporation's headquarters at 1211 Avenue of the Americas. The New York streets were strangely familiar, thanks to a diet of *Law & Order*, but faster and nosier, more colorful, more hectic.

The night before, I'd arrived at a small, gray-painted Upper West Side apartment owned by the *Post*—where exchangees got to live—and I'd decided to go to work on foot just in case I got lost on the subway. The journey only took twenty minutes—but then I'd found myself speed walking to keep pace with everyone else.

1211 was one of three identical silver towers that shot up from the west side of the avenue, and it stood imposingly in front of a paved concourse with concrete pillars at its entrance. On one side of the building, facing 48th Street, TV monitors blared out Fox TV and a red news ticker tape flashed out the day's headlines. "Man in black robes has last say: Courtney Love back to rehab." Fox—also owned by News Corp.—had the lower floors of the forty-four-story building, and the *New York Post*'s editorial office was on the tenth.

On arrival I had instructions to find Anne, who oversaw the exchange program and ran all the practicalities and finances of the paper.

Ken Chandler had popped in just to say hello, and after he dashed off, Anne signed forms for me to get my reporter's ID card. She explained that I was to be put on "General Assignment" for the City Desk, which handled all the hard news in the paper.

"Um, you do know I only worked in features before," I said. I hoped they'd all been warned I had no shorthand, no experience, not a blind clue.

"Don't worry, you'll pick it up. Get a pager from Myron on the copy desk, then find yourself a free terminal. We'll soon get you busy."

Anne's office was one of several small, windowed rooms which ran along the edge of a long, low-ceilinged area that was the main floor of the *New York Post*. And Condé Nast this place was not. The room was filled with rows of cluttered desks, each holding four or five computer terminals surrounded by piles of old newspapers, notepads, faxes, discarded coffee cups, half drunk Poland Spring bottles, unopened mail, family photos, press releases, and all sorts of other unidentifiable crap.

Between some of the rows of desks were banks of filing cabinets which were also strewn with old papers, pretzel boxes, trays brimming with stationery, packets of salt and plastic cutlery saved from food takeouts, phone books, other books, video tapes, festering flower vases, and mugs. And the floor hadn't escaped the mayhem either. The carpet around most terminal chairs was covered with crates of old notepads, stacks of fading newspapers, old jiffy bags, shoes, umbrellas, even kids' toys.

Anne cheerfully told me this chaotic scene was home to the City side of the *New York Post*—where all the reporters for news, business, and the Page Six gossip section sat, as well as all the editors, sub-editors, and layout guys. At the far end of the long room, she pointed out a huge glass-sided box that was the editor's office. Around the corner were sports, features, and the conference room where all the twice-daily news meetings were held, she said.

As I stood in her doorway taking it all in, a group of men in suits strode past, holding what looked like printed lists of that day's news. One glanced at me as he passed, as if subconsciously registering a new face. He looked about my age, the youngest of the group, and had a ruddy Irish-looking complexion and an unusual mop of curly brown hair. I flashed a polite smile at him but he'd already walked on. Then I went to find Myron.

The copy desk—which was the center of administration at the *Post*—was in the middle of the room, adjacent to an arena of marginally less cluttered computer terminals where, Anne told me, the city editor, his two deputies, and the morning assignment editor sat. Next to them was the Photo Desk, where the photo editor and her assistants handled the pictures for the paper and assigned photographers to jobs. Behind the copy desk, stacks of the three editions of the day's *Post* where piled up next to a shelf offering the other papers—the *New York Times*, the *New York Daily News, Newsday*, the *Wall Street Journal, USA Today*, the *Village Voice*, the *Washington Post*, and the *International Herald-Tribune*. Jammed all over the wall behind the copy desk were New York bus maps, a subway map, an array of yellowing torn-out front pages, tatty notices, a large page-a-day calendar, and a clock. Above that was a bank of six decrepit TV screens with the volumes turned down and closed captioning on, beaming out CNN, FOX 5, NY1, MSNBC, ABC, and Spanish soaps.

Myron was easy to spot—a meticulous-looking, mustached man with glasses wearing a white shirt and jazzy tie tucked neatly into his trousers. Myron was a thirty-year veteran at the paper, and, as I soon discovered, ruled the copy desk with an evangelical zeal for protocol, reigning over a rotation of "copy kids." They manned the phones and fax machines, ferried around proofs, fetched food from the lobby, and were at the editors' beck and call—all hoping to graduate into reporters one day.

"Er, Myron?" I tried not to interrupt him while he was answering phones and shouting out the names of editors and reporters that callers had asked for. "I'm Bridget, the new exchange person. Anne said I should come see you."

"Welcome to the *New York Post*," said Myron curtly, but not unkindly, when he finally looked up. "Here's your beeper. Wear it at all times, even if you get a cell phone. Wait, I'm testing it now."

He handed me a pager and then punched a message into a mini-keyboard on his desk. Two seconds later the black device buzzed and flashed COPY DESK. THIS IS A TEST!!!!! He beamed at it, thrilled with his own efficiency.

"Notepads are here, today's newspapers are behind you, yesterday's newspapers are in a box under my desk. But if you borrow them, you have to bring them back. Food menus are in this drawer, reporters' cell numbers are listed in the 'group list' displayed by every terminal, extensions are on another list. Tell me if there isn't one by your terminal, because there should be one by every terminal. Stringers' numbers and other useful numbers are in the Rolodex. When you sit down, tell me where you are sitting so I know your extension in case I need to put calls through to you." He snatched up one of the phones.

"*New York Post* City Desk. Hold. John Mancini, Ken Lovett, line two," he barked.

He was no longer listening, so I collected myself a new notepad and made my way back along the rows of desks.

Most of the terminals were still empty. I chose a vacant one three rows back from the copy desk and editors' arena so I could see what was going on without giving the impression I thought I was important.

I sat down and looked at my new notepad. It had *New York Post* emblazoned on the front in the tabloid's distinct black, slanted block lettering. Next to that was a red circular portrait of Alexander Hamilton, who founded the paper in 1801.

I took a deep breath. The *Post* was the oldest continuously published daily newspaper in the United States, and now here I was—a real live reporter for it! But I still didn't know what the fuck I was actually supposed to do.

Over the course of the day, the floor gradually got busier as reporters arrived back from assignments and other employees, including the copy editors and layout guys, ambled in to start later shifts. I idly looked out for Clark Kent candidates, but it soon became clear there was not much in the way of sex symbols in this office.

Most reporters looked as disheveled as their surroundings and came in clutching foil containers of steaming food which they devoured with particularly un-sexy gusto whilst tapping away at their computers. Scoffing down meals at your desk, I quickly discovered, was an integral part of *Post* life.

Some reporters who noticed me timidly sitting there like the new girl in school came over to introduce themselves—including Tracy Connor, a jolly woman a little older than me with short dark hair. She told me she'd been on the exchange to London.

"So, settling in okay?" she asked brightly.

"Yes, I think so. But I've never actually done it before," I whispered.

"Oh, you'll work it out soon enough. This is the *Post*. It's all about the zippy intro," she said.

Zippy intro?

Tracy went to her desk and returned with a battered book called a New York Street Planner, which looked like a hideously complicated version of the "A-to-Z" maps we had in London.

"And you're gonna need this," she said.

Then nodding across at the editors' arena, she pointed out the city editor, John Mancini, a chirpy, energetic man I had already noticed striding around the office cracking sarcastic jokes in an exotic-sounding Brooklyn drawl. Next to him was Stuart Marques, whose jet-black, slicked-back hair and sharp suit made him look like he'd just stepped out of a 1950s mob movie. He was the former city editor, now the managing-editor-for-news who was so fanatical about the *Post* that he got up in the middle of the night to edit copy, she said. And next to him stood a guy with a graying goatee and pony tail wearing faded black jeans and aside from a spotted bow tie, he looked like he'd just walked out of a Neil Young concert. Tracy said he was Steve

Marsh, who handled most of the stories involving the Shack, the *Post's* office at the New York Police Department headquarters, where three reporters were constantly posted to elicit on-record and off-record information from cops.

"Stu, Mancini, and Steve—they're cool, but they're insane," she added.

"Cool," I echoed back nervously. They all looked it. Cool. Insane. And foreign, in every sense of the word.

Stuart shouted out Tracy's name, and she rushed back to her desk to grab a notepad before going to talk to him. I flipped through the baffling Street Planner. I felt like I was waiting to be called on stage when I didn't know my lines.

Then at 4:36 P.M.—just as the room was heating up into a quiet frenzy of concentration before deadline—my first assignment came.

"Yo, yo! Sounds like we got someone under a subway. Union Square five minutes ago," came a call from an assistant on the photo desk, who was stationed next to the permanent murmur of the police scanner. (I later learned that this gizmo, tuned to the emergency services frequency, was also standard equipment in photographers' cars, enabling them to hear about accidents, fires, and crimes the moment they happened.)

"4 train uptown. Sounds like a minor."

The editors' arena burst into action. The assistant at the photo desk began furiously making calls to photographers, and Steve Marsh shouted to Myron to get him the Shack. John Mancini jumped up, scanned the room for reporters, and spotted me—alone at my computer like a sitting duck.

"You, what's your name? You free? I need you to get down to Union Square right now."

Union Square. Shit. Where the hell was that?

Mancini was already heading towards me. I got up, scrambled to put my notepad in my bag, and looked around wildly for a pen. With shaking hands I tried to attach my pager to my belt.

"4 train platform. Someone's been hit by a subway car. Could be a kid," said Mancini, now at my desk. "You're the new exchange reporter, right? I guess you know where Union Square is?"

"Er, is it on the orange line that goes into this building?" I decided now wasn't the time to mention that I'd never been on the subway before.

"Fresh off the boat," he said, flashing me a cheeky smile. He walked back towards his office, which was next to Anne's, and returned wearing a tweed overcoat.

"You ready? I'll ride down there with you. I've got an appointment in that direction. If you don't know where you are going, Union Square is kinda complicated."

With that he swept out of the office with me hurrying behind him. We sped across the 1211 concourse, turned the corner, and went west along 47th Street, which hit the top of Times Square, then dashed across Seventh Avenue towards the N and R station.

"To find the downtown entrance, just look for the Olive Garden sign," said Mancini as he expertly dodged tourists ambling in droves along the pavement, all of them staring up at the multitude of signs, huge billboards, and lights.

Times Square! I'm in Times Square on an assignment, I thought. I am Lois Lane! Bridget, don't fuck this up.

We ran down the station steps, Mancini swiped me through the barriers with his Metrocard, and we just made a train. As the subway moved off and began to rattle under Manhattan, we sat down on two vacant plastic seats (much less comfortable than the London tube, but clearly easier to hose down) and I caught sight of my reflection next to Mancini's in the train window. I looked petrified. I wondered if I was the only reporter on the planet to be personally accompanied on her first story by her news editor.

At Union Square, Mancini led me through the maze of underground passages and ticket halls booming with the noisy arrival of subway trains. We speed-walked through commuters streaming in all directions and ran down to a platform which said "Uptown 4, 5 and 6."

Oh. I was expecting to see emergency workers, perhaps a bloody body, and a whole section of the station that had been cordoned off. Instead the dingy platform was crammed with New Yorkers waiting for trains as if nothing had happened.

I fumbled for my notepad, resisting the urge to ask, "What do I do now?"

"So try to find out what happened, start looking for witnesses," said Mancini, as if he'd read my mind. Okay. Hmm. Where did one start?

I desperately scanned the crowds. Some people stared up the line, others were reading newspapers or talking to companions—all strangers in their own unapproachable worlds. I spotted a matronly African-American woman near to us who had a pile of shopping bags at her feet and a fairly friendly-looking face. I scuttled up to her.

"Er, excuse me. The person under the subway train, I don't suppose you know what happened, do you?" I gabbled.

"Huh?"

"Um, I'm from the *New York Post* newspaper, and I heard there was someone under a subway . . ." I felt horribly self-conscious. Mancini was still standing next to me.

A silver train came rocketing into the station. The woman picked up her shopping bags, and everyone got ready to move onto the carriage. Shit, were all my witnesses about to disappear?

The woman took pity on me. "I heard some kid got her arm stuck." She nodded over her shoulder towards the other end of the platform. "You should go down that way. People saw it down there." Rather unnecessarily, I began to scribble this down in my notepad to look efficient in front of Mancini.

"So I'm taking off," he said. "Get some actual first-hand witnesses, then find an MTA official who can fill you in." MTA official? His expression seemed amiable, but I imagined he was already making a mental note never to send me anywhere of any consequence again.

Relieved I was no longer under scrutiny, I trawled the platform, trying to pick out people who looked like they might talk to me rather than punch me if I approached them. Some ignored me or said "no thanks." Others stared glazedly at me as if I was speaking in tongues. Apparently my perfectly honed "London girls' school–cum–hint of affected cockney" accent was proving problematic to decipher.

But after fifteen surprisingly exhausting minutes, I had managed to find out that a teenager, a girl, had gotten her arm, her sneaker, her whole leg, or her ankle stuck in the doors of an uptown 4 train. That she had been dragged under it, that she had fallen down onto the platform, that she had been tripped, and that she had walked away unscathed. I scribbled it all down in my notepad in my own special (also indecipherable, I later discovered) short hand. I had absolutely no idea which account was correct—if any for that matter. It was a fine start.

My pager buzzed: CALL CITY DESK, STEVE MARSH flashed the message.

I found a pay phone attached to a platform pillar and dialed the office's free phone number that Anne had given me. Exchangees didn't get cell phones.

"*New York Post* City Desk," came Myron's efficient tone.

"Oh, hey there, Myron. May I speak to Steve, please?"

"Who's this?" he replied officiously.

"It's Bridget, the new exchange reporter. I met you earlier." Hadn't he just paged me?

"Bridget Harrison. I need your last name, as there could be more than one Bridget calling in and then there would be confusion. Bridget Harrison for Steve Marsh, hold line two," he said without taking breath.

"So what do you have?" asked Steve. "We're hearing from the Shack this girl got her foot stuck, then got dragged along the platform, may have a broken leg. She's been taken to Cabrini Hospital emergency room. I need you to get there as soon as you can."

"That's pretty much what I've got." Well it was, sort of. "Um, where exactly is Cabrini Hospital?"

"Nineteenth Street, the north side of Union Square. Hurry and call me when you get there."

I left the subway and found myself on 16th Street, where I stood for several minutes trying to work out which direction *was* north and then began running for my life.

I eventually got to a modern hospital building with a parking lot to one side where I spotted signs to "Emergency." I pushed through a pair of double doors and found myself in a corridor off which there was a small, windowed waiting room that contained a gathering of ill-looking, pissed-off people sitting on blue plastic chairs. A TV blasted down a Jerry Springer show from the wall.

A Hispanic couple were arguing while a toddler at their feet industriously dug a set of car keys into the linoleum floor. Next to them someone—I couldn't tell if it was male or female—was hunched under a mud-splattered coat, their dirty jeans extending outwards across the floor. In another corner, a pudgy Indian woman sat ignoring her teenaged son who had one hand wrapped up in a bloodied dish cloth while playing a Game Boy with the other. None of them looked like they had anything to do with the subway girl.

Stumped, I lingered by the Coke machine, feeling as shifty as a flasher standing outside a girls' high school. If I told the woman at the inquiries desk who I was, would she throw me out? I wasn't sure of the protocol, but it felt strangely improper to be hanging around a hospital when I didn't need a doctor. I suspected they'd feel the same.

But how to find out where the girl was? Could I masquerade as a friend and inquire? But what if they asked my name? I guessed if the girl had a broken leg, she might be having an operation by now. I pictured her in an emergency ward surrounded by doctors. Perhaps her anxious parents would arrive soon and I could approach them. I began to work out what I might say.

"Hello there, so sorry to bother you. I heard your daughter just got run over by the subway."

Hmm, that didn't sound quite right.

A woman and two kids with school satchels on their backs walked out of the triage area. The two girls were giggling and munching on sandwiches. They must have been visiting someone. My stomach leaped at the sight of their food, and I suddenly realized I hadn't eaten all day. Maybe there was a cafeteria in the hospital. The trio pushed through the double doors and turned out into the parking lot. Shit, too late to ask them. I was going to have to get over my fear of approaching strangers if I was ever going to manage this job.

An hour later—it was now past 7 P.M.—I was still pacing in the waiting room and still starving. On Steve's instruction, I had called a writer in the office called Willy Neuman, who Steve said was "pulling the story together" and that I should "dump" my notes to him. Willy told me to read out the most exciting bits from my frantic interviews on the subway platform.

"Um, I had a spot of trouble working out who actually knew what had happened . . ." I said, realizing I was also having trouble working out what the fuck I'd written.

"Just give me the best of what you got. I'm on deadline," he snapped.

After I'd stumbled through some lines with Willy—taking guesses at the bits of my writing I couldn't make out—there was still no sign of the girl, so I called Steve again. He instructed me now to identify myself at the information desk.

The attendant, who had clocked me some time ago and was clearly wondering why some strange woman was pacing the emergency area with a pen in her hand, now looked me up and down expectantly as I approached.

"Um, hello there. Er, I was looking for a girl who came in. She got hit by a subway this afternoon," I said.

"Oh, she only had a scratch. She already left."

What? She'd left? I'd been guarding the bloody door for hours. She only had a scratch? I thought it was supposed to be a broken leg! As it hit me, I broke into a sweat. The kids with the sandwiches. How could I have been so blind?

I retreated forlornly. I was clearly in for an illustrious career at the *Post.*

I called Steve, took a deep breath, and told him the girl had left the hospital. I decided not to say she had walked right past me because I had taken it for given that she had a broken leg and would be lying in an operating theater with half her bone showing, and so had disregarded the perfectly healthy girl her age striding along and laughing with her friend.

"Hmm, so she must have slipped out of another exit then?" asked Steve suspiciously.

"Guess so," I said, going as red as the Coke machine.

"Then you might as well pull out."

I put the phone down. What an utterly incompetent start. Steve and John Mancini were probably already in Anne's office arranging to have me shipped back to London. That or they'd give Myron a secret sign to put out a warning to the other editors: *"Do not send out new exchange reporter Bridget Harrison on anything important!!!"*

Then in my despair I had one sudden thought. With nothing to lose, there was always the option of begging. I had tried this on a boy who had tried to dump me once, and it had worked.

I returned to the desk window and told the nurse I was a reporter for the *New York Post*. I said I was aware that hospital staff couldn't give out patients' numbers, but might she consider—in fact could she *please, please, please,* help me out and call the girl's mother and pass on the number of my colleague at the paper who was writing about the accident. I had no number of my own.

"We think it would be *so* important to interview her—just to make sure a terrible incident like this doesn't happen to anyone else," I added, amazed at the sound of my sincerity.

The nurse looked at me pityingly—clearly wondering how I could bear to have such a degrading job.

"I'll see what I can do," she said. I scribbled down Willy Neuman's name and the main *New York Post* number, wanting to jump through the window and kiss her.

The following day as I walked to work and spotted the front page of the *Post* at a newsstand on the corner of Seventh Avenue, I wanted to kiss her even more.

GIRL'S SUBWAY TERROR; DRAGGED WITH FOOT IN DOOR, it said.

A twelve-year-old girl thought she was moments from death yesterday when her foot got stuck in the door of a rush-hour subway train and she was dragged—kicking and screaming—for 120 feet.

"I thought I was going to die!" said Margaret Schultz, who miraculously escaped with just a few scrapes and bruises in the horrific incident at the Union Square station.

The girl's mother had called Willy Neuman. I had my first "wood"—the term reporters use for the front page because front pages were once printed with wooden letters. And I vowed never again to let my own take on a situation stop me from seeing reality.

I had learned my first lesson in New York—when it comes to predicting the actions of other people, you should never take anything for granted. It was a mistake I was to make over and over again.

A hooker on Seventh Avenue

It took three weeks at the *Post* to begin to get a grip of what General Assignment (or GA) reporting entailed—and that was rushing off at a moment's notice to an obscure part of the city where something had happened, rushing up to strangers to get them to tell you about it . . . and a lot of waiting around for the relevant strangers to appear. To be effective you had to be pushy and patient, direct but ingratiating. You had to obey orders from the City Desk but also think on your feet. I meanwhile was still having problems deciphering my Street Planner and making my accent understood.

My shifts began at 10 A.M., so my orders usually came from the morning assignment editor, Marilyn Matlick. She, along with Vern Shibla—a thirty-five-year veteran of the Photo Desk—arrived at the office at 6:30 each morning to assemble the city news and picture lists. Marilyn put on the list stories in the day's papers which required follow ups and new stories drawn from police reports of crimes, accidents, and other *Post*-worthy events that had occurred overnight.

News for the list also came in from the Associated Press and Reuters wires, a constantly moving ladder of stories filed from around the country and the rest of the world, and also from the AP "Day Book," which detailed the day's upcoming events. Marilyn also talked to the Shack and to other reporters with beats—those who covered the Manhattan, Queens, Bronx, and Brooklyn courts; Long Island; the political reporters stationed in Washington, Albany, and City Hall—to check what was going on.

NYPD officials released the names of people involved in accidents and crimes—unless they were minors, victims of sexual assault, or had died—in which case relatives had to be notified first. And it wasn't hard to track people down. The addresses of all New Yorkers who had drivers' licenses were available on a database which the *Post* had access to. Beyond that the researchers in the *Post*'s clippings library could run more extensive searches to get the numbers and addresses of anyone in the country, along with the details of their family members and neighbors, the places they had previously lived, and the properties they owned. Useful for us, alarming for them.

GA reporters had to call in an hour before their shifts began. Often when I called Marilyn at 9 A.M., she gave me the address of a family who had been involved in a crime or accident—or sent me to the scene to search for witnesses.

Then I was usually out most of the day "running" and would "dump" to "rewrite"—the seasoned writers in the office like Tracy and Willy Neuman, Bill Hoffmann, Andy Geller, and Kate Sheehy, who'd been at the paper for years. They took information from everyone working on a story and put it together. But if had I been sent out early on a small story, I'd come back and write it myself—usually with help from Tracy.

On quiet mornings, I came into the office to wait for an assignment—and like the case with the subway girl, you never knew what was going to break next. In my first three weeks at the *Post,* I was sent to a subway derailment on the 5 train on Lexington Avenue, where I had to pounce on people emerging from a sweltering train in which they'd been stuck underground for an hour. I went to a project in the Bronx where a twenty-one-year-old Guyanan girl who'd won a writing scholarship to the United States had been crushed to death trying to climb out of an elevator that had stalled between two floors. I went to Henri Bendel, a posh store on Fifth Avenue, where Monica Lewinsky was launching a handbag line. I went to the national cat show in Madison Square Garden. And I went to the home of a stewardess from Queens who had just returned to the U.S. after being subjected to days of abuse in a Beijing prison for being a member of the Falun Gong movement.

On that last story, I'd run out so fast in the morning that I'd put on an old pair of smelly socks, thinking I could get away with it as I was wearing boots—only to be asked to remove my shoes as soon as I arrived at the woman's door. I sat through the interview surrounded by eight Falun Gong members, going redder and redder as the stench of my feet wafted around her elegant sitting room. Yes, you had to be prepared for anything.

Away from the office I was also getting used to approaching strangers. I had been given the names of "cool people" to ring up when I arrived in the city—Olly, a friend's girlfriend's cousin; Ben, the old family acquaintance of a work colleague; and Jodi, the ex-roommate of a girl I knew at school who'd lived in Brooklyn after college. As soon as I mustered up the courage to call and introduce myself, I noticed how differently things worked in New York.

Back home it was considered a bit annoying to have to look after random "mates of mates" from out of town. Arrogant Londoners usually assume they'll get stuck with a weirdo all night if they offer. But New Yorkers, who live in a city made up of outsiders, simply tell you to join their plans without worrying about the fitting in.

I called Olly first. He suggested I meet him for a drink that same night at Milanos, his favorite dingy Irish bar on Houston Street, the busy throughfare that cuts across downtown Manhattan separating SoHo from the Village. It was a blissful ten minutes by subway from the office in Midtown. I left a message for Ben, and two days later he called back asking me if I wanted to join him and three friends for dinner in a couple of hours at a French bistro on the Lower East Side called Le Pere Pinard.

It felt weird accepting their last-minute invites, as if it proved that I was a friendless loser—which of course I was. But when I later admitted this, both laughed at me, explaining that in New York people only ever made arrangements three hours ahead of time—any longer and someone was bound to be flaky and fuck up the plans.

And that was another difference I quickly noticed about New York. Thanks to the efficiency of the subways, the cheapness of cabs, and, in Manhattan especially, the relatively small area to cover, everything could happen at short notice. Forget making dinner-party plans a month in advance like people did in London.

So when Jodi called me back on my third Saturday in New York and, in an appealingly husky drawl, invited me to a "Pimps, Players,

Playboys, and Prostitutes" party she was throwing at her place in Park Slope, Brooklyn, that night, I decided not to be insulted by the lack of notice—and accepted.

"But you'll be okay that I don't know anyone, not even you? I don't want to be a burden," I said.

"Don't be crazy. Can't wait to meet you. Just make sure you're in costume. Otherwise we won't let you in."

So that evening I found myself sitting in a taxi going to Brooklyn for the first time in my life, heading towards a party full of strangers, dressed as a hooker.

Embrace the unknown! I told myself as the cab clanked over the starry lit Manhattan Bridge and headed down a busy highway that carved through a low-rise jumble of wood-framed houses, warehouses, and squat, red-brick apartment buildings.

"You have boyfriend?"

"Huh?" I looked up to see the taxi driver eyeing me in his rear view mirror.

"You have husband?"

"Yeah, he's in England."

I nervously inspected my outfit again. I hoped the ensemble of my scarlet minidress (care of the teen favorite store, Miss Selfridge in London), plus black fishnet stockings, strappy high heels, and a diamante Bunny Girl choker, all hastily bought from Ricky's costume shop at Columbus Circle, would be appropriate for a roomful of strangers. I wondered if I'd got a little too carried away with the blue metallic eye shadow and fake lashes. What if no one else had bothered with a costume—or they'd changed the theme to Librarians and Accountants?

"You ever had Pakistani boyfriend?"

Oh, for God's sake. I glanced at the cabby's ID medallion, which proclaimed him to be Mohammad al-Fayed. Presumably no relation to the owner of Harrods.

"Yes, in fact, I have had a Pakistani boyfriend. A very nice one called Omar Sheik when I was eighteen. He was at my brother's school." Why was I even getting into this?

"Ahhh." Mohammad al-Fayed nodded vigorously.

We turned off the main road and onto a long street lined with tatty looking stores—we passed a pizzeria-slash-Chinese takeout, a combination I never knew existed.

"So who make better lover: Pakistani man or American man?"

I kept my eyes fixed outside. Hopefully we were nearly in Park Slope. In my hand I clutched a scrap of paper torn from a *New York Post* notepad bearing Jodi's address.

"Pakistani man, right?" said Mohammad, contentedly answering his own question. "Yes, yes, we make very good lover. The best!"

I ignored him for several blocks.

"You want new Pakistani boyfriend?"

"Look, I'm going to a fancy dress party, okay? I don't normally look like this, and I don't want any other boyfriends. How much longer is this journey going to take?"

"We arrive soon," he said, totally unperturbed by my outburst. And sure enough, to my relief, we pulled up at the corner of Seventh Avenue and President soon after.

"Keep the change," I said tersely and handed over thirty dollars.

"Next time, you can be my girlfriend, yes?" he said, still beaming merrily as I slammed the door and hurried away.

I found myself in a dark, unfamiliar street and pulled my coat around me as I tried to get my bearings. It took me a while to spot Jodi's house number on the opposite side of the road on the gate post of a brownstone—the typical hundred-year-old, brown-brick family houses you find all over New York. She'd said her apartment was on the top floor, and I looked up and saw there was a red light on in a window, but the curtains were closed and I couldn't see movement or hear music. No one else was going into the house.

What to do? The taxi clock had said 21:27 when I'd got out. I had no desire to be the dorky early party arrival. Perhaps I needed a little liquid courage right now—and it was way too cold to stand in the street. Seventh Avenue looked like it had some action on it. I headed off to find the nearest bar.

Minutes later I was in the Santa Fe Grill, an unnecessarily brightly lit Mexican restaurant, where several smug-looking couples were sharing fajitas at shiny pine tables. Suddenly feeling self-conscious, I perched atop a bar stool, keeping my coat on to cover up the prostitute ensemble, and ordered a drink. After all, in New York it was perfectly acceptable to quaff a margarita alone in a sports bar. But I still felt like a saddo.

Two burly guys at the other end of the bar began shooting looks my way. I concentrated hard on an American football game on the TV in one corner. For the first time since moving to New York, I suddenly wished Angus was with me.

Angus. I took a huge gulp of my drink. We had tried to call each other regularly, but already we seemed to be struggling for conversation. Or was that just me? But then it was hard to relay every detail of my new life over the phone—there was so much to tell already and he didn't know any of the people or places I was talking about anyway. And it was exciting to be totally self-sufficient for a change. I hadn't really had time to miss Angus. Or maybe I just hadn't.

Sad for a moment, I drained my margarita. I ordered another and started to feel a bit better. I was worrying too much. Angus was coming to visit me the following weekend. Everything would be back to normal when we saw each other. And it wasn't like I fancied anyone else. No potential Clark Kents around, not one.

Jodi's party was in full swing when I returned to President Street with the fire of two margaritas in my belly. Now I could hear a Bee Gees song thudding out of the upstairs window of the brownstone, and the front door was open with a sign saying "Players This Way!!!"

I took the stairs two at a time and boldly knocked on the apartment door. A petite girl in a Dolly Parton wig, wearing a pink-check, knotted shirt and white denim hot pants opened it and fell upon me like a long-lost sister.

"Bridge, baby! I'm Jodi. *Sooo* excited you could make it!"

She swept me into a melee of afro wigs, sequined midriffs, furs, and feathers boas. I needn't have worried about my own costume efforts.

Jodi took my coat, then paraded me through the party introducing me as "Bridge the Brit." Someone fetched me a cup of punch, I was handed a joint. I found myself surrounded by a circle of guys, all asking what had brought me to New York.

I gabbled on grandly, telling my story and my fascinating adventures at the *Post* (I left out the Madison Square Garden cat show in case that sounded a bit lame). Yes, this was more like it. No longer was I Miss No-mates, fodder for letchy taxi drivers, drinking alone in a bar. Now I was the exciting mystery girl in the red dress—Lois Lane, intrepid reporter—who all the boys wanted to talk to. Okay, so I was also quite drunk.

With the small apartment crammed with new faces—and the fact that I was starting to see double—it was a while before I came across Deklin. But I had an instant party crush when I did. He was standing at the back of Jodi's kitchen wearing a panama hat and a shiny red sports coat over his bare chest, breaking up chunks of ice in a bag by whacking it on the side of the sink. He had black, curly hair and beautiful, thick eyelashes that flicked in concentration as he swung the bag. He caught me staring and smiled, displaying a slip of a gap between his perfectly square, straight, white front teeth. There was a lot to be said for American orthodontics. My night was getting better by the minute.

I walked over, pretending I needed some juice out of the fridge. He introduced himself immediately—quite different to the self-effacing manner that so many blokes had in London. In fact, I wondered if I'd ever gone to a party before where I'd spotted someone cute and got to talk to him so easily. Or maybe Deklin just wasn't that fussy.

He told me he was an illustrator from Boston who'd moved to New York the year before.

"So what's your costume?" I asked as an excuse to gaze at his athletic-looking chest.

"I'm a Venice Beach pimp. I know I look like a total jerk with my bare chest out, but Jodi told me my costume sucked and literally ripped off my T-shirt when I arrived."

"No, really, it's fine," I said, making a mental note to congratulate Jodi later.

I told him that thanks to Jodi, the fancy-dress Nazi, I'd just spent half an hour alone in a Mexican sports bar looking like I was cruising for business.

Deklin laughed. I felt like the wittiest woman in the universe.

He asked what brought me to New York, and I proudly told him that I was a reporter at the *New York Post*. He said he never read the filthy right-wing rag, and it was pro the Yankees, rivals to his beloved Red Sox. I decided now wasn't the time to mention that I didn't have a clue who the Red Socks were.

"Seriously, though, it's a pretty ballsy thing to move out to a new city and get into a crazy job like yours." He actually looked genuinely impressed. "And to turn up to a party on your own when you don't even know the host."

"Well, it's important always to give things a go, right? You should always feel excited by life and seek new adventures," I said.

Impressed by my own grand philosophical statement, I smugly weaved my way back to the other room, where most of the party was now dancing on Jodi's bare living room floorboards. I shimmied in a corner, looking mysterious, confident, and sexy—*a la* exciting girl in red dress—and it didn't take long for Deklin to join me. He was holding a strawberry popsicle.

"Thought you might want this. I found it in the freezer," he said handing it to me.

I looked at him and took a slow lick.

"Where's yours?" I said.

"It was the last one, but we can share it if you like," he said. And then I knew he was up for it.

Eventually we flopped down together on a sofa. On a table next to us, a computer screensaver showed pink and orange fish swimming in never ending circles.

"Nice aquarium," I said, for want of a better line.

"If you can't face going all the way back to Manhattan tonight, I live down the block," was his.

"Maybe you should kiss me first," I said, lunging at him with a partly opened mouth.

He suddenly sat forward. I toppled into the space behind him.

"Um, I feel kinda high school kissing you on this sofa," he said, as I found myself snogging a cushion.

It was a sign I should have noticed, but I was still cowering into the sofa.

Deklin pulled me back up, insisting it had been cute.

"Maybe we should just get out of here," he whispered.

Deklin told Jodi he was going to walk me to the cab dispatch office on Seventh Avenue. I thanked her for the best party I'd been to in years and we stepped out onto the brownstone's top landing. Now we were alone, Deklin took my face in his hands and kissed me slowly at first, then increasingly hard. I moved back against the wall at the top of the stairs. He leaned into me and the chemistry jumped between us, mixed up with the thrill of tasting someone for the first time. Manhattan, it was a long way home.

Deklin's apartment consisted of two small rooms at the back of another Park Slope brownstone three blocks from Jodi's place. On the wall was one solitary black-and-white picture of a silver Airstream campervan framed by palm trees, and elsewhere in the room an Apple Mac and loads of boys' sports stuff, including a long board, an American football, and a baseball bat and glove. Looking at the strange American stuff made me feel like I was in a teen movie—though I hoped not one in which the girl who goes home with the sexy boy then gets chainsawed.

I sat down on Deklin's bed. He took my coat, then chucked his, and we flopped backwards together, rolling towards each other in a drunken haze.

Kissing him was delicious, and soon he pulled my dress over my head—leaving me lying in dainty black Dior bra, knickers, and garter belt from Paris. I'd put them on at the last minute to get into hooker mode, with no intention of showing them off.

Deklin sat up and looked down admiring me, stroking my waist. Then he laughed and shook his head, saying he couldn't believe that he was the one who'd got to take the Brit girl home.

"I hope it wasn't a competition," I said.

He punched the air.

"Yeah, babee, yeah! And *I* saw it off."

Oh, no. It was that classic moment in bed with a stranger when they suddenly do something cringey and all their sex appeal threatens to vanish. I prayed that would be his last Austin Powers impression.

He got up to go to the bathroom, and now alone, I suddenly became aware of what I was actually doing. The sight of the delicate black underwear against my pale skin made me think of the time I'd worn it after the oyster night in Saint Germain with Angus. We'd stayed in a rambling old hotel, and the bedstead had banged against the wall when we had sex, so we'd thrown a pink shiny eiderdown onto the floor and carried on there.

Deklin flushed the toilet. I felt sick. I reminded myself it was probably not the best idea to start reminiscing about vacations with one's boyfriend while in bed with someone else. But it was too late.

Jesus, I had been away from Angus for less than a month, and here I was already. I looked around at Deklin's unfamiliar stuff. A book titled *Joe Humphrey's Trout Tactics* sat by his bed with a transistor radio on it. Ironically, it was precisely the kind of book Angus would enjoy.

But then Angus had nothing to do with this. This night was just another New York experience, no different than running around on the Union Square subway platform or walking through Times Square. Oh, who was I fooling? I should be getting up right now and calling a cab back to the Upper West Side. Then again, it was 4 A.M. on a freezing winter morning.

Deklin came back into the room in his boxer shorts. I turned to the wall, pulling the covers around me. He got into bed behind me and kissed the nape of my neck.

"Aa-ah, cold hands," I said, cursing myself again as my body tingled pleasantly with goose bumps. I decided not to think about Angus until the morning. Or to worry about the small fact that he too would be in New York in four days' time.

"So, who are better in bed then, English or American blokes?" said Olly, draining his pint of Guinness and turning to me with his toothy smirk.

"Don't ask me," I replied. "Nothing happened. Honestly."

It was now Sunday afternoon. I'd made it back from Park Slope a few hours before, and dreading a lonely, hungover night of self-loathing in the *New York Post* apartment, I'd called Olly again. He had immediately summoned me to his second favorite drinking spot—a bricked basement bar on 5th Street called The Scratcher.

Three-quarters Irish, Olly had already been in America five years, living in a railroad apartment in East Williamsburg and commuting to work at a pharmaceutical company in Hackensack, New Jersey, in a ridiculous electric blue, 7.5–liter, 1973 Buick Electra 225. He spent most of his spare time in Milanos, Scratcher, or the Mars Bar on First Avenue, usually with his best friend, Ken, an earnest Duke graduate from Seattle who worked on the arts pages of the *Wall Street Journal*, and Agnes, a tomboyish backpacker from the British Midlands who tended bar at The Scratcher.

"American men are better, no question," said Agnes, removing Olly's pint glass and placing a fresh one under the Guinness tap. "I'll tell you why—because American men are into performance, while English blokes don't give a monkey's. An English man will happily get pissed, stagger into bed with you, attempt to get a shag, then roll off and be asleep in half an hour whether he's successful or not."

"You're right on," said Ken. "Americans want to be the best they can be at whatever they do. It's the same with our attitude to sport and work. We think about it, we read books on it, we put in the effort. Not like you lazy-assed Brit guys."

"You taking the piss?" said Olly.

"Not at all," said Ken. "An American will stay up all night trying to make a girl come, but mainly to satisfy his own ego."

I thought back to that morning. Deklin and I had simulated sex for hours, kissing and writhing and grinding our bodies together, and just about resisting temptation to go the whole way. Luckily Deklin had said he only felt comfortable making love to girls if he was in a serious relationship, and of course I'd heartily agreed.

But my encounter with Deklin had been incredibly sexy. And now Agnes and Ken came to mention it, his technique was spot on—he knew all the ear-, neck-, and hair-stroking like he'd just read February *GQ*'s "Ten top tips to turn on a woman." But I knew my thrills hadn't come from Deklin's slick bed manner, but from the fact that the handsome stranger I had wanted at a party had also wanted me.

My guilt returned. But then perhaps it was quite normal to fancy other people, even in a serious relationship. Angus himself had once said a friend of his who'd got married had warned him that the most shocking thing he'd found about newly married life was how much he still desired other women. And here I was alone in a new city, with a mission to seize the day and try new experiences. . . . Yes, I could make every excuse in the book. But deep down I knew that if I had so quickly betrayed Angus, something was probably wrong. Going to New York was one thing. Jumping into bed with the first guy I fancied at a party was quite different.

Scarface in
mom-and-tot stickup spree

General Assignment reporting was a job that kept you permanently in suspense. You might spend at entire day sitting nervously at your desk, thinking the editors had forgotten you existed, and the next you'd be hauled out of bed to rush to the scene of some bodega holdup or apartment fire and might not get home until midnight.

The *Post*'s legendary, if eccentric, night editor Mike Hechtman, who named his cats after the transit system—Metrocard and MaBSTOA— took over from John Mancini in the evenings and had no qualms about keeping reporters out late on stories. His favorite saying was that no one deserved to be an editor unless they'd done their time on the street, no one was too good to cover a fire, and there was no such thing as a martyr on time-and-a-half (our overtime pay for working beyond our seven-and-a-half-hour shift, which we often did).

But the joke amongst *Post* reporters was that typically the days you wanted to be busy, you ended up sitting around. And the times you were desperate for a quiet day in the office, you'd get dispatched to some godforsaken corner of New York.

The day Angus was due to arrive from England was one of the latter. I was woken by my pager buzzing, followed two seconds later by the shrill ring of the apartment phone.

"City Desk, hold for Marilyn Matlick," came Myron's voice.

"Hi, we got an arrest on a parolee who robbed three moms on the J train by putting guns to their babies' heads," said Marilyn, the morning assignment editor, in her efficient tone.

"Jermaine Barima," she said, giving me a double number address on 174th Street in Queens. "I think that's St. Albans. Photo is on the way. This guy, he's got a major rap sheet: five previous convictions for robbery and weapons possessions, and numerous arrests. Broke parole last month and had evaded an arrest warrant until last night. They got him after he snatched a gold chain from a woman at Church Avenue, jumped onto the tracks, and tried to hide under a train. You got all that?"

My scribbles were as illegible as ever.

"Um, I am going to where this bloke lives?"

"That's the address the Shack gave us. But don't worry, he's in Central Booking. See who's there, though. Ask them what they think of their son, brother, cousin, or whoever they are sticking up kids."

She put the phone down before I had a chance to ask about subways to St. Albans, so I turned to my new bible—Tracy's Street Planner.

174th Street turned out to be a swathe of residential roads beyond the end of the subway near Hollis, the tough neighborhood which had spawned one of the first rap groups, Run–DMC. Tracy had explained that the double numbers in Queens addresses referred to the cross street and then the house number on the block. After much frowning to get my head around this system, I reckoned that I could get the E train to the end of the line at Jamaica Center, then walk for half a mile. I hadn't yet learned the trick of getting the photographer assigned to the story to pick me up at the nearest subway station en route.

The photographer sent out on this story was Rick Dembow, a *Post* old timer with a greasy mop of dark hair flecked with gray at the temples and a Long Island drawl. As I eventually trudged around the corner at 109th Avenue, he flashed his headlights at me from across the street. I flopped into the passenger seat of his white Honda. It stank of menthol cigarettes.

"How you doing? You're the new exchange reporter, right?" He flicked his cigarette out of his open window. "Apologies for the mess in the car."

"No worries," I said, looking at the collection of old coffee cups, loose pages of the *Post*, and crumpled up McDonald's bags at my feet. "Got a light?"

I had been meaning to give up smoking the moment I got to New York. But then the main lot of a reporter—waiting for something to happen or chasing something that had happened—made it almost impossible not to smoke. And of course smoking was vital for on-the-job bonding, which was very important.

Rick lit my cigarette and pointed out of my window towards a tatty, brick, semidetached house. Rust-colored bars fortified the front door and its two ground floor windows. A garden path ran up the side of a muddy lawn where a kid's pink plastic tricycle lay abandoned on its side.

"That's the address. I tell you this guy's a sick motherfucker. One of the women he robbed pointed him out in a line up yesterday evening. He's got this big scar down his right cheek, and they make him repeat the line he said to her on the subway. He had his gun jammed into her kid's temple. He says, 'Shut that little bitch up, or I'll blow her brains out.' When the lady heard him say it again, she started freakin' out. Said it brought the whole ordeal back."

Rick produced a crumpled photocopy of a photo.

"That's him on the perp walk late last night. Keep it if you like."

A perp walk was the made-for-the-media moment when cops took suspects out of the police precinct into a squad car to be driven down-town to be booked by the courts. To show off their conquests, cops usually told the snappers when it was going to happen and gave them a couple of seconds to get a clean shot.

This picture was of a scowling man with narrow, pointed cheek bones hunched into a sweatshirt. His right cheek had an ugly seam running through the middle that looked like a knife wound. I hoped he wasn't about to turn up at 174th Street any time soon.

I put the picture in my bag and took a drag of my cigarette. In the confined space of the musty Honda, my stomach turned from the smoke.

"So should we ring the doorbell then?"

"Nah, done it already. There's no one home. Gotta sit tight, see who appears. Chances are they're down at the courts now, but this guy ain't makin' bail."

I noticed Rick's camera was sitting ready on his lap.

We sat in the car for the next two and a half hours, intermittently smoking. To pass the time, Rick told me about his new thing—Match.com. His friend had recently gotten married to a woman he met online, so as Rick was a divorcee who worked long, unsociable hours at the *Post,* making it impossible to meet women, he'd decided to give it a go. After hours of late night searching on the site, during which he'd sent out dozens of introductory e-mails, he'd met three women face-to-face so far.

"And?" I was riveted. "How did that go?"

"Well, I can tell you right off the bat, those women online, they don't look anything like the pictures they post," he said, lighting another menthol Parliament and flicking his match book onto the cluttered dashboard.

"You turn up, and sometimes you can't even recognize them. Guaranteed, they always look older—and usually a lot heavier than their pictures too."

Rick said the most recent candidate he had met for dinner had been a divorced advertising executive, who'd claimed to be thirty-five but he estimated was at least five years older. Still she had seemed sweet—until she'd glugged back a whole bottle of wine before their pizza had even arrived. By the end of the meal, she'd gotten catatonic and tearful, telling him how lonely she was. He'd practically had to carry her out of his car and into her home.

"She was gone. Lucky for her I wasn't a date rapist. Didn't return her e-mails after that, cut her off. Single women in New York, there are so many of them. They get past their prime and they go crazy in the head. You don't wanna go near them."

Oh God, may I never be that woman, I thought to myself. I felt a sudden rush of love for Angus. I would see him in just a few hours' time.

Suddenly a middle aged woman wearing a long brown raincoat and fur-lined boots rounded the corner from 109th Avenue and turned down the garden path to 109-xx. We were both out of the car in seconds. I reached her as she pulled out the keys to her front door. Rick was right behind me.

"Mrs. Barima? Mrs. Barima, do you have a moment?" I said, my heart beating with adrenaline.

She didn't turn around.

"We're from the *New York Post.* Would it be possible to talk to you about Jermaine?"

"I ain't got nothin' to say," she replied as she quickly shoved her keys into the three locks on her door, keeping her back to me.

"But you're his mom, right?" said Rick.

She turned for a second, his camera flashed in her face. She put her hand up, swearing.

"If you use that picture, I'll sue your damn newspaper." The door slammed in our faces. Rick shrugged.

"Guess she ain't got nothing to say."

We returned to the car. Twenty minutes later a lanky teenager also approached the house, walking with a hunched swagger, the crotch of his jeans slung low. I got out of the car, catching up with him.

"Excuse me, do you know Jermaine?" I said.

The front door swung open, the mother was back on the steps.

"Hey, you leave my boy alone. You better stop hassling people!" she screamed. A man appeared from behind her, then came stomping down the path towards me. I instinctively backed towards the car. The boy ducked into the house.

"You heard the woman. She said get off this property," the man snarled, now a few inches from my face. He was stocky, with bulges of steroid-pumped arms that were bare under a blue Disney World T-shirt. That was all that I noticed, my heart was pounding so fast.

Rick pushed me aside, confronting the guy with his camera in one hand. "Hey, you fuck, who the fuck are you talking to? Are you proud your son's a filthy piece of shit?"

"I said get the fuck off my property or I'll break your neck and your camera," said the man.

"We're not on your fucking property. See this sidewalk, it's public property. I can stand here all fucking day if I like," shouted Rick, furiously pointing at the ground. "And if you don't wanna talk to us, you can read about that piece of shit in the paper tomorrow."

"Well, thanks for your time, sir," I said, relieved that the man seemed to have a modicum more restraint than Rick. What the hell was he thinking?

The man stomped back into his house. Rick threw open his car door, dumped his camera on the driver's seat, and lit a cigarette.

"Gotta rile them up. Sometimes it really does the trick, and you get a great quote or photo," he said, exhaling loudly and glaring at the house. "I been on this job twenty years. I tell you, this city is full of scumbags."

I tried to disguise my shaking hands. That was the thing about reporting. You never knew what was going to happen next.

My pager buzzed, with instructions to call Steve Marsh. I borrowed Rick's phone.

"So what you got on the baby mugger?" he asked.

I recounted the morning, saying I thought it was distinctly unlikely that we would get any more quotes. Steve then gave me a new address, a fifth floor apartment off Avenue Y, near Coney Island in Brooklyn.

"The Shack thinks his girlfriend might live there," said Steve.

Coney Island was miles away, but I presumed I'd drive there with Rick and felt excited about the next leg of our adventure. But then Rick called his desk and was told to meet a different reporter covering an armed robbery in a bodega in Astoria. As he rushed to start his car, my trepidation came back. Hopefully Jermaine's girlfriend would be less scary than his parents.

Rick dropped me at Jamaica Center, and clutching my Street Planner, I embarked on an epic, hour-long, three-line subway trek from east Queens to southwest Brooklyn. When I finally emerged at the Avenue X stop, I found myself on a long, desolate street overshadowed by the raised iron tracks of the subway line. Adjoining it was an ominous industrial area that was filled with boarded-up warehouses. It was now close to 3:30 P.M. I had about half an hour before it began to get dark.

I tried to affect nonchalant bravado as I headed towards Avenue Y. The last time I came to Brooklyn alone I'd got lucky with Deklin. This time I felt like I'd be lucky if I survived with my life.

Avenue Y led me into a huge area of brown-brick apartment buildings that seemed to stretch for miles. I supposed my address would be in one of them, and I cautiously followed the numbers on the blocks, getting further from the road. I wondered where the nearest pay phone was. With no mobile phone, I would be screwed if something happened.

I passed a play area where a gang of high school kids were slouching and smoking weed on swings. They all stared at me. I shot a fierce look back at them as if to say "Yeah, and? I come here all the time."

Striding on purposefully like we had been taught to do in self-defense classes at school, I eventually came to the address I was looking for, an eight-story building with a black front door. The crescent of reinforced glass at its center had been shattered and the metal intercom lock was broken, which allowed me to push the door open.

The foyer was almost pitch black. I stood for a moment holding the door open behind me to keep the light, wondering if I should go on. The place stank of cigarette butts and urine, and there was a dimly lit elevator which was half open, revealing walls that were covered in graffiti. I had no desire to get stuck in that. On the far side was a door that I guessed might lead to stairs.

I took a deep breath, glanced back outside to check no one was following, then made a dash for the stairwell. My footsteps sounded loud and conspicuous in the half-darkness as I made my way upwards.

I picked my way past old condoms and broken glass. For protection I put my hand in my bag and clutched a pen. But then this wasn't the movies. What was I going to do? Pull off some kind of Bic neck jab if I came face-to-face with a mugger wielding a knife or a gun?

I reached the fifth floor and a dog began barking, snarling and scraping behind an apartment door. I jumped back, staring at its pacing shadow in the crack under the door and feeling irrationally afraid to pass. Fuck. I hated this. This was a nightmare. Why didn't I just go back to the subway and tell Steve that no one was home at the address? No one would know. Then I could go home and get ready for Angus.

But I was almost at the apartment now. What kind of saddo would give up? And here I was, after all, actually doing the job I'd dreamed of all my life. I just hadn't imagined it to be quite as lonely as this.

I comforted myself that no matter what, soon I'd be with Angus, telling him stories of my daring. I rang the grubby bell of 5x, praying no one would answer.

I heard a bolt slide. I took another deep breath and steeled myself for hostility. An elderly woman clad in a claret-colored, velour track suit answered the door. She had pale brown skin and a roly-poly figure and wore a gold cross amongst several gold chains around her neck. She looked at me, surprised.

"Um, hello," I stammered. "I'm a reporter from the *New York Post*. I was wondering if you knew Jermaine Barima."

"The *Pos*'? Sure, Jermaine's my son-in-law. Come in, I've got some coffee in the pot. So where are you from?"

"Er, England," I said, taken aback. The gun-toting thug was her son-in-law and she wanted to have coffee?

"Hurry up. You don't know who's lurking in them stairwells," she said. I stepped through the doorway, in no doubt that she was right about that.

We entered her sitting room, which contained a purple chenille sofa and armchair, both decorated with colorful crocheted quilts. A pile rug was littered with toys: a red New York fire engine, Star Wars figures, some robot-like action men. A delicious smell of chicken soup wafted from a galley kitchen half hidden behind a sliding door.

It was incongruously cozy compared to the grimness outside. The woman went to the kitchen and returned with a mug that read "I ♥ Coney Island." I took it out of politeness, and she insisted I sit down.

"Their boy, I look after him while my daughter Lizette's at college," she said, smiling at the toys on the floor. "So anyway, what about Jermaine?"

Shit. Maybe she had no idea that her son-in-law had been arrested for armed robbery. And she'd just made me coffee. What the hell was I going to say?

"Er. Well . . . "

She smiled at me, waiting. I felt myself starting to sweat.

"I'm afraid he's been arrested."

"For what?" She looked genuinely surprised.

I looked into my coffee. How was I going to put this?

"Um, well, it seems he's robbed some women by putting a gun to their babies' heads . . . "

My light tone made me sound like a teacher informing a parent their kid had been playing hooky from school. But still the sentence rang out, sounding utterly surreal in the warm, homely room.

"Jermaine? No, it must be someone else. Jermaine would never do anything like that." She folded her hands in her lap, satisfied that she had cleared up my silly misunderstanding. "Jermaine, he's the most wonderful son-in-law. He's so good to my daughter and their son. And he sends me flowers on Mother's Day."

Now *I* was confused. How could the mother-in-law of a man with a rap sheet dating back his whole life not know about it? But this woman was talking about him like he was a saint. And surely no man with a young kid of his own could put a gun to the heads of other children? The Shack must have made a mistake with the address. I felt a wave of relief.

"You know what, we must have got the wrong Jermaine," I said, smiling. "I'm so sorry to have bothered you."

"Well, it was nice talkin' with you anyway. You don't often get people from England around here," she said.

I put my notepad back in my bag and got up to go. Then my heart stopped. On the woman's window ledge I noticed a photo—proud parents with their son. I went to look at it more closely. A distinct scar bisected the father's face.

Now I remembered the photocopied picture of Jermaine Barima. I pulled it out and handed it to the woman.

"This is Jermaine, right?" My voice was high and shaky.

"Yes, that's him!" She sounded proud for a second—and then she looked confused. The phone rang, making us both jump.

"That will be my daughter now. She's coming by to drop her son off." She answered it. "Lizette, there's a woman from the *Pos'* here. She says Jermaine's been arr—" She stiffened. Then she looked at me, all friendliness extinguished from her face.

"My daughter says you had better get the hell out of her house," she growled.

"Sure, look, I'm really sorry about all thi—"

"Now! My daughter said I can' talk to you no more."

I left my coffee cup on the floor and fled. She slammed the door behind me. The dog behind the door barked again as I hurried back towards the stairs, cursing my stupidity. Thank Christ I'd spotted the picture. Once again my first impressions were totally wrong.

I opened the stairwell door and came face to face with a lanky woman in a blue metallic Puffa jacket holding a toddler in one arm. We each knew immediately who the other was.

"Yo, reporter, who gave you permission to come into my house?" she screamed in my face.

"Well, your mum did." I scrabbled for my notepad, fighting the desire to run for my life.

"Yeah? Well you got no right to go snooping about Jermaine. He's a good person."

Fuck, where was my pen?

She pushed past me. I found it at last.

"Er, just wondering if you could give me your full name?"

"Fuck you, I'm not talking to no ho' reporter." She started up the stairs with the toddler still in her arm.

"Yeah, well, don't you think that sticking guns in babies' faces is a bit fucking extreme?" I shouted after her.

"Fuck you, bitch!" she shouted back.

I wondered if Rick's rile-them tactics ever actually worked.

But then at least I had got something. Thanks to this woman and her mom, I could call Steve Marsh with some quotes and go straight to meet Angus. By the skin of my teeth I had avoided the chance that night editor Mike Hechtman might have kept me in Coney Island half the night.

Date with destiny in romantic Brooklyn eatery

The shuttle bus from the Howard Beach subway station lurched and swerved around the long-stay parking lots, heading for Terminal Four at JFK. I smiled out into the darkness, thinking about the last time Angus and I had met at an airport.

It was at Stansted a year before and he'd found me at two in the morning, sprawled asleep on a bench after I had staggered off a hopelessly delayed flight from France. I had burst into tears with happiness when I saw him (something I rarely do).

It had been my birthday, and my parents—travel writers—were fact-checking a guidebook on the southwest of France and had thought it a wonderful idea that I go join them for the weekend. And it was wonderful—as wonderful as it ever is being stuck in the back of a steamed-up car on a driving holiday in the rain.

True to form in my parents' company, I had not been gracious about having a nice weekend away. I had regressed straight to adolescence, fuming in the back seat amongst a pile of maps and tourist pamphlets because my dad insisted on eating old bananas in the car. Meanwhile, they ticked off local sights and towns on their list with all the gusto of a young couple on honeymoon.

The parental pact had been that I could fly back from Carcassonne Airport in time for a big birthday dinner at home in Shepherd's Bush. But no sooner had I excitedly buckled up my window seat than the captain announced the plane was "broken" and we would all have to return to the terminal.

Seven hours later I was still sitting in the airport's stale, smoky canteen, waiting for a new plane to arrive, dreaming of axe-murdering anyone who'd ever worked for Ryan Air. I'd called Angus first to warn him that I might be late for the dinner, and then later to tell him to cancel it. To stop me turning the axe on myself as well, he'd promised that however late I eventually flew in, he would drive to Stansted to pick me up. In the end I'd landed at 1 A.M., only to be paged by airport staff who told me Angus had left me message to say he'd broken down on the motorway.

So I'd lain down on a metal bench in the desolate arrivals hall waiting for him. When he finally arrived—as exhausted and pissed off as I was by this point—I sobbed in his arms with love for him. He had brought a mini–chocolate cake and a half bottle of Dom Perignon, and we had my birthday party in the car, speeding back down the motorway to Kentish Town.

The Arrivals area at Kennedy was as desolate as Stansted when I got there a miraculous half an hour early. The hall that had been bursting with passengers when I'd nervously lugged my suitcase across it on my arrival in New York twenty-six days before was virtually empty.

I sat down on a row of seats to wait and noticed some crumpled pages from a discarded *Post* strewn underneath me on the floor. I moved them with my toe, hoping to spot my byline on the story I'd written the day before—about a Queens double-amputee who'd won $17.5 million in the New York Quick Pick lottery and planned to buy himself a new pair of legs with the money. The headline had been LOTTO WILL HELP HIM WALK AGAIN! But I couldn't see it. Only pages from Sports were there. Yeah, I usually chucked those too.

I gazed at the white wall that separated the rest of the world from America and thought about all that had happened since I'd emerged through there myself. A month in which I had already seen the insides of three New York hospitals, had been to all five boroughs (which some Manhattanites never do their whole lives), had covered several unfortunate accidents and crimes—and had committed my own crime of spending the night with someone else.

The memory of Deklin's dark eyes and eyelashes up against my skin flashed into my mind. Again it hit me how quickly I'd managed to trash the trust of a boyfriend I was supposed to love—and maybe even marry. All that time I'd told myself being away for four months was nothing—and I'd already derailed my old life.

How would I react when I saw him? I felt so different from the restless, unfocused person I had been when I left London. Now he would be here in the flesh, stepping into my new, independent life.

I decided that the "Airport Test" was a good way of telling how you really felt about someone. Surely that very first instinctive moment I spotted him would tell me if he was The One. Would my heart soar, would the very sight of his face make me feel complete? But then at Stansted, hadn't I felt like that? And I'd still buggered off to New York.

Transatlantic passengers began to appear from behind the wall: tired-looking couples pushing trolleys, businessmen with folded suit bags slung over their shoulders, New Yorkers coming home, Brits coming on shopping holidays.

And then I saw him, leaning over the bar of his trolley in his old, soft, navy overcoat as he weaved through the throng. His thick, fair hair had grown a bit and was pushed back from his large brow. His creamy skin looked typically fresh.

So there he is, I thought. What, hang on. Was that it? Where was my thunderbolt? Where was my moment of truth?

"Hello, gorgeous," he said in his soft voice as he approached, still slouched over the trolley. And then we were hugging and smiling like reunited couples do. I held onto the bulk of his coat, letting its lovely familiar smell wash over me. He lifted me onto tiptoes to kiss me. I loved Angus. Of course I did. But the moment which was supposed to tell me if he was The One had gone. And I still didn't know.

In the taxi back to Manhattan, I leaned against his side as we sped along the Van Wyck Expressway, past the dark ends of tatty suburban avenues like the one on which I had begun my day with Rick. I prattled on, paranoid there shouldn't be any silences between us so soon after we had been reunited.

I told him about how I'd had to break up a fight between Rick and a thug he'd taunted to get a good quote, how I had braved the most notorious housing project in Brooklyn (well, it might have been), and how I had had to break it to a grandmother that her son-in-law had pointed a gun at babies' heads.

"Gorgeous, I really am proud of you," said Angus. "You must be so happy that you're finally doing what you've always wanted to do."

"Well, I'm not actually very good at it yet," I replied. Angus rolled his eyes as if to say "you haven't changed," and looked away from me out of his window. I immediately felt annoyed. I _had_ changed.

"So, what's been going on back home?" I asked.

"Not much." He shrugged. The documentary he was working on about kids around the UK celebrating their birthdays was going okay. There'd been the stag weekend in Amsterdam during which our friend Ed had fallen in a canal. Isabel, one of our mates, had begun dating a film star and had flown out to Vancouver to stay with him in some flashy penthouse while he made a movie. She kept calling everyone from her Jacuzzi on the fifty-first floor of a skyscraper overlooking the Pacific and talking about how she was making Hollywood babies.

"Fucking hell, that's so typical," I said. "I'm afraid my life hasn't been so glamorous."

I warned him that the New York Post apartment was in a bit of a lame part of town, stuck in a wasteland of new building developments off Eleventh Avenue, and was less lavishly furnished than a Holiday Inn. My view was of another half-built skyscraper owned by Donald Trump, but if you craned your neck out of my bedroom window, you could see across the Hudson to New Jersey.

"I've come to see you," said Angus, and we hugged again a little awkwardly on the shiny, fake-leather taxi seat.

We hit the stretch of the Long Island Expressway that mounted a long overpass across Queens before dipping towards the Queenstown Tunnel, and the panorama of Manhattan suddenly rose up ahead of us like a movie set. The white, starry jumble of apartment buildings and office towers twinkled under the indigo-orange sky, spliced by the spikes of the Empire State and the Chrysler Building. We both instinctively leaned forward.

"God, that is an incredible view. You could never get tired of it," said Angus, chirpy again. "New York is the business. You're so lucky to be living here."

It suddenly hit me that he was right. I was unbelievably lucky. Not just to live in New York, but to have as the sole requirement of my job to discover and document all the yet-to-happen events caused by the millions of people going about their lives, all encased in that magical view up ahead.

"I don't think I've ever felt happier in my life," I said. And we fell silent.

"Meet any good people yet?" he asked.

"Did I already tell you about Olly?" I said, guiltily looking straight ahead.

That night we stayed up making plans. Angus, who'd been to New York several times, wanted to visit his favorite building, the Flatiron. He also suggested the Guggenheim, where he said there was a mind-blowing exhibition by a cutting-edge South Korean artist who did things with TVs. With just a little less sophistication, I said I wanted to go on *The Beast*—a powerboat I'd read about that had teeth marks painted on the front of it and that jetted up and down the Hudson while everyone screamed. Angus raised his eyebrows and said he thought that only ran in the summer. Trust him to know.

The next day we got up early, and to show off how native I'd become, I suggested we "go grab bagels" at the The Coffee Pot on Ninth Avenue. I made a big show of attaching my pager to my belt.

"The office might need me at any time," I said grandly.

Then after Angus was settled at a table in the cozy café which smelt of cinnamon and fresh coffee, happily flipping through the *New York Times*, I rushed to a deli and threw down a quarter for the *Post* to show him my story.

Police arrest "scarface" in mom-and-tot stickup spree was splashed over page five, and my name was among several bylines. He read the whole thing while I watched proudly.

"Nice one, Bridge," he said. Then he turned the smudgy pages of the rest of the paper with a quizzical look on his face, stopping at the headlines: DEPRESSED DENTIST IN DEATH LEAP, BRONX DUMPSTER HID GRUESOME SECRET, HAS E. SIDE SEX FIEND GONE TO W. SIDE?

"Okay, so it's not quite the *Guardian*." I suddenly felt crossly protective over the grungy *Post* office and the collection of oddballs who worked there.

"Relax, Bridge," said Angus. "It's a cool paper, even if it is a bit in-your-face."

A bit in-your-face? It's a tabloid in the most in-your-face city in the world. What the hell do you expect? I wanted to shout. But even I knew that picking a fight within twenty-four hours of his arrival would not go down too well.

We decided to save our official sight-seeing activities for Sunday, and headed into SoHo. The afternoon brought bright spring sunshine, and the narrow streets bustled with shoppers wandering in and out of the multitude of boutiques and galleries, squeezing past each other on the pavement past hawkers' tables laden with NYPD, FDNY, and Yankees hats, black-and-white portraits of the city, fake pashminas, and photocopies of famous movie scripts.

On Broadway, Angus spotted a black-and-red flag attached to a brick building at 670 advertising the Leica Gallery—and having considered buying one of the cult cameras for a while, he wanted to go in and check them out. Inside and up the stairs was a counter displaying an array of the cameras, and past it a small room was filled with black-and-white pictures of parkscapes taken by some obscure Czech photographer. Angus got straight into conversation with an irritating hipster girl behind the counter, so I idled in front of the photos.

Not that she was that pretty or anything, but I could tell she was sucking up to him because he had an English accent. What was so special about Leica cameras anyway? These pictures looked like any clichéd arty landscape snaps to me.

Suddenly my pager buzzed, giving me a start as it vibrated on my belt. I snatched it from its plastic holder; CALL CITY DESK, STEVE MARSH, said the green message strip, and instantly I was pumping with adrenaline. There must be an emergency, a big breaking news story. The office needed me! I looked around the gallery for a pay phone.

Angus was now studying some lenses the girl had got out for him. I touched his arm, announcing I'd been paged to call the office and would be back.

"Cool," he said, not looking up from the black contraptions.

Back out on Broadway, in the sunshine and the clamor of traffic again, I darted through the crowds to a sidewalk phone on Great Jones Street, buzzing with excitement as I hammered the *Post*'s free phone number into the silver buttons.

"Ci-dy-desk," came the drone of a copy kid stuck inside on a Saturday.

"Hello, Bridget Harrison for Steve Marsh," I said importantly.

"Hold."

"Yup?" Steve sounded hassled when he came on the line.

"It's Bridget. You just buzzed me. Do you need me to come in?"

"Wow, that was quick. No, don't need you today. I was just doing the schedule. Can you work next weekend?"

"Oh." I felt like some overly keen wannabe. "Of course. Well then, jolly glad I didn't have to chuck in my day off—"

As usual I found myself talking to a ring tone.

Guiltily disappointed, I turned back towards the gallery and stepped into the path of two guys who were strolling up the sidewalk. I immediately recognized one as the young editor I had seen on my first day at the *Post*. I had since found out he worked on the business section. Today, instead of a suit he was wearing an old black leather jacket and dark jeans and was holding a plastic bag with records in it. But it was impossible to miss that distinctive mop of hair.

"Hey, it's Bridget, right?" he said. "I'm Jack. I don't think we ever got introduced in the office. This is my friend Mike."

Mike was taller than Jack, with spiky, short dark hair. They looked like the cool college boys who'd skipped out of class. I shook Mike's hand.

"Bridget's over from the London *Times* on the News Corp. exchange program," said Jack. I was taken aback. He knew all about me already?

"Man, you British people are crazy," said Mike. "I went on an exchange to London when I was in eighth grade, and they sent me to live with this insane family in a place called Maidenhead. They spent the entire time force-feeding me with black pudding and beans on toast for 'my tea.'" He said "tea" in a phony but not bad cockney accent. "And then in the evenings, everyone went to the pub and had fights."

I laughed. My eyes were drawn back to Jack's.

"Yeah, well, we do like our pigs' blood—and our closing-time punch-ups," I said.

"So what are you up to?" asked Jack. His eyes were pale blue and he had a direct, steady gaze that seemed to twinkle. I realized I'd lost awareness of the busy street around us.

"Actually, I was just calling the office, so it's funny I bumped into you. I got paged, thought I might have to go in . . . but they just wanted to talk about the schedule."

Shit. Did I actually say the word "schedule"? These boys didn't want to know about my boring schedule.

"Um, how about you?"

"Just been music shopping." Jack gestured towards the carrier bag he was holding. "Found some incredible old jazz 12-inches. Now we're headed to sink some Old Fashioneds in a great bar we know on Commerce Street."

"Old Fashioneds. They're something whiskey-related, right?" I said.

"Yeah, bourbon, Angostura bitters, sugar, and orange zest. What more could you wish for on a Saturday afternoon?" He paused almost imperceptibly. "Join us if you like."

I felt myself about to go red, although I didn't know why.

"Um, actually, my boyfriend from England is over. He's just up over there in the Leica Gallery. I should go find him."

"Oh, Leicas. Evidently people go crazy for them. It's those pin-sharp German lenses." I couldn't tell if he was joking or not.

"It's all a mystery to me," I said.

"Well, enjoy the rest of your weekend," he said.

They moved off, merging back into the crowd as they ambled up Broadway. Jack took out a cigarette as they walked, and the curls on his head bounced as he dipped his head to light it without stopping. I watched puffs of smoke wisp out behind his black jacket until they turned the corner. Only then did the sound of the traffic seem to start up again.

The River Café, nestled in an old boat under the Brooklyn Bridge, had an amazing view of Manhattan and was the most romantic restaurant in New York, I'd been told by several people when I was planning for Angus's trip. Its write-up in *Zagat*, the city's famous restaurant guide, promised: "All occasions are special ones at this beautiful, barge-based Brooklyn waterside escape, a fabulous date place (even with your husband) thanks to that priceless view."

Shame the write-up didn't add: "all occasions, that is, apart from breaking up with the love of your life, in which case the waiters will be unsympathetic, the whole restaurant will be able to hear you crying, and your money will be wasted because you won't be able to stomach the food."

Angus and I had missed Valentine's Day while I'd been away—and on his last night in New York, I wanted to take him out somewhere fancy as my treat.

That evening we'd got dressed up and I had refused to tell him about my surprise destination until we arrived. But I regretted my choice the moment we walked into the restaurant's austere foyer and were greeted by a pinched maitre d', who looked us up and down and said, "You have reservations?"

"I think you have us mistaken for the pizzeria around the corner" is what he meant.

But *Zagat* was right. The view from the restaurant was, in the true meaning of the word, awesome. The whole place was geared towards a wall of windows which looked back across the black ripples of the East River to lower Manhattan, which shot up out of the water on the other side. Countless night-lit office windows looked like stars on a painted canvas, linked to the vast arc of the Brooklyn Bridge which reached out directly above us, thousands of tons of iron and brick. To the south, the twin towers of the World Trade Center dominated the night sky.

But like walking into a restaurant with a prix-fixe deal on Valentine's Day, there was a couple at every table, their seats arranged—as if at a race track—to face towards the view. The place was almost silent, except for the clink of cutlery and the murmur of self-conscious conversation.

We shuffled into our seats and a sommelier presented Angus with a booklike wine list, which he began leafing through distractedly. A single red rose in a crystal vase sat between us. I wondered how many diamond rings had been whipped out at this very table. I now wished I'd picked a busy East Village bistro for our dinner. We could have done with the bustle of strangers to lift our mood.

Tired from two days of sightseeing, we had spent Angus's last afternoon wandering in and out of shops again—both silently aware the hours were ticking before he had to leave. Now it felt like we'd spent the whole weekend trying not to be irritated by each other, rather than savoring our precious moments together. Our increasingly obvious uncertainty about the future had lingered between us, unmentioned. I'd even begun to wonder if my mishap with Deklin had been such a mistake after all.

The inevitable "what the fuck are we doing?" conversation finally began over the main course. But when I spoke the words, I still felt like they'd come from nowhere and regretted them.

"So, do you think we should be worried that after almost two years of going out with each other, at our age, we have no idea if we want to get married?"

Angus put down his fork and ran his hand through his hair. The creases around his gray-green eyes seemed to deepen. For the first time since he'd arrived, I suddenly saw him as my confidant again.

"You want the truth?" he said. "It seems you've . . . we've both found it very easy to live without each other for a month. And I admit it has been quite tough being in each other's company again for twenty-four hours a day." He paused. "But if you want me to tell you what I think that means, Bridge, I honestly don't know."

I looked down at my roast duck confit with truffle honey and fennel pollen pan sauce and my appetite evaporated. Once we had enjoyed these kinds of conversations—analyzing and discussing our big life dilemmas. But now the topic felt evil and raw.

"But you've missed me, right?" I said.

"Have you honestly missed me?"

I glanced back across the river to Manhattan.

"Yes of course I have, I mean obviously I have . . . "

"But . . ." he said.

A waiter sidled over to refill our glasses and Angus waved him away.

"I dunno, it seems like this past month . . . so many things have happened. Getting used to a new city and everything."

Then the adrenaline of honesty took over.

"Maybe I haven't missed you as much as I should have."

Angus dipped his head and took a swig of his wine.

"Truth is, Bridge, I've been pretty busy too, and probably haven't missed you as much as I could have."

"Oh."

"But it's not about that." His voice turned gentle. "It's about how you imagine a future for yourself that may actually make you happy."

I looked back across the black water to the bright façade of Manhattan again and imagined all the adventures that might be waiting for me there. More madcap news stories at the *Post*, other sexy strangers at other costume parties, afternoons drinking American cocktails with Jack and Mike. A scary thrill welled up in me.

Across the table from me was a life of safety and stability, a destination I felt I could predict. Out there was a gamble, a risk. But just how big a risk? I had no idea.

The next words came out before I'd realized I would say them.

"I want to see if I can stay on in New York after my four months is up. I want to know I really lived in this city."

Angus didn't flinch, he pushed back his plate and picked up the wine bottle and carefully refilled our glasses with the 1996 Pinot Noir he had chosen.

"Then I think you've answered our questions about us," he said.

And then I knew my world had turned on its head.

No, no, I wanted to shout, *I take that back! I'm not actually sure! I don't know what I'm saying!* But it was too late.

"You know, Bridge, I just don't want to be with someone any longer who's always got their eye on something else," he said.

Now silence gaped between us as we both tried to take our words on board. I felt sick.

"So . . . bearing in mind that breaking up is always a bitch," he said eventually. "Maybe we should at least think about executing that while you are still away."

"I guess it would be sensible to get used to that while there's no chance of us bumping into each other at the weekend at parties," I replied. Oh God. I was losing my future husband and I was talking about parties?

Now all our moments together began rushing through my mind. The night we had first shared a bed together—a mattress on the floor at a mate's place after a costume party (ironically enough). The first time I had gone to his father's home in Gloucestershire and we'd sat on a stone bench in his garden talking about our families, suddenly noticing it had got dark and the lights on in the house made it look like an enchanted castle. Another weekend there when I'd left him getting in logs to make a fire and had taken his old BMW to buy milk and cigarettes at the garage and had been furious at the way the check-out girl dithered because it delayed my getting back to him. The many times I had imagined the day I would go into labor with his baby and he'd be there telling me to breathe.

Now he put his hand over mine on the table. I blinked back tears and his own streamed down his cheeks. The waiter came to remove our barely touched entrees. We ignored him, while he tried to ignore us.

Angus asked for the bill, and I tried to fight the panic as I realized time was still moving forward indifferently, and in a few hours he would be leaving for London. The waiter took my debit card quickly, clearly hoping the sobbing couple who was putting a damper on the night would hurry up and push off.

We waited for a taxi by a gas heater in the restaurant's empty summer patio. He held me tightly as my body heaved with suppressed tears. But he didn't suggest that we reconsider.

A few hours of shallow, miserable sleep in the apartment later, my alarm went off at 5 A.M., and he got out of bed quickly and put on his clothes. I heard him brushing his teeth in the bathroom and wondered if this would be the last time I'd ever witness him doing this.

When he was ready to go, I got up and walked with him to the elevator on my floor, looking at the brown-and-yellow striped carpet all the way. He kissed the top of my head.

"I'll ring you tonight when I get back," he said. Then the elevator pinged, he stepped inside, the doors closed again, and he was gone.

I went back to bed and lay in the silvery light of the New York dawn, staring at the ceiling. My head swam with vertigo. Had I just made the most liberating—and mature—decision of my life? Or had I just lost with the ping of an elevator the greatest boyfriend, future husband, father of my children I could ever have had?

So, what brings you here tonight?

....

"Tilly, it's me, Bridge. How's it going?"

Angus had departed less than a miserable week before. I had woken way before my shift was due to start at the *Post*, and I needed to hear a comforting voice.

"Hey," came my old friend's reply. "That's so weird. I was going to call you. I've got some news."

"Oh, yeah?" I'd been hoping the conversation could be all about me.

"I'm pregnant. With twins! Can you believe it!"

What? Pregnant? *Tilly?* The vertigo I felt when Angus left now returned as I struggled to focus on her news.

"Shit, Tils, um, that's amazing . . . "

The worst thing about friends telling you they were pregnant was trying not to sound the way they expected you to sound—envious, disorientated, and strangely betrayed. And for some reason I was.

Tilly and I had been friends since university, and we'd lived together at my place in London for the past three years. She and her boyfriend Andrew, her former boss at a TV production company, had started seeing each other the same month that Angus and I had got together. She'd only just agreed to buy a house with Andrew. She'd always promised she was in no hurry to move to the "next stage."

"My pill fucked up, it was an accident. But now it's happened, we're actually unbelievably excited. Can you imagine, Bridge, I'm going to be huge."

"Wow, congratulations, really."

"I want you to be godmother. You're the only person I know whose family actually goes to church. When are you coming home?"

"Uh, soon." I didn't feel like mentioning that I was thinking of trying to stay on in New York.

"Hey, I forgot. Didn't Ang just fly out to visit you? Did you guys have a good time? Do give him my love and tell him the news."

"Yes, yes, I will." Tears began to fall down my cheeks again, but they weren't for Angus this time or over Tilly's babies. It suddenly felt like our lives would never be the same again. A lot could happen in four months when you were hitting thirty.

"Tilly, I gotta go. Let's speak soon. Don't drink, okay?" I suddenly felt desperate for a vodka and tonic myself.

I put the phone down. Fuck it. So what if it was only eight in the morning? I went to the freezer and took out a bottle of Stoli and slowly poured a measure in a glass. Then I filled it with flat tonic from the fridge and drank it in one go. So everyone else was moving on. I would move to AA.

Three hours later, I stood swaying on the concourse outside work, craning my neck to look upwards from the base of 1211 Avenue of the Americas. The vertical stripes of concrete and glass zoomed up like rail tracks to the bright blue spring sky high above. I felt decidedly ropey now, no thanks to my vodka breakfast. But, I sternly reminded myself, I was still lucky enough to be living in New York.

For the past seven days I had tried not to think too hard about the long-term implications of Angus's departure—nor the list of New York pros and cons I'd made in Jamaica. "*Lose everything and end up lonely spinster with cats???*"

Yes, best forget that. After all, I was now a reporter for the *New York Post*. It was 11:10 A.M., and up there, ten stories high, in the left-hand corner of the building, the morning meeting was taking place, the time when the editors or deputies of each section—news, photo, sports, features, business, Page Six, TV—presented their lists of the stories that were panning out that day.

I had passed Jack, the guy from Business, on his way there, and I'd flashed him a smile, thinking of our friendly encounter on Broadway. It was the only positive thing to have happened that sad weekend, and I hoped Jack and I could become new mates. But this morning he'd barely registered me.

New Yorkers were a tricky lot to work out, I decided. They could be amazingly friendly and welcoming, but once they were onto the next thing, they seemed to forget they'd ever met you. But then Jack probably had his head full of the day's fresh news.

The morning meeting was the time when the editors got their first impressions of what the following day's *Post* would contain. Meanwhile, as a news reporter, I got up each morning with the exciting feeling that I had absolutely no idea where I would be by the end of the day. Which was fitting, as I had no idea where my head was either.

I ran my fingers over the laminated surface of my new green press pass that hung around my neck.

"Police Department, City of New York. Working Press," it read. "Bridget Harrison, *New York Post,* is entitled to pass police and fire lines wherever formed." So what if Tilly was having twins? She didn't have one of these.

"Bridget. Light! If I don't get some nicotine inside me, I'm going to literally throttle someone." I jumped to see Paula, a manic Ohioan who worked on Page Six, tossing her streaked, blonde, blown-out hair off one raccoon fur–swathed shoulder. She seemed to have a wardrobe crammed with such unusual work accessories—as well as hundreds of pairs of vintage shoes bought on eBay. Most mornings, in fact, Paula swept through the office like she was heading to the front row of a Versace show—unless she was hungover, and then she staggered in with a hoodie over her head, looking like she'd slept the night in a dumpster.

"You've only been in work an hour. Surely things can't be that bad." I handed her my Union Jack lighter. She fired up a Marlboro Light.

"No shit, I tell you, if I get one more call from Paris Hilton's flack bitching about this item we're going to run, I'm going to go to her office in person and ram my phone down her throat. Half of Lotus called us to say she's dancing on the table and flashing her cooter.

Then her flack tried to tell me she was, and I quote, 'wearing her G-string backwards, Paula.' What, like she wanted a cooter wedgie or something? I mean, gross."

"So Paris has a reputation for dancing with no knickers on, right?" I had already caught the New York bug of being obsessed with socialites and celebrities whom I had scarcely given a thought to back home. Reading Page Six was so contagious you'd need antibiotics to come off it. It was the reason why most Manhattanites bought the *Post*.

Paula shrugged. "What makes me so mad is that Paris only does it to get attention, and then she has the nerve to start complaining about being written about."

"That does seem a bit rich," I said.

"No kidding. FYI, Page Six helped put that girl on the map. Anyway, what's up with you? Didn't you just have your boyfriend over?"

"Sort of. He did come over, but now he's gone again and he's not my boyfriend anymore."

"That sucks," said Paula.

"Yeah," I said. "And my best friend is having twins."

"Now that would really suck." She exhaled some smoke in a flourish and waved it away with a manicured hand. Then she noticed my glum expression.

"You know, there's no point in having a long-distance relationship with anyone. Just forget about him. You're in New York now, honey. It's a whole crazy singles playground out here."

Which didn't sound comforting at all.

"So what are you up to later?" I chanced, desperate to stay busy. Even Olly was probably getting sick of me by now.

Page Six was deluged with invitations to film premieres, product launches in department stores, shop openings, book previews, charity galas—a never-ending round of PR–driven socializing which was all aimed at getting media coverage—and the greatest prize was a mention in Page Six.

Each evening Paula, her cogossiper Chris Wilson, and their legendary boss Richard Johnson would divvy up who would go where, depending on the likelihood of celebrities or good contacts turning up. If a guest list for a party was flexible—which it usually was for Paula—she might take me along, usually at precisely one minute's notice.

"You got plans?" she'd say, stopping at my terminal on her way out in a mask of foundation and eye shadow.

"Um, not really," I would reply.

"Okay, come with me to Henri Bendel," she might say. "There's a Fendi autumn collection launch, and then a party for *Glamour* magazine afterward with awesome goodie bags. I've got makeup in my drawer. We have to go now."

But this evening Paula's schedule was already packed.

"I've got drinks at six in Langan's with Ken Sunshine, Ben Affleck's flack, followed by dinner in Nobu with Monica Lewinsky, and then it's the season premiere of *The Sopranos*. Hon, I'd take you, but Richard and Chris are both coming, and the rep at HBO is freaking over numbers."

"No worries," I said as we turned to head back into the office. "Guess I'll have a quiet night in."

A quiet night in? No way. This wasn't what I had sacrificed a potential husband for, I told myself as I sat on the sofa in my apartment later that evening, wearing my coat in front of the switched-off TV. The microwave clock said 19:43. All I needed was the courage to get up and go.

On my way home from the office, I'd remembered that Wednesday was the evening Jodi tended bar in her neighborhood Park Slope watering hole, Great Lakes, and her friends often gathered there. At the fateful costume party, several people had told me I should "definitely come down some time."

Suspecting that if I stayed in another night I might start to contemplate slitting my wrists in the shower—not a good look for your employer's flat—I'd called Jodi and left a message, asking if she'd be at the bar that evening. She hadn't called back, but I decided I ought to chance it anyway.

And if I was honest, it wasn't Jodi I was after. Deklin had left me a message the previous week saying the party night had "knocked his socks off"—whatever that meant. Now maybe I could cooly swing into the bar and knock his socks off again. After all, at this moment in time distraction was key.

With the aid of my Street Planner, I worked out that Great Lakes on Fifth Avenue at First Street was probably more than forty minutes on the subway from my stop, Lincoln Center, with a change at Union Square to the N and R line. No problem. After all, in London, traipsing across town on the tube to meet friends was perfectly normal.

But to travel by subway in New York, I realized too late, you not only had to know whether you were going uptown or downtown. You also had to work out by studying the complicated subway map just which numbered or lettered train on a color-coded line was local and which was express.

Over an hour and a half later, I was still sitting on the N and R between Union Street and 4th Street in Brooklyn, cursing that I had stepped into a train that stopped at every single station possible between Union Square and west Brooklyn. By the time it crawled into Union, it was already 9:30 P.M.

"Oh well," I told myself, slapping on a bit more lipstick as I eventually climbed the subway stairs to the street. At least I knew the people I was going to meet this time.

But not quite as well as I thought I did, as it turned out.

I pushed open the door to Great Lakes to find an impressively long bar with tatty old wooden stools running its length. Then I stopped, confused. All of them were empty.

A lone couple with their backs to me were deep in conversation at the other end of the room, and the barman was definitely not Jodi, even without the blonde wig from the party.

It *was* Wednesday? Yes. Then where was everybody? I walked up to the bar feeling like a dork. But after coming all this way, I couldn't face the subway again quite yet.

Then to my relief, when the barman came down to serve me, I did recognize him from the party—he'd been wearing a black leather corset and feather boa last time.

"Hey, there," I said, not feeling as confident as I sounded. "I met you the other night at the pimps and players party. Er, I was the English girl, Bridget."

"Oh hey, yes, I remember you." He looked a bit surprised to see me—and not in a good way.

There was a pause.

"So . . . is Jodi not working tonight?" I asked.

"Jodi's sick—she got so trashed last night she said she'd hurl if she even looked at a bottle of alcohol, so I'm covering for her."

There was another pause.

"I'm Jason, by the way."

"Hey." I now sounded as unenthusiastic as he did.

He paused again, then nodded towards the couple at the other end of the bar.

"The others are down there. Well, at least Kai is, Jodi's roommate. I guess you met him the other night?"

"Oh, sure," I said, cheering up, remembering Kai as the friendly, bare-chested, half-Japanese website designer who bore a huge, sexy fish tattoo on his shoulder. I forged down the bar to greet them.

"Hey, guys, it's me, Bridget, the English girl from the party!" I said.

"Oh. Hey," said Kai. Did he also look suspiciously uncomfortable? I cursed the gods of paranoia and plowed on.

"Er, I hope I'm not intruding. Jodi said come down, so I thought I'd just pop by," I said, ignoring the fact that it was hardly a pop from the Upper West Side to Park Slope. "Fancy another drink? My round."

"No . . . you're not intruding at all," said Kai, looking distinctly like he was lying. "Actually, I'm doing good for a drink. I'm not sticking around too long. By the way, this is a friend of mine from, er, school, Melissa."

Melissa was pretty and petite, almost swallowed up in a baggy sweat top that said "Yale" in big white letters. She had the sexy, long-dark-brown-hair/blue-eyes combo I'd always envied in other women and automatically hated them for. But we shook hands and I beamed at her, vowing to stay true to my motto that it's more important to act friendly to strange girls than strange boys, even if you don't really mean it.

"Sooo," I gushed. "I met all these guys at Jodi's mad party the other day. It was amazing. I turned up like a total loser, knowing no one, and they welcomed me like a long-lost sister. You'd never get that kind of treatment in London."

"I've never been," said Melissa. "But I lived in Milan for a year, and they're pretty much the same there too, until you get to know people. And you have to speak the language. Otherwise you're totally screwed."

I pettily declined to ask if she could, even though she actually seemed very nice.

"Yeah, everyone made me feel really welcome . . . "

Why was Kai exchanging looks with Jason, who was hovering nervously behind the bar? I stumbled on. "Jodi, Kai, Jason, Dek—"

"Hey, how about a round of shots!" said Kai, leaping off his bar stool as if he'd just been hit with an electric cattle prod.

"Jager? Tequila? Jas, what you got for us?"

"Shots? Are you kidding me? I thought you were taking off," said Melissa.

"Well, I just remembered, we have to drink to Jodi's health—as long as we don't end up in the same state she's in," he said.

Jason began lining up glasses with great show and filling them with Jagermeister while Melissa and I looked on reluctantly.

"Yeah, anyway, I wish I'd made it to that party," she said.

"Well, there'll be plenty more," said Kai. "I tell you, Melissa's the shot queen. There was this time once in school when she drank an entire roomful of frat boys under the table. Mel, you should tell Bridget that story."

"Jesus, Kai," she replied, turning back to me, rolling her eyes. "Anyway, I missed the party last week because I was in Maine, but Deklin said it was a blast."

"Deklin?" I said.

"Yeah, my boyfriend. Maybe you didn't meet him. He's an illustrator."

Boyfriend? My eyebrows shot to my forehead before I could stop them. I glanced at Kai and Jason, who were focusing very hard on measuring out the shots. Now I got it. They'd all seen me all over Deklin that night—and they didn't know the half of it. I felt like the biggest slapper in the universe.

Melissa looked at me expectantly.

"Um, Deklin . . . let me think. Yes, I think I did get introduced. He was dressed as a Venice Beach pimp, right, or something?" I tried to keep my voice the same pitch. "He had a great costume."

"Actually, I didn't see it. We had a fight. He was supposed to come with me to Maine. I was visiting my sick grandmother."

Oh, no. Oh God. So I'd as good as shagged her man while she was tending the dying.

"Um, I'm sorry to hear that."

Silence descended and I became desperate not to appear suspicious.

"Well, actually everyone at the party had great costumes. You know, people really put in a lot of effort, wearing wigs, sticking sequins on their bodies, sewing things . . ." What was I saying?

"C'mon then, girls, throw them down. Here's to Jodi," said Kai like an angel of mercy.

"To Jodi," I mumbled.

At that moment the bar door opened again. We all looked around. Deklin was standing in the doorway. Oh, great. Fucking fantastic. Maybe I could crawl to the ladies loos and drown myself in the toilet bowl.

Melissa leaped off her chair and ran to him. Jason, Kai, and I all studied our empty shot glasses. I wished I could order Jason to pour me out ten more.

Deklin walked towards us with Melissa's hand clamped to the waistband of his jeans. I forced my mouth into a smile. Our eyes met for a moment before he looked away, giving me a sheepish half-grin. I saw the sexy gap in his snow white teeth and felt like punching them out.

"Hey, guys. Wassup?" he said lightly.

"Hey," we all replied quickly in unison.

"Dek, this is Bridget. She's from the UK. I guess you guys met the other night?"

"Hey, Dek," I said evenly. "I think I remember you. The Venice Beach pimp, right?"

"The girl in the red dress," he said.

"Yes, that was me."

"Good to see you again."

"Likewise."

We all stood there.

"So, what brings you down here tonight?" he said.

Because you fuckers all told me to come down, and you forgot to mention you'd be here with your girlfriend.

"Oh, you know, just avoiding a quiet night in." Why, oh why, hadn't I opted for one?

We all managed to get through another twenty minutes, making small talk while Deklin kept his arm remained fixed over Melissa's shoulders—as if to remind me not to utter some clanger.

Admittedly, I could have warned him that I was planning to make a guest appearance in Great Lakes, but he—much like me, in fact—had never let on there was someone else in the picture. Suddenly it dawned on me why he had avoided a public snogging session at the party.

Eventually, after what seemed like a lifetime of fake joviality, we decided to call it a night and all trooped out of the bar together. I bid Deklin and Melissa a cheery wave on the sidewalk and watched the two of them stroll up the same hill towards his brownstone that he and I had stumbled along gleefully less than fourteen days before.

So now in one week I had lost my own boyfriend and been slapped in the face by someone else's.

"Nice one, Bridget," I said out loud as I turned to embark on my long journey home. I had to hand it to karma.

I didn't know it yet as I sat on the subway trundling back to Manhattan, but I'd just received another key piece of training for my new future life. The ability to act with blank-faced nonchalance towards someone with whom you had been in bed days before was a regular part of being single in New York.

Decapitation—
hey, it happens all the time

....

"I need you to go to Erminia on the Upper East Side. It's one of the best restaurants in the city," said John Mancini, appearing at my desk just as I was shoving the larger half of a Wendy's chili-filled baked potato into my mouth. It hadn't taken me long to catch the no-lunch-break habit of feeding over my keyboard.

"O-kay," I mumbled, my cheeks bulging. I grabbed a pen, ready to take down his instructions.

"The owner's been decapitated, found lying in a pool of blood on the kitchen floor. They think one of the employees attacked him with a meat clever."

"Right." I nodded, munching hard, writing "meat clever" in my pad. It was now six weeks since he'd witnessed my first shaky attempt at news reporting on the Union Square platform. I was desperate to show the city editor how far I had come along.

"East 83rd Street. They found him with the meat clever on his chest and a 12–inch carving knife lying next to him. Sounds like it was some scene."

"Sure, I'll get there right away," I said, swallowing the rest of my potato almost whole and getting up, my hand automatically checking for my pager on my belt.

"Take a cab. It's a great story," he said. He flashed me his cheeky grin. "Hope I didn't put you off your lunch."

Decapitation? Hell now, why would it?

"Erminia ristorante Italiano" looked like a rustic little cottage, squashed in at the end of a row of elegant townhouses on the south side of East 83rd Street, just off Second Avenue. It had ornate curved grates on its windows, lace curtains, and ivy climbing around its wooden front door, next to which signs said "American Express" and "Proper Attire Required." Today the quaint façade was ruined by yellow NYPD crime-scene tape, which zigzagged rudely across its entrance, barring anyone from going inside. Two stocky, uniformed cops with particularly large bottoms crammed into their blue-black nylon trousers guarded the sidewalk in front of it.

I pulled my NYPD reporter's tag out over my jacket where it could be seen and strode straight up to them. This time I was going to get the scoop.

"Yes, hello, I'm from the *New York Post*. Can you tell me what's been going on here?" I said authoritatively, like Sherlock Holmes.

"Ma'am, can you please move off the sidewalk?"

"But I'm from the *New York Post*," I waved my magic "Access-All-Areas" press pass at them. "I hear there's been an—"

"Ma'am, I'm not tellin' you again. You gotta move off the sidewalk."

What was he doing? Practicing to become a nightclub bouncer?

"But I'm from the media," I said.

"This is a crime scene."

Well, I thought that was the point of my being here, I wanted to say. Five minutes into a "great story" and I was stumped again.

I retreated to the north side of the street opposite the restaurant and stood there like a lemon. What was I supposed to do now? I reached for a cigarette.

"Hey, hey, Lady Bridge, good ta see yah again!" came a voice I recognized.

Rick, the *Post* photographer I had worked with in Queens, had emerged from a dry cleaner's on the corner of Second Avenue, across the road from Erminia. Was this some happy coincidence that he happened to be dropping off a suit?

"Hey, Rick, what are you doing here?"

"Well, waddaya think? I'm here for this nutty homicide. I'm hearing the guy had his head swiped clean off."

"Oh, right, of course. Mancini didn't mention anything about a photographer."

"Are you crazy? What good is your stuff unless we got a picture? The dead guy's still inside, but I'm gonna get him when they bring him out. Some family should be turning up soon too. Word is they're driving in from Queens—Flushing, I'm hearing."

"But how do you know all this? Those guys won't tell me anything." The cops were still giving me the evil eye from across the street.

"Ah, you can't waste your time with those bozos. There's a detective around somewhere. He's the one you need to talk to. Think he just went to get coffee," said Rick, shifting the weight of the two cameras he had slung across his shoulders. "Meantime, those Chinese people in the laundry, they saw the guy they think did it leaving the restaurant this morning. You should go talk to them."

"Right, okay," I said, putting my unlit cigarette back in its box and getting out my notepad. Thank God for Rick.

I walked to the corner and entered the dry cleaner's. It was a tiny place with one small Formica counter strewn with safety pins. Behind it a tiny woman with her hair in a bun was ironing a shirt, in amongst rows of pressed clothes that hung on rails, covered in plastic wrappings.

"Hello there, I'm a reporter from the *New York Post*. I gather you know something about the murder in Erminia," I said pleasantly.

"Huh?" She jabbed a shirt sleeve with her iron and didn't look up.

"The murder in the restaurant over there." I pointed back through the window at Erminia's door. "Did you not see someone come out this morning?"

"Sorry, no understan' English," said the woman, still not pausing from butchering the creases in the shirt.

"But didn't you just speak to that man who came in, the guy with the cameras?"

What was wrong with me? Did I have "Do not talk to this loser" stamped on my forehead?

"Look, I'm from a newspaper and it's vital I get some information."

"Maybe when my husban' come back, he help you," said the woman in a way that made it sound highly doubtful that he would—and that the conversation was now terminated.

"Well, thanks anyway." My special charm was working wonders.

I made my second retreat in less than ten minutes and rejoined Rick, who was puffing merrily away on a Parliament with one eye on Erminia.

"Get what you needed?" he said.

"Um, not exactly," I said.

He pointed his cigarette up East 83rd Street in the opposite direction to the dry cleaner's.

"There's your guy. He's the detective."

A sturdy man in a beige raincoat was leaning against a black Lincoln, talking to a woman with choppy blonde hair. She wore a neat black suit with a short skirt. Her hand rested on the car next to him. They looked like couple having an office affair who'd arranged a sneaky liaison by the water cooler.

"Who's that he's talking to?"

"Michele McPhee, *Daily News* Shack reporter. Been on this beat for years. She's got the whole lot of them in her pocket. They'll tell her anything."

"Oh, great." And I couldn't even get a Chinese dry cleaner to look at me.

I contemplated striding over to get in on the conversation, but an attack of English politeness prevented me from butting into what was clearly a private tête-à-tête. I decided to wait my turn and get the information from the detective after Michele McPhee had finished.

Five minutes later they were still chatting away, and now Michele McPhee had begun scribbling industriously in her notepad, nodding with interest, presumably over every last detail of the decapitation. And I still knew nothing.

Then she shut her pad and touched the detective's sleeve in thanks. But before I could rush over, the detective got into the car and pulled off down the street.

Fuck, fuck, fuck.

Worse, Michele McPhee then turned her back to Rick and me, pulled out a cell phone and began talking into it while reading from her notepad. She was dumping the whole scoop back to her office already. This was a disaster.

When she'd finished, she sauntered over to us, tantalizingly tucking her pad back into her bag.

"Hey, guys, great story, right?" she said mildly.

I wanted to throttle her. Instead I had no option but to prostrate myself at her feet.

"Er, hi. Look, I'm Bridget, a new reporter for the *Post* from the exchange program. I don't suppose you could tell me what's going on."

She smiled. Was it false? I couldn't tell.

"I've heard about that exchange. They have you people all the time. You from Australia?"

"No, England." *Can't you tell the difference, you annoying cow?* I wanted to say.

I looked at her, my notepad poised.

"Well, there's not much to repeat. The owner got his head taken off, they think it was an employee, happened this morning around eleven thirty," she said.

Yeah, like that took twenty minutes of smooching with the cops to write down, I wanted to scream.

"Didn't the detective say *anything* else?" I said imploringly.

"Not really," she said lightly.

"Thanks," I said. For nothing, I thought.

My pager buzzed on my belt.

CALL CITY DESK WITH UPDATE, said the message. Cool, and my update was: "I've been blown off by two cops, a detective, a Chinese dry cleaner, and a *Daily News* reporter who got the scoop under my nose—and I've only been here fifteen minutes."

But before I had time to call, a blue van emblazoned with "Medical Examiner's Office" pulled up outside Erminia. To my relief, the detective's Lincoln pulled up behind it.

Rick threw down his cigarette and swung one camera off his left shoulder. And this time I didn't hesitate. I walked straight over to the car, cornering the detective as he hauled himself out of the driver's seat.

"Hi, I'm from the *Post*. Can you please just tell me what's going on?" I said, sounding like a petulant child.

"Lady, you'll have to wait," he said, trying to get past me. He was at least six-foot and solid from the neck down. He probably moon-lighted as a bouncer just like his uniformed pals.

"No, look, please, you have to understand. I'm new to this job, I'm about to get fired. You just chin-wagged with the *Daily News* for twenty minutes. You've gotta give me a break and tell me the low-down," I said. Wow, suddenly I was talking in lingo.

The detective studied me like I was a small spider flailing in his soup.

"Okay, here's what I can give you. But this is the last time I'm saying this, and it's all off-record—you got that?"

"Of course," I said, not sure exactly what that meant.

"It's the owner of the restaurant, his name is Nick Orobello, he's sixty-two. He was found this morning around 11:30 by a linen deliv-ery guy. The delivery guy came to the back entrance and knocked on the door but when there was no answer he went to get a coffee. He came back fifteen minutes later and noticed the door was ajar. He found Orobello on the floor in the kitchen. It was a pretty horrific scene. Suffice to say if you get your head taken off with a meat cleaver, there's a lot of blood."

"Do they have a suspect?" I said grandly, like I asked that kind of question all the time.

"We're looking into the kitchen porter. He was the only one sched-uled to be here this morning. Some Albanian kid. It sounds like they had argued about wages in the past. But that's only a theory at this time. As far as it officially goes, the case is still under investigation. No more than that, okay?"

"Yes, sir," I said. He seemed to like the "sir."

"Guess you don't see this kind of thing too often where you come from," he said with a flirtatious twinkle. He had fair but thinning hair and not unattractive Germanic blue eyes.

"No, sir, not so much."

His voice dropped to a conspiratorial tone.

"If you guys stick around, they'll be bringing the body bag out later and you can get some shots. And if we do pick up the perp, he'll be in the 19th Precinct. But I'm telling you now, his wife is about to arrive, and if you hassle her or try to take pictures of her, I'll have you all arrested. You got that?"

"Yes, sir, thank you."

Hurrah. Now it was my turn to call the desk.

"You know what, I once dated a broad looked just like her," said Rick a little later as we watched a middle aged woman with long, dark, tied-back hair emerge from a Town Car that had pulled up in front of Erminia. She was followed by a younger woman who resembled her wearing a denim jacket, jeans, and high heels.

"Which one, the old woman or the chick?" asked Joey—another snapper among several reporters and photographers who had gradually been gathering on the north side of East 83rd Street like vultures to a carcass.

"The old one, unfortunately," said Rick to Joey, repeating what was clearly his current obsession. "You ever tried that Match.com? I tell you, man, you scroll through photos of all these broads who look all cute and young, then you go to take them out on a date and they're more like fifty. I'm giving up on it any day now."

"So you still haven't had any luck in cyberlove then, huh?" I said as we all watched the action unfold across the street.

The older woman was now clinging onto the younger woman to steady herself. Her face was red from crying and she held her hand up to it, clutching a raggedy tissue. The two were staring towards the restaurant doorway but looked unsure as to whether they would go inside. The detective was talking to them, his head bowed in sympathy.

Joey pointed the long lens of his camera in their direction from his hip and surreptitiously clicked off a round of pictures.

"Ooh, yeah, I got that great. Tears, the lot," he said.

"Anyone for coffee?" said a photographer standing behind us. "I'm doing a run, there's a great bakery on the next block."

"Hey, how about getting me a couple of donuts. I ran out on this job without eating lunch," said Joey.

"Orders, any other orders?" said the photographer as if he was going to fetch beers at a ball game.

He returned with a tray and we gathered around, diving in.

"Man, you can't beat a job on the Upper East Side. They don't make donuts like this in the South Bronx," said Rick happily.

I emptied a packet of sugar into my coffee, then looked back towards the miserable gathering outside Erminia. I was suddenly struck by how surreal the situation was. On one side of East 83rd Street, we were acting like we were on one big jolly picnic. On the other, a family's world had just fallen apart.

"Heads up, here it comes," called a photographer, chucking his donut as two suited detectives and two men in medical examiner's jackets emerged from the restaurant and went to open the back of the ME van. The pack of photographers and cameramen surged forward with their lenses up.

The two ME guys went back inside the restaurant and then reappeared, carefully carrying a trolley-like stretcher up the steps of the restaurant. On top of it, a white plastic sack the length of a man was strapped down, wider in the middle and tapering off towards one end. At the top of the steps, the men placed it carefully down and wheeled it towards the van.

A strange hush descended, leaving only the sound of the cameras clicking in time with their flashes.

The wife stood motionless while the younger woman held onto her arm. She looked at the stretcher for a second before turning away, tears soaking her face. The detective stood between them and the ME van, as if it was his futile duty to protect them from the horror that had already happened.

"D'you think the head's coming out separately?" said one reporter, standing behind me. "I heard it came clean off."

I'd arrived outside Erminia shortly after 2 P.M. By 6:30 P.M. the body had gone, as had the family—without anyone getting near them. I had dumped my notes—the details I'd got from the detective and some other tidbits reporters had shared. Even Michele McPhee had warmed up over the afternoon and had confided to me that some kitchen staff had complained recently over a pay dispute. I felt bad that I'd thought evil things about her. I'd also tried the Chinese dry cleaner's again and

got the same fuck-off response, then trawled all the shops on Second
Avenue, some of whose owners knew Orobello. They described him as
"a gentleman" and someone "without a mean bone in his body." I assumed I was done at that point. Oh, how little I knew the *Post*.

"You still outside the restaurant?" said Mancini when I called him
to see if I could go home.

"Yes, I'm just round the corner on a pay phone."

"Great. Head back there. Get people's reactions when they turn up
for dinner."

"Huh?" Was he having a laugh?

"Erminia's a great restaurant, one of the best in the city. I bet quite a
few people had reservations, and I doubt the staff had time to cancel
them. But it's unlikely the kitchen will be open tonight. They've got
some scrubbing to do first."

I put down the receiver and placed my head against my hand on the
top of the metal phone. Gad, no, please. I couldn't face it. I just wanted
to go home. Then I took a deep breath and picked up my notepad.

Another hour went by. Dinner time, I reckoned, would begin at
7:30 P.M., so I stood around smoking cigarettes, chatting to a young,
serious reporter from the *New York Times* who wore a blue cable-knit
sweater and jotted tiny, neat notes in his pad like he was fathoming
long equations. Not like my maniacal scrawl. Several camera crews
stuck around too, preparing to do live feeds in front of the restaurant
for the evening news.

I spotted two potential diners from fifty yards away, crossing
Second Avenue diagonally down towards the south side of East 83rd
and holding hands. They were in their thirties. He was wearing a cashmere coat and preppy loafers. She had porcelain skin and pale blonde
hair that wisped prettily on her shoulders. They looked set for a romantic night out in a cozy Italian eatery.

I darted across the street towards them, followed by the *Times* reporter, and cornered them just as they turned onto East 83rd.

"Hi there. Just wondering if you had dinner reservations at Erminia
tonight?" I said, sounding like an overzealous maitre d' who'd decided
to greet guests halfway down the block.

"Yes, we do," the man said, taken aback as we blocked their path.

"I'm afraid Erminia's closed. There's been an . . . incident." I said.

"What's happened?" said the guy, suddenly taking in the rabble of camera crews patrolling outside the restaurant.

"Well . . ." I stammered. Sometime soon I was going to have to get better at this.

"There's been a homicide. The owner was killed in the kitchen this morning," said the *Times* reporter.

The woman gasped, putting her hands to her face.

"Oh my God, that's terrible," the guy said, putting his arm around her protectively. "This was one of our favorite places to eat."

I scribbled his quote in my pad.

"Yeah, it was a pretty bad scene. He was decapitated, so it's taking some clearing up," said the *Times* reporter.

"Well, did they get the guy who did it?" The man looked around as if someone were about to leap out from the proverbial bushes on Second Avenue.

"They've got a good idea," I said. I took their names.

"Well, honey? Should we call Primavera? It's still early, we might still snag a table there," said the woman, reaching in her bag for her phone.

"Good idea," said the guy. And off they went. No point in letting a grisly murder stop you from tucking into a $100-a-head dinner on the Upper East Side.

Next I spotted a portly man in a gray flannel suit heading purposely towards our corner. I suddenly had a nose for these people. I stood politely blocking his path and asked him if he was heading for the restaurant.

"Yes, excuse me, I'm late. The owner is my cousin, can I help you?" he said impatiently.

It was as if the word *cousin* had been megaphoned down the block.

Two TV crews came running over, female TV reporters wielding microphones with their cameramen in tow. Another three spotted the action and rushed over too.

"Please, what is this? What's going on?" He was now surrounded.

"You've heard the news—about Mr. Orobello?" I said.

"What news? Really, I'm in a hurry. I'm late for a meeting with him right now." He looked frustrated, and his path was still blocked.

I swallowed hard. I was about to change this man's life forever and he didn't even know me.

"I'm afraid Mr. Orobello's been killed. It happened this morning," I said. "I'm really very sorry."

Like hunters who'd snared their prey, the cameramen flicked on their lights, beaming them in his face. He put up his hand to shade his eyes.

"I . . . I don't understand. I only spoke to him this morning." The circle tightened. This was great TV news in the making.

"Sir, can you give us your name?" ordered a reporter from Fox News.

"I'm his cousin . . ." he said, trailing off. His confusion was now turning to panic as he computed that such a gathering of the media proved this was no joke.

One reporter shoved out her microphone and switched to a sugary TV tone—"And tell us, you are Mr. Orbello's cousin, what did this man mean to you?"

Tears welled up in the man's eyes and he reached his hands out towards the restaurant.

"Please, please . . . I have to find my family. I have to find out what's going on." He broke through and stumbled away from us.

Like a school of fish with a collective conscience, we all turned to follow him, then stalled in a moment of self-awareness. If one went, we'd all have to go.

"Better give the guy a break," said someone.

"This is awful," I said.

It had turned into a chilly night by the time I got back to Avenue of the Americas. Mancini had told me I'd done a good job and could head on home, but I'd left my keys on my desk in my hurry to get out the door earlier—which seemed like a lifetime ago.

Although I'd covered quite a few fatal incidents by now, this was the first time I'd been present when the bad news had been broken to a victim's loved one, let alone had to do it myself. I wondered what the Orobello family were doing now. Was it left to them to clean it all up?

Deep in grim thoughts, I trudged across the 1211 concourse, then suddenly spotted Jack. He was standing by a pillar, smoking a cigarette and reading a page proof. Despite my early hopes of making him my new work buddy, I'd hardly seen him over the past couple of weeks. I'd been out on stories most days, and whenever I passed him on the tenth floor he looked too preoccupied to approach.

In no mood to be ignored tonight, I pretended I hadn't seen him and tried to stride past him into the lobby. But he noticed me first.

"You're here late," he said.

"Just back from a story." I stopped. "You haven't got a spare cigarette have you?"

"Sure." He offered me a Camel Light from his packet and cupped his hands to light it for me. After the emotion of the day—and the past two weeks—the brief kind gesture suddenly made me want to burst into tears.

"You okay?" he said.

"I've been on this really sad story, a guy got murdered in his restaurant. I ended up breaking the news to his cousin who turned up for a meeting with him and didn't know about it . . ." I exhaled deeply. "The whole media pack was around him and none of us cared. Fuck, I felt crass."

He looked at me kindly. I noticed his blue eyes again—and the same strange twinkle that I'd seen on Broadway.

"Well, I'm sure he would rather have heard it from you than any of those Rottweilers on the beat," he said.

"But it was really awful. How do you get used to that kind of thing?"

"Death knocks—I guess the thing is never to get used to them. If you do, that's when you know you're jaded."

"I suppose." Suddenly I had an overwhelming desire to ask him to give me a hug.

"Look at it this way," he said. "You'll wake up tomorrow and you'll go on another story, and you'll get just as absorbed in that one. Caring is what makes a great reporter."

He paused. "And from what I've been hearing, you've been doing a great job since you came over."

"Really?" I had been doing a great job? Me? For the second time, I also felt oddly pleased that he seemed to know all about me.

"Yes, really." He smiled. "And just remember, you work for the greatest newspaper there is, in the greatest city in the world. Getting out on the street and witnessing life, that's what it's all about. No point in being stuck in the office all the time, like me."

He did look pretty washed-out.

"Actually, I'd better get back in," he said, chucking his cigarette. "We're still closing our section."

"Thanks for the smoke," I said.

"Any time." He turned and swung back through the revolving doors.

I watched the back of his suit as he headed towards the elevators. I already found myself wanting to catch him alone again.

Good-bye, Shepherd's Bush . . .
Hello, East Village

Apocryphal tales and too much TV lead us to believe that big life changes happen in one huge moment of drama: the morning you dump your husband's fried eggs in his lap and announce you're eloping with the pool cleaner. The day you suddenly chuck in your 7 A.M.–start office job to do tantric yoga in India. The one time you look down at a pregnancy test and there are two pink lines instead of one.

But in reality life is more likely to change course through a sequence of small epiphanies. A chain reaction of events—some prompted, some out of the blue—which gradually nudge you down a new path.

The sequence which took me from a four-month "last hurrah" in New York to becoming its newest English transplant began that night in the River Café when Angus and my faint indecision about each other suddenly precipitated the end of "us" altogether.

The next nudge came shortly before the end of my stint as a *Post* exchangee, when the editor, Xana Antunes, called me into her office and said she'd heard I wanted a permanent job at the paper.

Xana was a smart, instinctive Scot who'd earned Rupert Murdoch's respect and ear while turning the *Post*'s business section into a must-read on Wall Street. Promoted to editor in her mid-thirties, the attractive, soft-spoken woman had been considered an unusual choice compared to Murdoch's other bullish tabloid greats, like former *Sun* editor Kelvin MacKenzie and Australia's Daily and Sunday *Telegraph* editor-in-chief Col Allan—who would later take over at the *Post*.

But Xana had been tasked with dragging the inky, ragtag *Post* into the twenty-first century—revamping sections to make it easier to navigate and, crucially, making it more appealing to women. Millions were being invested in state-of-the-art, color printing presses based in a massive new plant in Hunts Point in the South Bronx. The aim was to fire up the paper with brilliant color pictures; luscious, money-making, ad-filled supplements; and juicy female-oriented features pages—a strategy that had already helped the *Daily Mail* pull ahead of the competition in the UK. The entire look and feel of the 200-year-old tabloid—which was as famous for leaving its readers' hands covered in black smudges as it was for its screaming, punned headlines—was about to be transformed.

I think Xana—who'd first moved to New York to set up the *Evening Standard*'s Wall Street bureau—saw a little of a kindred spirit in me. A British woman who'd fallen in love with the exhilarating whirl of New York news and who was crazy enough to stick up a finger at settling down back at home.

"So you really want to give up your life in London and move to New York at your age?" she said from behind her huge desk as I dawdled respectfully in the doorway of her glass-walled office. As usual, she was sucking a lollipop gleaned from the tenth floor's candy basket outside Anne Aquilina's office, which was restocked every hour to stamp out any attempts at healthy living in the office.

"Look, I know half the people who come here on the exchange say they don't want to leave," I said. "But I'm absolutely serious. There's nothing I want more than a permanent job on this paper."

Why I was actually saying this now, I wasn't entirely sure. I'd just returned from a hellish morning spent skulking around the burns unit of New York Presbyterian Hospital, wondering why anyone would want a job on any prying tabloid.

That day we'd been tipped off that the author Kurt Vonnegut had been rushed for treatment after setting fire to himself and his East Side apartment with a cigarette. After getting past the hospital security guards by using my best disguise—my English accent—I'd suddenly arrived in the hushed, spooky ward where the only sounds came from the peeping of ECGs and the murmur of stricken relatives at bedsides.

So what was I going to do now, I'd wondered? Storm up to a blistered, near-dead version of the famous writer for a cozy bedside chat?

Still, I'd gingerly poked my nose behind several curtains, hoping to come across what was left of him—until a matronly African-American nurse had marched over and asked me what the hell I thought I was doing.

Rules at the *Post* were that we had to identify ourselves if we were challenged outright in a hospital. So I told her—as if it was the most normal thing in the world—that I was from the *Post* and was just popping by to see Mr. Vonnegut because we were all "big fans" back in the office.

"He's gonna make it," she had replied curtly. Then she'd had security throw me out.

But now, safely back in Xana's doorway, I watched her cheerfully swiveling in her chair to admire her beloved Midtown out of her office window, and I felt both desperate not to let her down and completely inspired by her.

I realized that from the moment I had arrived in New York, I had found it a blessed relief to be away from the claustrophobic rush to nest back home. In London it had felt like the dreaded 3–0 was as good as stepping one foot into middle age. Here in single, too-busy-to-settle-down New York, being thirty was practically considered as youthful as being twenty-one—after all, there was always Botox.

In London I'd fretted about where I should be in my career . . . in fact, in my entire life. Here (despite more screwups than the City Desk knew about) I got up each morning feeling that if I tried hard enough, anything was possible. Not that I had any big plans to be editor of the *Post* one day. Getting to be Lois Lane for a little bit longer was enough for me.

"Stuart and John tell me you've been great since you arrived here, and enthusiasm is indispensable at this paper," said Xana with a wave of her lolly. "And with all the changes coming up, I think your experience of British newspapers would come in very useful here. I just wanted to let you know that if something does come up, I'll see what I can do."

And that was that. The ball was in motion.

Another less pleasant nudge came later that week when I woke up in the corporate apartment on Eleventh Avenue, glued to my sheets in horror after a nightmare that I'd arrived home at Angus's flat in Kentish Town to find him making French toast for a new girlfriend.

As soon as I could move again after the trauma, I'd looked at my clock. It was 5 A.M.—10 A.M. in London—so I'd leaped out of bed and dialed his mobile.

"Hey, it's me," I'd said, not comforted by his slightly impatient hello. "Sorry to call, but I just had this horrible nightmare that you had a new girlfriend and I came back and you were making French toast with her in your kitchen," I'd stammered.

I could almost hear him rolling his eyes.

"Well, I don't have a new girlfriend, so don't worry about it. And I can't stand French toast," he'd said flatly.

"But am I totally mad to be trying to stay in New York? Am I making some terrible life mistake?" I'd wailed.

There was a silence—as if in the emptiness he'd said: "I'm not sure if this is actually my problem anymore."

"Babe, it's your call, not mine." He paused again. "But as far as you and I are concerned, we've already made that decision, remember?"

Oh, yes. A lot had happened since I made my little list on that Jamaica beach. I was already on the path of no return. One which I now just had to pray wouldn't end up in lonely spinsterhood—or involve cats.

I arrived home in London from the exchange in early June. Thanks to Xana, the offer of a job back at the *Post*—and the precious gift of a three-year L1 work visa with it—materialized shortly after. And this time around it was too late to start having doubts.

The summer then passed in a whirlwind. I formally gave notice from the features department at the *Times*. Sandra, my editor, and Gill, her secretary, raised their eyebrows at my decision but—like my resigned parents—took the attitude that if I was desperate enough to go back to New York, I was doing the right thing (and hopefully I would come back soon).

I found new tenants to live in my house in Shepherd's Bush. Tilly was now blissfully ensconced in her own heavily mortgaged terraced house in North London with Andrew—and growing steadily more huge with her twins. My other housemate, Kathryn, was a rising star at Channel Four and was also buying her own terraced cottage in London near the Harrow Road. I calmed my nerves over the fact that my life was now hurtling in a whole different direction by hosting endless "last" sessions in the pub.

As it turned out, Angus and I spent more time together than expected over the summer, due to the gang of mutual mates we still shared. As our breakup had been so ridiculously practical, we made a huge effort to be "great friends." We even fell into bed together on occasions. But we never forgot that I was going again. For how long this time, I didn't know.

Three days before the morning of my flight back to New York, Angus booked us a good-bye weekend in the plush Somerset country house retreat, Babington House. In a giant four-poster bed on our last morning, he presented me with a leather-bound photo album which he had filled with photos of us and our friends, depicting our two years together. Paris, Italy, Cap Ferrat, Jamaica, a cricket match at his dad's estate, the day trip to visit my parents on a barging holiday. In the front of the album was a hand-written message which said: "Angus and Bridget 1998–2000. I will always love you. Angus xxx." I cried until I could no longer breathe. He held me tightly, suitably touched by my response.

Then my time in London ran out—and before I could think about it anymore, I was back in Brooklyn again, ringing on the doorbell of Olly's railroad apartment in East Williamsburg on a steamy September night. I was clutching a bottle of Jameson—a present in return for his letting me sleep on his sofa while I hunted for an apartment. I intended to down the whole lot myself.

Part Two

Single on Sundays

A rabbit hutch with a view

"Excuse the dog. He's kinda sick, but he usually makes it to the poop tray," said the girl with purple hair. She stood in an old apartment building on Malcolm X Avenue in Harlem, holding a bowl of Fruit Loops covered in M&Ms.

I looked downwards and gingerly stepped over a motionless hound that could have passed for a sewer mop—in appearance and aroma—and followed her into, well, a cave.

"There's no window, as the apartment backs onto the inside well of the building. But that makes it real quiet, which is a good thing because there's some pretty crazy people livin' in this place," she said as I peered into a dingy bedroom smaller than the average prison cell. Most of the space was taken up with an enormous, blue, square water bed. I cautiously planted my bum on a corner and the bed rippled like an overweight belly in need of a stapling.

"The last guy left it, and it's real comfortable, I heard," she said, taking another spoonful of milk coated M&Ms while I tried not to hurl.

I'd been warned that apartment hunting in New York was akin to having your energy, money, and domestic aspirations sucked out of you by a swarm of vampire bats. But having to pay $800 a month to tread in dog shit, sleep on a cube of cellulite, and cohabit with someone who had the eating habits of an unsupervised five-year-old was surely taking the piss?

Or perhaps not.

"This one's in an awesome neighborhood. Totally up and coming," said Jed, a suspiciously bouncy real estate broker, as he led me into a dank building on Stanton Street just south of Houston Street that reeked of boiled cabbage. Great, my prospective neighbors had similar culinary abilities to me.

Five-B was a railroad apartment (named that because the rooms linked from one to another in a row) that was so small, "rail car" would have been a better description. The walls were open brick, which did work in its favor—and were in fact the only thing that worked in its favor. The bedroom, "sitting area," and kitchen were one long, narrow cell divided by sliding doors. If you bent over in the bathroom, you'd give yourself a frontal lobotomy with the sink.

"Great, right?" said Jed, turning on all the lights to battle the gloom.

A slow, ominous whoosh noise reverberated down from the ceiling above us. It sounded like a dead body was being dragged across the floor. We both looked up, alarmed.

"Neighbors!" Jed shrugged. "Everyone's got them in New York. This place is $1,800, plus one month's rent broker fee and a month deposit. And I'm tellin' you, that's a steal."

So that was $5,400 up-front to live in a moldy hovel underneath a murderer in the Lower East Side. And to think I'd ever been rude about the soulless yet comparatively palatial *Post* corporate apartment on the Upper West Side. That, alas, was reserved for exchanges—and I was about to be *Post* staff!

Indeed, as I spent my first week in Manhattan searching for a place to live before I returned to work, I was quickly seeing for myself the reason why few people entertain at home in the city. It's well known in New York that you can be friends with someone for years without ever sitting down at their dining room table—and that's probably because they don't have one.

Thanks to endless stingy apartments built for immigrants—and the fact that the island of Manhattan has a finite amount of space—even the city's chicest residents bed down in exorbitantly expensive rabbit hutches.

I was already resigned to spending half my monthly income on renting a place one twentieth the size of my house in Shepherd's Bush, but I still couldn't bear to give up the fantasy that in New York I'd live somewhere a little bit cool. What if someone from England wanted to come and stay?

"Forget Manhattan, live in Brooklyn," Olly and Paula (still Queen of Page Six) both advised me during my first week back. Indeed, Olly's narrow railroad apartment felt vast compared to the rip-off apartments I'd seen—and he only paid $1100. But East Williamsburg was still a bit of an urban war zone late at night, he admitted. Meanwhile Paula paid $1300 for a spacious, sunny, top-floor apartment in Cobble Hill, one of a strip of neighborhoods that ran from Brooklyn Heights to Park Slope and that were rapidly being gentrified.

Days after I arrived back, Paula summoned me to her place, saying she had a bag of clothes she was about to give to charity. Having a passion for hand-me-downs because they saved me from my own lack of style and taste, I went over like a shot.

Before knocking on her door I had a quick peruse of her patch. Cobble Hill and neighboring Carroll Gardens consisted of leafy streets lined with brownstones off the two main drags, Court Street and Smith Street, which boasted an array of new trendy ethnic eateries, funky bars, and old-style ale houses. Everywhere, young professionals sauntered around looking like they would burst with smugness at their fabulous neighborhood. And the F train meant it took less than fifteen minutes to get to Manhattan. I was almost won over.

But later as I rummaged through Paula's stack of castoffs—an outrageous Diane von Furstenberg pink snake print vest, two pairs of Juicy Couture cords that were annoyingly too small, and a host of heartmeltingly soft Alice + Oliver cashmere—I spotted the twin towers of the World Trade Center out of her window in the distance. They just seemed too far away.

"To afford to live in Manhattan, you have to have roommates. And I don't know about you, but I just could not cohabit with someone again—yes, that sweater's a definite, it looks amazing on you," said Paula, sprawled on her sofa in a tank top that said "Eat Me" across her boobs while I modeled an alarmingly tight, purple Cynthia Rowley roll neck.

"Once I lived with this Jesus freak. Every time I came home with a guy, the creep would shove 'no sex before marriage' flyers under my door. Talk about a passion killer," she said.

But after much agonizing, I decided to stick to the standard advice for New York newcomers—which was that you should live in Manhattan for at least a year so you're in the action—and then be boring and move to the 'burbs.

When it came to what part of Manhattan to live in, I wasn't fussy at first. But I was told that the coolest was anywhere below 14th Street—which meant the East and West Villages, the Lower East Side, and Tribeca.

But you had to be stacked with cash—a la Gwyneth Paltrow and Sarah Jessica Parker—to afford anywhere in the West Village, and because of Tribeca's proximity to Wall Street, it was full of young guns in suits. Moving uptown, Chelsea was the gay quarter, and the Upper West Side was Mecca for young families (therefore best avoided at all costs). Going East, Gramercy was also prohibitively expensive, Murray Hill was packed with young couples in high rises, and to live on the Upper East Side you had to be a millionaire and be able to cope with streets full of old ladies distorted by plastic surgery. I liked the sound of the East Village best.

"'Allo, so I'm Pierre," said Pierre, sounding like Gerard Depardieu and looking me up and down as I stood in the corridor at apartment 6N, East 7th Street between Avenues B and C. I'd found him on an e-mail message group called "Quentinsnyfriends." It had been set up by an industrious Brit—called Quentin—to help out newcomers to New York.

"I'm Bridget, great to meet you," I said, hoping it was only a joke that the French and the Brits couldn't get on. "So I guess you've had loads of people about the room?"

"Sure we 'ave, of course," said Pierre with a Parisian shrug as I walked into a sunny modern apartment. "Quentin 'as many friends."

There was a smart brown sofa with matching chairs under a window at one end and a spotless kitchenette at the other. Pierre, who was wearing an orange Lacoste tennis shirt over brown-tailored trousers and loafers-minus-socks, suited the place well.

"It's my friend Roman and I. We want someone cool, who will, you know, fit in with us and make the apartment feel like 'ome," said Pierre.

I liked the sound of that, despite the fact that it was more anally tidy than an operating room and had little evidence of human inhabitation.

"So I'll show you to the room first," he said.

He went to the windowed end of the apartment and opened a door that was partly obscured behind a humongous TV. My moment of elation was dashed.

"Jesus, $1400 for this?" I stammered, looking in an empty white box which would have barely enough room for a double bed and table.

"It's very tough, I know, but what can we do? We split the rent fairly three ways," said Pierre. "This is the price for the East Village now, and it's a nice building with a doorman. But, wait, you must see the wonderful terrace."

His accent made it sound like he was showing me round *un terrace* in Cannes.

We went up a flight of wooden steps behind the kitchenette into his bedroom—which was significantly larger than mine for his "fair" third of the rent, I noticed. But as he led me through onto the terrace, I forgave him everything.

The space was some 15 by 10 feet and looked out across the tree tops of Tompkins Square Park half a block from the apartment to the entire panorama of Midtown. The Empire State Building rose like a silver space ship bang in the middle of a jumble of building blocks. To its right, the white-specked Chrysler stood like its wingman. This afternoon the September sky was a glorious blue.

"Wow," I murmured. "This is amazing."

"Of course," said Pierre.

Suddenly I was on charm offensive.

"I have to tell you, I'm really laid back. I've had flat mates all my life. And I've got a lot of girlfriends here already," I lied. But perhaps this would reel him in.

"You know I'm here in New York to make money. I don't want to 'ave a girlfriend. They make life far too complicated," he said.

I wasn't actually offering you one, I wanted to say. I tried a different tack.

"I love buying provisions for the fridge," I said.

"Oh, our fridge is empty. In fact, we don't 'ave any food. We only do take-outs."

Well, that sounded good, as I couldn't cook either.

"And do you have any rules, like smoking or anything?" I asked.

"Sure, of course, we all smoke," he said, producing a packet of Marlboro reds and popping one in his mouth.

"You haven't got a spare one, have you? I just ran out," I lied. I hadn't smoked since I'd left New York in the spring, but it was surely worth sacrificing my lungs just this once for a bit of French-style bonding.

We stood admiring the view of Midtown again. The cigarette tasted acrid and gave me an unpleasant head rush. I exhaled hard.

"You smoke weed?" he said.

"Sure," I said.

"Great!" he replied.

Something told me I'd found myself a place to live.

Hanging out with
the "plus one"—me
....

New York, according to the U.S. Census Bureau, has the highest density of single men and women in America. I'd read that there were 2,563,986 women compared with 2,080,881 men between the ages of twenty and forty-nine in the city when I arrived. That was half a million more women—plus me! Not to mention the old adage that half the single men in New York were also gay.

But in my first six months back in New York, I decided not to worry too much about distracting things like the difficulties of finding a boyfriend—and my pending spinsterhood. My thirtieth birthday had passed without hysteria (drowning myself in tequila at Milanos with Olly). My reporter's life at the *Post* was all-consuming, and I had Olly and his friend Ken to hang out with (Agnes had given up on finding a guy in New York and had gone to be a diving instructor in Honduras). Paula still took me to PR parties at a moment's notice, and there were always Pierre and Roman for company, though I usually found them in a stoned heap on the sofa—a state they transformed into nightly within an hour of returning from their respective French banks, where they worked as currency traders.

And unlike London, New York was an easy place to be on your own. Everywhere, it seemed, were singles like me: people happily sitting on park benches in Tompkins Square Park, reading books while the homeless crazies wandered by; girls pottering around in my deli on the corner of Avenue A and 7th Street, buying late-night meals for one; roller-bladers cruising around Central Park in the blissful solo world of their Walkmans. It was even acceptable to go to movies alone—indeed it was considered a necessary escape from New York's thronging population for a couple of hours.

I quickly became used to pitching up to places on my own—telling myself it was all part of my rich, new New York life to be a lone urban explorer. Not that arriving solo at parties was always that enjoyable— as I decided one evening as I found myself with my back pinned to the wall in a small, crowded gallery on Crosby Street, clutching a plastic cup of sangria.

I had been invited to this particular party by Ken, through his contacts at the *Wall Street Journal*. "It's going to be a real downtown scene," he'd said. "The art will be great. This is a crowd you have to know."

I had neglected to convey that a gallery full of hipsters fawning over recycled packaging material was not the kind of scene I wanted to know—not even in brave, new New York.

In the middle of the room was a haphazard stack of wooden crates, all painted electric orange, around which a terrifyingly trendy array of people dressed in cargo pants, shredded sweatshirts, and ripped jeans were greeting each other with weird handshakes. They all looked like they skateboarded and nipped down subway tunnels to do a spot of graffiti in their spare time.

With still no sign of Ken, I pushed my way through the crowd towards a sangria tub, where a statuesque girl wearing a zany head scarf was ladling out drinks.

"Great art," I said pleasantly as I stuck out my cup.

"The art's dope," she said, eyeing my neat, gray office skirt and powder blue T-shirt as if I were the most uncool thing she'd ever seen.

Which was probably fair enough. Her outfit consisted of a white ribbed singlet that revealed a flash of bright yellow bra and jeans split up to her thighs, under which she sported gold fishnet stockings paired with pink, spray-painted boots.

But determined not to be intimidated by the party, I spotted a cute guy standing in a corner—he looked like the singer Beck. I strolled over and pretended to be taken with a piece of driftwood he was admiring. It was labeled "Excrement."

"Do you know the artist?" I said grandly, as if we were standing in front of a Rothko at the Tate Modern—rather than a piece of wood masquerading as poo.

"No, I just play music for the graffiti crowd," he said, glancing side-long at me.

"Ahh, so you're a DJ?" I said, ignoring his "why is this chick talking to me?" tone. Perseverance was everything in this town.

"Dude, nobody DJs anymore. I'm a selector."

"Oh, right. So what do you select?"

"Vinyl."

Was I missing something here?

"Making great music doesn't take skill, it takes vision. That's why you've got to select, not mix. That's why graffiti is great art. An empty paint can is a symbol of defiance, just like selecting new wave punk music is. That's what it's all about."

O-kay.

He turned away to greet a friend before I could ask what he had been smoking—and did he please have any more.

Giving up on Ken, I headed back outside. There I immediately recognized a guy standing in a small group smoking cigarettes on the sidewalk. At last, a party pal! He was another friend of Olly's, a graffiti artist called David whose tag name was NATO.

I'd met him back in the spring, and he'd done a drawing of a stick man in my Union Jack Filofax, including his cell phone number and a note: "Come back soon, hot Brit chick. David."

"Hey, it's David, right?" I said, walking up to the group. He looked like his mother had just called him squitty-bot in front of his friends.

"It's Nay-tow," he drawled.

"Oh. Sorry. I'm Bridget, remember me? Olly's mate from England."

"Oh, yeah." He could not have sounded more disinterested.

I stood at a loss. Neither he nor his three friends looked like they were going to help me out.

"You don't have a spare cigarette, do you?" Oh, the glorious crutch of smoking.

He handed me one and lit it at arm's length.

"Thanks, Da— Er, Nato. Well, anyway. So guess what? I'm back in town, and this time for much lo—"

"Bridge, nice to see you again. I gotta run. People are looking at my art," he said, touching my arm and turning back to the gallery.

I was left holding my cigarette alone in the potholed street. I threw it on the ground, thinking of the lesson Deklin had taught me that excruciating night in the Great Lakes—just because a New York guy has expressed interest in you on one occasion, don't assume he will the next. And in this city, business always came first.

Like any other metropolis, New York had a plethora of scenes—and in Manhattan, thanks to its compact geography, they were comparatively easy to spot. There were the hipster, arty, downtown types like those at the Crosby Street party. They hung out in the Lower East Side and tended to freelance in the city's massive creative industry—photographers, stylists, website designers. Then there were the button-down shirt, banking types, who frequented the flashier bars in Midtown, places like Tao, a pan-Asian restaurant–cum–nightclub on East 58th Street, and The Peninsula Hotel rooftop, where martinis were a hair-raising eighteen dollars. On weekend mornings in the West and East Villages, and in Pastis in the Meatpacking District, you could spot the well-heeled Euro crowd—Pierre and Roman among them—all furiously air-kissing and brunching in expensive shades. Meanwhile uptown, the Upper West Side was a hub of young Jewish parents, many who grew up in New York, pushing strollers to Central Park after stopping at Barney Greengrass for cappuccinos and omelettes. Over the park on the East Side were the perfectly blonded and manicured Upper East Side women and their Waspy, pastel-wearing benefactors.

Then on Friday and Saturday nights, Manhattan filled up with "Bridge and Tunnelers," those who came into "the city" for a big night out, traveling through the Lincoln and Holland Tunnels, or on the Path Train, from Jersey—or over the four bridges that cross the East River from Brooklyn and Queens. They were snobbishly avoided by Manhattanites and scorned for their tacky outfits and drawling Tri-state area accents. For Manhattanites, Thursday was party night.

There was also an ever expanding group of Brits in New York—many of whom worked in magazines, the media, and fashion. And they terrified me.

Of course when anyone asked me if I hung out in the ex-pat scene, I retorted that I had come to New York to get to know Americans—not people from the Fulham Road. But in actual fact I was straight-up intimidated by the incredible confidence and glamour so many Brits seemed to acquire the moment they stepped off the plane. English girls like Plum Sykes, and her equally chic sister Lucy—who worked respectively for *Vogue* and *Marie Claire*—were treated on the Page Six circuit like they were movie stars. I only ever went to parties as someone else's "Plus One."

Meanwhile my interest in household bonding had dwindled the moment Roman had installed record decks in the living room, on which he liked to practice at five in the morning when they came back, paralytic, from their favorite nightclub, Centrofly. It was all very well being a lone urban warrior—but maybe looking for a boyfriend wouldn't be such a bad idea after all.

From "great date" to new fate

······································

I stood panicking in front of the changing-room mirror in the Banana Republic at Rockefeller Center, looking at myself in a cherry-red, stretchy top which gave me hefty cleavage. Was it subtle-yet-sexy? Or way too tacky for a first date?

I didn't have much choice. I had less than fifteen minutes until I was supposed to meet a total stranger in the Whiskey Bar nine blocks away, and the dainty, white linen shirt I'd planned to wear was ruined by an ominous, oily green stain.

That morning I'd left the house sporting freshly washed hair and wearing the shirt with my new Seven jeans, ready for my first-ever blind date. Not long after, I'd learned my first dating lesson—do *not* wear to work what you're planning to wear for the night.

I'd got to the office and was sent straight out to Hunts Point, a bleak corner of the South Bronx mainly frequented by crackheads, hookers, and truck drivers, to track down a priest who'd heard a confession that was helping with the acquittal of two men wrongly convicted of murder. Just as I'd walked out of the nearest subway stop to his church on Longwood Avenue, a big splat of stinking, green goo had slapped me on the head. Yes, that's right: indiscriminate, viscous, steaming goo.

"*What the bloody hell?*" I had shouted out loud, jumping backwards and looking up. It was sliding through my hair and down the back of my shirt. Another splat had coated the inside of my bag. It was greasy, like vomit mixed with grass. One whiff of it made me gag.

It must have been chucked from one of several apartment windows above the subway entrance—presumably on purpose. With no other option—and the priest to find—I'd walked to a diner across the street and locked myself in a grimy bathroom, where I tried to get it all off with a tissue.

Out in the Bronx until early evening, I hadn't had time to go home and change, but I wasn't about to go on a date and explain that my oh-so-glamorous job as a *New York Post* reporter involved shit bomb attacks. A dash to Banana Republic had been my only option.

My blind date's name was Daniel, and he'd written me this e-mail:

Hello, Bridget: I enjoyed reading your recent article about being an unmarried Brit in New York. I'm a 32-year-old investment banker, good-looking, intelligent, and a lot of fun. I have green eyes and dark hair, and I'm a GREAT DATE!!

Earlier that week I'd written a witty review of a book titled *The Marriage Plan: How To Marry Your Soul Mate in One Year or Less*. It basically told women to treat getting hitched like getting a job—draw up a plan of action, get everyone you know on the case, and broach the "M" word on the first date, which all sounded a little extreme. But I was amazed that a reader had bothered to write in.

Liking the sound of his green-eyes/dark-hair combo, I'd e-mailed back on the pretense that I was curious to know what constituted a "GREAT DATE!!" After all, moving to New York was all about being able to do this kind of thing—meeting the types of guys I would never have crossed paths with had I stayed in London.

In the UK, blind dates were still considered desperado, period. Unlike New York, where it was normal to court strangers over several dinners, at home most people got together when they were shit-faced at group events like house parties or in the pub—and then mainly with people they vaguely knew already. This was exciting new territory for me—and hopefully I'd have a New York boyfriend out of it by the end of the night!

I legged it up to the Whiskey Bar, arriving at precisely four minutes past eight, tingling with nerves. The inside of the bar was dark as midnight, and I peered at the groups of people sitting on low sofas in delightful anticipation of my first sighting of Daniel. Then I saw someone hailing me from the bar.

Shit. Was that him? I waved back. Through the gloom I saw what looked like a stocky version of Nicholas Cage, but more square and wearing a turtleneck. Not exactly the chiseled champion of my fantasies.

But then, I told myself, it was unlikely that the first sight of any blind date could live up to the image created in one's head. Or did they sometimes? I was new to this game.

I walked over, trying to look enthusiastic anyway, wondering how many other people had had a similar disappointment in the first few seconds of a date. From the way Daniel heaved himself off his bar stool and kissed my left cheek whilst looking past me, it seemed he might be experiencing it too.

"So, Bridget from the *Post*, good to meet you," he said flatly. "You look kinda different from your picture."

Oh God, no. Wasn't that what Rick the photographer had always complained about? I'd never imagined it could happen to me.

"Do I?" I said, fighting the urge to apologize. Next to my book review there had been a photo of me sitting in Langan's, the *Post's* local bar, trying to look winsome over a martini. I had had my hair blow-dried straight for the occasion. Now my hair was curly—and, okay, a little disheveled from my day in the South Bronx. But surely I didn't actually look older—or, horror—*fatter*?

I didn't fancy asking. Instead Daniel asked me what I wanted to drink and turned back to the bar to duck the awkwardness that was already crashing down between us. I tried to imagine that he was simply an old friend I hadn't seen in a while.

Our drinks in hand, he then ushered us to a low table which had two armchairs opposite each other. I sank down. The chair was unexpectedly deep. Sprawling backwards and self-conscious of my now prominent cleavage, I tried to relax, or at least to appear relaxed.

Suddenly I felt it was my responsibility to justify the fact that he had asked me out.

I took a big suck through my drink straw. So I would just have to make up for his disappointment in my appearance with my conversational skills.

"You'll never guess what happened to me this morning," I began. "I went on a story in the South Bronx, and someone tipped a bucket of green goo out of a window onto my head!"

"Oh, yeah?" Daniel's eyes flicked from my chest to the crown of my head.

Shit, Bridget, what did you tell yourself? Don't mention the slime. Quick recover, recover.

"Oh, no, it's fine now. You can't smell it on me or anything. But the really weird thing was that it was impossible to work out what it was."

Daniel looked as if he didn't want to have to think about what it was.

"So does that kind of thing happen to you often?"

"Oh, no, this was a first for me, but then I'm pretty new to the job. I do know a group of reporters once got a bucket of human shit thrown at them when they went to the home of a man who caused delays for hours on the Metro North one night because he got his arm stuck in a train toilet trying to retrieve his mobile phone."

"You're kidding, right?" said Daniel, shifting in his chair to get further away from me, as if my very presence might cause a similar fate to befall him.

Yes, indeed. Why exactly was I talking about toilets and human shit?

"So anyway, um, enough about that. I guess you're quite an expert on dating, right?" I said, draining my drink.

"I've been on a few." Daniel was still pinned to the back of his chair, looking at me like I was a madwoman.

"I know you said in your e-mail you were a great date, but have you ever been on any really terrible ones?" I contemplated adding "and where does this one sit on the scale?"

"Well, there was this time when I took a girl to the Moon Dance Diner for BLTs and she ordered extra bacon—that was that pretty gross."

Huh? What the fuck was wrong with an extra order of bacon on a date? I couldn't ask. Maybe he was Jewish and would be offended I hadn't somehow known that.

I pictured him on his next date, relaying the story of how he'd met an English girl who turned up with parrot shit on her head and then talked about toilets. God, this whole experience felt so odd. Here we were sitting opposite each other, trying to chat like old friends, but both of us knowing that with every word we uttered, the other was quietly making judgments. And odder still, even though I already knew I didn't much like Daniel, I still desperately wanted him to like me.

After an hour of stilted conversation about his job and my move to New York, Daniel announced he'd made a reservation at Rue 57, a restaurant three blocks away.

"Great, that would be lovely," I said. How, I didn't know. But it seemed too rude to suddenly say I couldn't go.

Rue 57 turned out to be a large, posh, fakey bistro full of office types having work dinners. As we got settled at our table, a waitress brought the wine list, but Daniel turned it away and asked for a Bud Light. Disappointed, I asked for a glass of house white, remembering how Angus used to love to study the wine list before ordering us something delicious. Again it felt weird to be having a romantic dinner with a stranger.

Our drinks came and our food followed. He told me he lived in Murray Hill, came from Chappaqua, and had attended Yale. I excitedly asked him if he had seen Bill Clinton's house, and he looked at me like I was a sap. We moved onto European ski resorts—he'd been to Verbier on a trip with his bank. I told me I'd been there with an ex. I felt the twinge again, remembering the weekend Angus and I had spent there for Easter.

"So, do you know that great celebrity columnist, Cindy Adams? She often eats here," said Daniel, who I noticed glanced over my right shoulder every time a new diner walked through the door. "I picked this restaurant because I was thinking if she came in, you could introduce us."

"Um, I don't really know the *Post* columnists. They mainly work from home."

"Too bad," he said.

Bloody charming, I thought.

I tried another topic. "So have you seen that new film —" I stopped. Daniel leaned back, stretched out his arms, and did one great big huge yawn. I couldn't believe what I was seeing.

"Long day?" I asked frostily.

"Not really. But I should get home soon."

When the check came, Daniel resignedly flicked his platinum Amex card onto the table. I dug in my bag for my wallet, trying to avoid the green goo that still lingered at the bottom.

"I'll get this. I asked you," he said flatly.

We put on our coats as quickly as we could without being actively rude. Then we walked out onto Sixth Avenue, where Daniel stood in the road with his arm up to hail a cab. I wondered how to proceed. Surely we would at least make some pretense of staying in touch? In the UK, embarrassed politeness would have caused us both to go on and on about how we "must do it again soon."

Little did I know there was an entire New York Magna Carta of unspoken date rules already in place for just this kind of situation.

A taxi pulled up, Daniel ushered me into it.

"So you're going east too, right?" I said, moving over to make a place for him.

"I'll get the next one," he said and slammed the door. And that was it.

The cab pulled away, and I looked out through my window at the towering Midtown buildings, feeling deflated. How could I have gone from sitting down to dinner with a guy who I didn't even like to feeling hurt and dumped?

"Well, so much for green-eyed Daniel. Plenty more fish in this sea," I said to the passing streets. But my voice sounded very small.

"I mean, this bloke, he yawned. He actually yawned while I was talking to him. I couldn't believe it. What a dickhead."

"Honey, that's nothing. I once dated a guy who picked his nose and wiped it on his ass while we were having dinner in Nobu."

I was leaning against a filing cabinet strewn with invitations to movie premieres and cocktail parties. It was next to Paula's desk at Page Six.

"The weirdest thing was I knew I didn't like him as soon as we'd said 'hello' and he told me straight out that I didn't look like my picture," I said.

Paula looked aghast.

"Then excuse me, but why the hell did you have dinner with this guy?"

Paula's Vertu cell phone rang. She snatched it up, listened to it for three seconds, then cut in. "Clarissa, honey, can't talk. I'm just doing the list from the morning meeting." She tossed the phone and turned her attention back to me.

"We'd kind of arranged it," I said.

Paula sighed. "Bridget, I love you, but you have no idea what you're doing. Never, *ever* turn up to a blind date without an early get-out excuse. Do drinks, *then* only say 'yes' to dinner if you like the guy. It's the first rule in the book."

"What book?"

"Jesus Christ!" she rolled her eyes. "It's dating common sense. Otherwise you'll wind up getting stuck out all night with all sorts of jerks. Do you have the time and energy for that? No, you don't."

"But I was hoping this date might have turned into something."

"Honey, don't we all."

"Well, are there any other rules I should know before I continue in my quest for a boyfriend?" I asked.

Paula flicked her perfectly blown out hair to one side. "If you don't want to see a date again, don't call even to say 'thank you.' If you do wanna see a guy again, never, ever leave more than one message on his voice mail. Don't e-mail until he does, and don't e-mail back straight away. Avoid any e-mailing that might involve arrangements over the weekend, and do not ever talk about your emotions until you get beyond the third date—if you get that far."

"God, it all sounds a bit complicated to me."

Jon Auerbach, the *Post*'s Sunday editor, was standing near us, waiting to talk to Richard Johnson, who as usual was nodding secretively into his phone.

"Well, it's nice to hear someone experiencing our city for the first time around," he said.

"You think this is funny, Jon?" snapped Paula. "You're happily married, you have no idea. Going on a bad date is like having a hemorrhoid explode in your ass."

"*Jesus*, Paula," Jon and I both said.

Later, when I was back at my desk, Jon called and asked me to have lunch with him the following week.

Over a pile of mussels mariniere and French fries on Sixth Avenue, he then made me an extraordinary offer. He told me that he and Xana wanted to add a new female voice to the *Sunday Post*—and as I was a fresh face to New York, did I want to try writing a weekly column in addition to my news reporting job?

"What, would I have to write about city issues and politics and stuff?" I said in a blind panic. New York's system of city council members, borough presidents, and state representatives still had me utterly baffled.

"We were thinking more along the lines of your personal experiences—you know, with guys, friends, how you're coming to grips with the city. You could start by writing about that blind date," he said.

"Okay," I said doubtfully, the butterflies doing overtime in my stomach. This was the kind of job people on newspapers dreamed of their whole lives. And here it was being handed to *me*.

The following day I came into the *Post* office at 6 A.M., feeling like I was sitting down to take an exam. With shaky hands I opened a blank document and wrote:

What do you do when you go on a blind date—and are disappointed at first sight?

What do you say when you know from twenty paces across a dark bar that there's no chemistry, no spark?

Should you simply blurt out: "This isn't going anywhere, shall we end it right here?"

This question hit me head-on as I dashed into the Whiskey Bar on Central Park South, late for a blind date with a man I'd been fantasizing about for days . . .

Daniel the green-eyed investment banker ended up a hero after all. So much for Cindy Adams. Now I was a columnist too!

What's wrong with New York men?

I am a New York Post *columnist! Guys will want to know me!*

I stared at myself in the bathroom mirror at W 8 club on West 8th Street while a pack of girls who looked like *FHM* models jostled behind me wielding lip glosses and mascaras.

"Excuse me, excuse me, can I get in here, I need to check my color contacts, did you see that guy who just walked in, he was *totally hot,*" said a blonde girl with a name sticker marked "Candy" stuck between her pert boobs.

These women are my friends, my comrades in the city, I told myself. She barged me to one side.

Thanks to my new column, I'd been invited to a speed-dating night sponsored by *Jane* magazine and Kahlua. The "singles mixers" had become the latest fad in the city and I wanted to try one out, especially as back in London speed dating was still virtually unheard of.

At home the notion that you would line yourself up opposite ten men and spend a timed minute with each of them sounded so humiliating that a Brit would probably rather have opted straight for the arranged marriage. But in New York, where people liked immediate results—it made perfect sense.

And, I reasoned—as my date with Daniel had proved—if you can tell if you have chemistry with someone in the first sixty seconds, speed dating was an ideal way to avoid wasting a whole demoralizing evening with the wrong guy. Well, that's what I thought anyway.

I returned to the dance floor at W 8, where two long tables had been set up. At the bar, groups of girls decked out in various combinations of miniskirts and high-heeled boots were tucking into complimentary

Mudslide cocktails whilst eyeing the competition. Gradually the guys began to arrive, striding into the room like gladiators entering the Coliseum. They were a clean-cut bunch. These boys all looked like they had office jobs and gym memberships.

The hostess handed me a pen and score sheet and explained that you had a minute with each guy, then had to tick "YES" or "NO" next to his name, depending on whether you wanted to see him again or not.

"If both of you tick 'YES,' we give you each other's e-mails!" she exclaimed, beaming like Cupid himself.

I refrained from adding the minor point that a girl could also be dumped ten times in ten minutes.

We were called to start, and with palms sweating, I climbed onto a stool opposite Mike. And there went my big theory. As I stared across at his short, bankerish, dark hair and not-unattractive, square-jawed face, I couldn't work out if we had chemistry or not. Candy perched on a stool next to me and hoiked down her top so it rested a millimeter above her nipples. We both clocked a cute guy with thick, wavy hair, wearing nerdy-cool glasses a couple of stools down. He looked like Keanu Reeves. I hoiked my top down too.

"Go!" shouted the hostess, and the room descended into pandemonium.

"Right, so hi, yeah hello, so yeah, so how are you doing?" Mike and I shouted at each other above the din of couples around us. "Yeah fine, great, you? Oh sorry, no you start. Sorry, no. Go on."

We tried again.

"So you're Bridget, right?"

"Yes! How did you know?" Had he read my column and recognized me from my picture?

"It says it on your name badge," he said.

"Oh, right, of course, sorry."

"That's okay,"

"So, wha—"

"Time's up! All change!" shouted the hostess, ringing a handbell. God, a minute went quite quickly!

Mike shrugged, as if he'd just thrown a dud at a fairground ball toss but had plenty more balls in his bucket. He moved to the next stool, taking his score sheet with him. I tried to spot which box he was ticking for me, but he wrote behind his hand like the swot at school who thinks everyone is copying him. So I ticked "NO" for him on principle.

In Mike's place came Rich, who looked a lot like Mike—clean-cut and chiseled, in a pressed shirt. But he had an appealing smile. The cute guy was now opposite Candy, who was visibly simpering. I tried to ignore her and let Rich take the lead this time.

"Go!" shouted the hostess.

"Hi, Bridget."

"Hi, Rich."

"Hey, love your accent. Where are you from?"

"England, actually."

"Wow, that's great, I totally love that Austin Powers movie, *The Spy Who Shagged Me*."

"I haven't seen it."

"Oh. You should."

End of conversation. Pause. Shit. The seconds were ticking. Rich stepped in again.

"I'm thinking of visiting London in the summer."

"Great. Got an itinerary sorted?"

"*I'm not wearing any panties.*"

The statement rebounded between us. We looked around in horror. Candy was leaning across the table; her cleavage was practically in Keanu's lap.

"I have no inhibitions at all," she screamed over the din, then started to voraciously snog him. Rich looked gutted, clearly wondering why he hadn't got the same treatment from Candy.

"Er, where were we?" I said. "Yes, London. Itinerary. The city's got some amazing museums, and then there's Windsor Castle . . . and of course Stratford, where William Shakespeare was born. . . . "

Rich looked less than riveted. Even my eyes were glazing over.

"CHANGE!"

Rich shuffled off. I ticked "NO," because I was sure he would.

Next up was Keanu. His name label said, rather disappointingly, "Howie."

"Hey there, Bridget," he said, wiping Candy's slobber off his mouth.

"Hey," I said.

We had a sixty-second conversation about nothing while he played footsie with Candy under the table.

But all was not lost, I decided once I was safely back at the bar supping on my fourth Mudslide while a second round of speed daters screamed at each other. Forget what you said across the table, the most effective aspect of speed dating was finding yourself in room full of drunken people who were all there for the same thing. Perhaps sixty seconds wasn't long enough to work out if the candidate opposite you was your future husband, but it was ample time for you to decide whether to approach him afterwards.

A brilliant theory! I decided to put it in my column.

And, as if to prove me correct, when the speed-dating rounds ended, everyone stuck around. And just as I was avidly watching Candy ditch Howie for another specimen at the far side of the room, a sexy guy in a red shirt and natty charcoal suit appeared next to me.

"Hey, there, hope you don't mind me coming over to say 'hi.' I saw you earlier and was bummed we weren't in the same group."

He saw me earlier? I loved him already. His name badge said "Eddie." He had pale chocolate skin and eyes the shape of laurel leaves.

"Well, I might have had a reason to tick my 'YES' box if I'd had you," I flirted. "Though I have to admit this thing definitely turned out to be quite a laugh."

He looked confused.

"A laugh? Yes, I was laughing quite a lot, actually."

I tried to explain the translation.

Eddie told me he came from Virginia Beach and put feeds together for independent TV production houses that made programs for VH1 and MTV. I had no idea what that meant, but it sounded good.

"Listen, I gotta get out of here. I got an early meeting with some big clients in the morning, but I'd love to call you some time," he said.

"Sure!" I said, writing my mobile number on a napkin (now I was in New York proper, I'd invested in a phone). I resisted the urge to ask when did "some time" mean?

"Some time," it turned out to be two days later, was just in time to make a plan to go for drinks in his favorite club, Etoile, on a Thursday night.

"It's classy, international, and comfortable, and you deserve to be spoiled," he said on the phone.

That's a bit bloody cheesy, I thought, then scolded myself. Did I want a boyfriend or not?

He told me to meet him outside the Astor Place Starbucks at 8 P.M. This time I made sure I had time to go home and change after work. After the lack of success with the red Banana Republic stretch top, I chose as my outfit a sheer green vintage Versace shirt—which I'd found in Paula's castoffs bag—paired with the Seven jeans and black, high-heeled boots. It was a pleasing, subtle-but-chic combination, I reckoned. But not, I soon discovered, pleasing enough.

Eddie was ten minutes late. I spotted him crossing Lafayette from the subway stop, checking me out as I approached.

"Oh," was the first thing he said, bypassing the "Hi, great to see you."

"Hi, there," I replied, waiting for the "sorry I'm late." I leaned upwards anyway to give his smooth cheek an enthusiastic peck.

"I thought I told you Etoile was classy," he said, air-kissing back. "Are you sure you want to go uptown wearing that?"

That was a Page Six shirt. He, I refrained from pointing out, hadn't had the imagination to deviate from his same charcoal suit.

"It's not that you don't look great. It's just that the women in Etoile are very chic, sexy, and modelesque. I don't want you to feel intimidated by them," he continued.

Intimidated? I was a *New York Post* columnist, for fuck's sake.

"You are joking, right?" was all I could manage.

"No," he said, studying me again. "But I guess you look cute enough—in a cowgirl kind of way. That messy hair, it kinda looks like you've just been having sex."

This date was not starting well.

It didn't improve on the subway uptown. As I chatted away, trying to make Eddie feel pleased he'd come out to meet me, he suddenly cut in. "Hey, Bridge, turn it down a bit. Maybe the whole car doesn't want in on your life."

I went scarlet. Then under the bright 6 train lights he peered at me intently. I felt like he was counting every criminal stray hair and black-head on my face. I was glad I'd taken the virgin step of having my eye-brows shaped—despite the psychological trauma I'd endured as a maniacal Korean woman in Bloomie Nails descended on me with wax and tweezers.

"You know, you would actually be one hot chick if you made a bit more of an effort," he said.

"Brits just aren't into obsessive plucking, preening, and grooming, okay?" I snarled. He glanced down at my crotch as if suddenly imagin-ing the horrors that might be going on there.

But once in the door of Etoile on East 56th Street and in sniffing distance of a drink, my spirits lifted. Until Eddie took a mint from a bowl next to the cloak room and popped it in my mouth.

"Better stay fresh!" he said.

Fuck, I had halitosis too?

The rest of the evening passed bearably enough—for sitting at a bar with a guy who talked in obsessive detail about his line of work and checked out every other girl who walked past.

As we headed outside again, I steeled myself for the thanks-but-no-thanks good-bye. But despite his criticisms of me, Eddie, unlike Daniel, appeared more than willing to keep the evening alive.

"Wanna come back to my place for a nightcap?" he said. "It's on your way home."

"Sure, why not?" I said, wondering why I was agreeing to spend more time with a guy who'd annoyed the pants off me all night. Paula would have been horrified.

I'm doing this as research for my column, I told myself. But I knew that wasn't the reason. After several months alone in New York, I was beginning to crave affection—wherever it came from. Putting up with

Eddie still beat going home to find Pierre and Roman surrounded by half-eaten takeouts, comatose on the couch.

Eddie's tiny apartment was in Chelsea, and he took me straight through to his bedroom, skipping the nightcap. His room at least was peaceful—painted a trendy hotel off-white. We lay on his large double bed next to each other.

"I'm not shagging you, you know," I said, sounding like a school marm.

"I know," he said, leaning in to kiss the back of my left ear. I shivered at the touch of his soft lips. Maybe he wasn't quite so bad.

His shifted onto his right side to look down at me. I stared into his laurel leaf eyes. He reached into his pocket and pulled out his phone.

"I just gotta call my buddy, Curly. He lives in Chicago. He'll get such a kick out of this!"

What, did Eddie have a swinging gay lover?

No, but perhaps a frat boy one. As I lay drumming my fingers on the bed, Eddie had a five-minute conversation with Curly about a basketball game and the MTV deals. And then he got onto the subject of me.

"Man, I've got this English girl here. She sounds like something out of Austin Powers. She actually just said 'I'm not going to *shag* you'!"

That fucking film again. I felt like axe-murdering the infernal Mike Myers.

"You have to hear her accent." He shoved the phone into my hand.

"Er, hi," I said.

"Hey, do you English people really say 'shag'?"

"Well, I do."

"And what's that other one? *Blowk*? 'He's a brilliant blowk'? You say that, right?"

"We do say *bloke* for a guy, yes."

"And what about 'Wot's up gove-noor.' 'Please ser can I have some mo-ore'?"

Oh God, no.

"Um, I think you're confusing something you've seen in a couple of different films there . . . "

"Oh. So what slang word do you use for chicks?"

"*Birds* sometimes, I suppose." I looked at Eddie, wondering how long this linguistic adventure would have to go on. He was beaming at me like a proud parent on speech day.

"So, like, 'There is a bril-liont bird. I wont to sha-ag her'?"

"Something like that."

"Say 'groo-vy ba-beee.'"

I could no longer be polite.

"Curly, it was great talking to you. I'm handing you back to Eddie now, okay? I'm actually on my way out."

I saw Eddie a few times after that, mainly when he called out of the blue because he was passing through the East Village—and only when I felt like I could take an evening hearing about the minutiae of cable TV production deals while giving out lessons in English slang.

Then, out one Saturday night at a party with Pierre and Roman—in a loft on Bleecker Street—I met Tom.

Unlike Eddie, who got distracted every second by waitresses' boobs, the greasiness of my hair, or the constant ringing of his phone, Tom gave the impression he wouldn't notice if he walked into a wall.

I'd had a long night on the Absolut Tangerine. He wandered into me in the kitchen, shifted his smeared glasses on his nose, and telepathically worked out that I was single—and hammered.

Tom was tall and wiry—appealingly like Angus. He had blonde, shaggy hair and an exotic Southern lilt. He told me he was twenty-eight, from Georgia, and trying to make it as a screenwriter. I ended up sitting on a never-used slate breakfast bar, wrapped around Tom's neck.

"So where do you live?" I slurred when I knew the time had come to go home and pass out.

"Around," lilted Tom.

How much more vague could you get?

I took Tom home with me when I found out that "around" actually meant his uncle's apartment on 89th Street, where he was sleeping on the sofa. Back in the East Village, I showed him to my shoe box and went to brush my teeth. He was flat out and snoring by the time I got back.

The next day he suggested brunch in the Great Jones Café—an orange-painted shack on Great Jones Street that served Mexican food and stiff Bloody Marys. There we found out that we both liked obscure documentaries, late-night drinking, and long walks. It was like something out of the personal ads! We were actually getting on well until he mentioned that he was thinking of seeing a film later in the day.

"Oh, cool, I was thinking of going to the cinema myself."

He looked panicked.

"I'm not sure that's a good idea," he said. "It's Sunday night. I kinda need my own head space."

What did he think I was going to do, stalk him home to the Upper East Side?

After that, Tom phoned me from time to time to see what I was up to, but his vagueness never changed.

"Um, yeah, hi, it's me here," was his standard opening. "So I might be up for some kind of activity this evening. Not really sure yet exactly what I'm doing. But if you're having a couple of cocktails, I might be around."

We did make it into bed a few times, but I began to suspect Tom would say "sure, whatever" no matter if I offered to him a marathonic, Jenna Jameson sex session or told him I had a headache. So ultimately my enthusiasm waned. I found out later he also had an on-again, off-again girlfriend in San Francisco. "On-again, off-again" was a well-used phrase in New York.

I knew I was up against half a million women, but finding a normal guy was a little harder than I had imagined. I decided to write about my experiences with Tom and Eddie. Both seemed thrilled to be featured in the *Post*, no matter how I described them.

WHAT IS WRONG WITH NEW YORK MEN?

Am I just a nut magnet, or are all New York men abnormal? The two guys I've been casually dating leave me gazing to the heavens in despair.

One is so uptight, he criticized what I was wearing before he even kissed me hello. The other is so laid-back that if I offered to make slow, sweet love to him, he'd probably reply, "Yeah, sure, whatever." And he'd respond the same way if I told him to get lost.

By now I had tackled of range of world-changing subjects in my Sunday column: my nightmare roommates, going to parties when I didn't know anyone, the trauma of having my eyebrows waxed for the first time, the pros and cons of speed dating. If I managed to strike a chord, my e-mail box would fill up with people offering their own insights on life in New York. And the response, I soon noticed, was most enthusiastic when I wrote about my dating difficulties. It seemed half the city was as baffled as me over how hard it was to find a partner—something I'd never had to think about in London. And it was comforting to know that it wasn't just me who was landing terrible dates or sometimes feeling a little lonely.

Dear Bridget, I don't think anyone can know the true meaning of hell until they've experienced the dating scene in New York.

Dear Bridget, I saw your piece from the weekend about New York men, and I couldn't agree with you more. I am currently experiencing the exact same thing with a Mr. Laid-Back. So much so that after reading your column, I was convinced we were seeing the same guy. He doesn't work in the music industry does he?

Dear Bridget, I often blame my bad luck with romance on long work hours or not putting myself out there enough. But I think we should start to acknowledge when men aren't treating us the way they should be.

Dear Bridget, This city can really make one go mad sometimes. I have a love/hate relationship with it. I love everything it has to offer, but at the same time, you are constantly judged by others by how you look and what job you do. We are surrounded by these glamorous sticks, and men here expect all women to be like that. What happens if you're just a normal size eight?

Hi Bridget, Does the *Post* pay you to write about how hopeless you are to make other women feel better about themselves? Do you get fired if you do find a boyfriend?

What if he was The One?

"So why is New York the hardest city in the world to find love?" I exclaimed, sucking on an iced latte (my new thing) and draped over a chair in Brad Hamilton's office. "You want my explanation?"

Brad was a chirpy, sandy-haired Californian and the editor of Sunday Pulse—the features section of the paper in which my column ran. "Sure, hit me with it," he said.

I'd thought about the e-mails from readers I'd got and the attitudes of the guys I'd come across in the city so far. I had also started talking to women about being single in the city. I'd noticed how common it was to see groups of girls out together having dinner—but with no guys. *Sex and the City*-style girl bonding played out nightly in every Manhattan restaurant and bar.

I produced a torn piece of paper on which I had written my new grand theory about single New York life.

1. New York is a city of opportunity and outsiders, and people come here to try and make it/make money. This makes everyone v. self-centered and means careers come first. Love and romance are never, ever allowed to hold you back.
2. Peoples' industrious attitudes towards their careers affect the rest of their lives. Dating has an allocated window. If a date doesn't work out to your highest expectation quickly, cut your losses and move on.
3. Not only are there half a million more single women in New York, guys have a wide age range to pick from—say 21 to 45—making the competition v. stiff for women.

Even if a guy's on a date with a smart, beautiful woman, he knows there are plenty more where she came from.

4. Smart, beautiful New York women feel they deserve to be treated a little bit special, especially with all the work they put into staying in the competition. To guys this can translate as "demanding."

5. Singles of both sexes who have become used to this cutthroat dating environment become jaded and defensive—making it even harder to have a relationship.

"But you know what," I said, folding up my piece of paper again. "I think what it's really about is plain old geography."

"Geography?" said Brad incredulous. Perhaps I hadn't told him it had been my degree in college.

"In London people like to be in couples, because it's a pain in the arse to go out. Here it's much easier to be footloose. You can jump from party to party every night without even breaking into a sweat. So if you're having a drink with someone and it's not fun, then it's easy to move to something better. If you're a guy out on a date and your friend calls to say he's in an apartment full of hot women, you can nip over later and check them out too. And if you hook up with someone, you can go home with them with the knowledge that you can leave just as quickly."

"Surely you're not suggesting that an efficient subway system and cheap cabs can have that much effect on love?" said Brad. He was thirty-seven and had been with his girlfriend for ten years. They lived in the ground floor of a brownstone in Carroll Gardens and had a hot tub in the garden. No wonder he didn't think about that kind of stuff.

"Don't underestimate the passion-killing effect of a long, sobering journey home with a stranger," I said, thinking of one I had endured in the UK from the West End to Kingston. During the ride, my vodka-and-tonic goggles de-misted, and I found myself sitting next to an ac-ned twenty-four-year-old I had mistaken for a tanned snowboarder.

"Back in London, the time it takes to get anywhere means you have to make a plan and stick with it. In New York you can chop and change in an instant—so why commit to anything, least of all a relationship?"

Brad nodded slowly. "I do see what you're saying."

Bloody hell, I was an anthropological genius.

The following day I was back on my news reporting duties and had been assigned the illustrious "weather story." An unseasonal storm was heading for the city—with a threat of freak flash floods. But as usual I couldn't help flicking to my inbox every half an hour to see if any more fan mail had arrived. I wondered how much Cindy Adams got each week.

So I noticed immediately when an e-mail from Angus popped up mid-afternoon. It was a mass invitation to a screening in London for the first drama he'd directed for the BBC. I grabbed my phone and dialed his number. We hadn't spoken in a while. He didn't even know about my exciting new column.

He answered on the second ring. I plowed in before he had a chance to speak.

"Babe, that's amazing about your film. You must be *so* excited. God, I'm proud of you. I'm so sorry I can't be there for the screening."

"Hi, gorgeous." He sounded like I'd caught him off guard. "Yeah, I am pretty stoked. So how's it all going in New York?"

"Oh, you know. Fine, up and down," I said. "I've got a column! I write about all my new experiences in the city. And now I'm writing the weather story. But forget that, I want to hear about the film. Did they totally love it?"

He paused. I sighed. After dealing with Tom and Eddie, talking to him made me feel like I had come home. At least he could conduct a normal conversation.

"Look, Bridge." He suddenly sounded formal. "I've been meaning to call you, actually."

"Oh?"

"I wanted to tell you before anyone else did. I've started seeing someone."

My insides heaved. The rest of the office fell away.

"It's India. I think you've met her a couple of times. We've been casual for a while, but now, well, it's a bit less casual."

India? . . . "a bit less casual" . . . what did that mean? . . . I remembered her as a pretty hippie artist who'd once been on a group weekend away with us.

"She's lovely," I managed.

He paused again.

"She's a very cool lady. I'm sort of excited." It was the worst thing I'd ever heard anyone say.

I swallowed hard, feeling tears wrenching from the pit of my stomach.

"Hon, I'm really happy for you. It's getting near deadline. I've got to go. Let's speak soon, okay?"

I ran through the office to the elevators, blind to everyone, and went straight to the newsstand in the lobby to buy cigarettes. Once outside I squatted on the floor with my back against the concrete of the building for support. My fingers shook as I tried to strike a match. *"Casual, now a bit less casual?"* I knew it had to be serious for him to tell me about it.

I smoked, taking deep breaths. The traffic on Sixth Avenue suddenly sounded loud and fierce—the honks and screeches reminding me that I now lived in a city that stopped for no one.

Suddenly I realized I had still imagined that I would return and marry Angus some day. But why on earth had I assumed he would wait? Now here I was, miles from home, cracking jokes about my disastrous dating life in a tabloid newspaper while his sincere, true love had turned to shine on someone else. God, what had I given up? I felt physically sick.

I looked at the time. Shit. Deadline was approaching and I hadn't even started to write my story. I forced myself to stand and walk back inside. Now I felt like I was heading into a future that I had totally fucked up.

My phone was ringing when I got to my desk. For one joyous moment I thought it would be him telling me he'd made a huge mistake. I snatched it up.

"*Angus?*"

"Hello, National Weather Service here. You called about the precipitation outlook for this evening and tomorrow?"

Not Angus.

"A depression forming over the Great Lakes area is likely to move over into Pennsylvania and to the outer counties in New Jersey and upstate New York later today. When it hits the current high pressure zone over the city . . . "

I tried in vain to focus. Maybe "a bit less casual" still wasn't that serious.

"Does that mean there could be flooding?"

Angus and India. Even their names sounded good together.

"There's a likelihood of flash flooding early tomorrow, especially in the upstate counties. We're warning drivers to take extra precautions on the roads, which would be useful to mention for the public if you are writing an article."

Angus was in love with someone else, and I was a warning drivers to take extra precautions on the roads.

"Vodka and tonic, please, Joe," I said an hour later as I heaved myself onto a bar stool in Langan's and lit yet another cigarette.

"So, what did you have goin' on today, then?" replied the Irish barman as he plunked a lime in my glass and filled it with the soda gun.

"The weather story. There's a storm heading for the city, with a likelihood of flash flooding." Oh, and, yes, the guy I always thought I would marry one day is now in love with someone else.

I took a huge swig of my drink. Already I felt like I had spent a near lifetime in Langan's.

Tonight the place was quiet. A football game flickered down from the TVs at each end of the long bar, watched by gatherings of men in suits, fresh from the News Corp building. Paula was perched on a stool in the far corner, gesticulating wildly at a tanned guy with blonde highlights—probably an agent or flack in from LA. Next to her, Steve Dunleavy, the *Post*'s legendary columnist—and former news editor—who drank like a fish, was propped up at the bar with a cigarette dangling from his leathery hand. In the restaurant area at the back of the

---

bar, a party of middle-aged Midwestern tourists, fresh from Times Square, were sitting around one of the red checked tables, munching on platters of fried finger food.

This bar was a second home to people who worked at the *Post,* who came in after their shifts to bitch about their days. Dunleavy—who was a friend to every firefighter and cop in the city—would hold court in his Australian twang, slurring increasingly as the night went on and telling tales of the road when journalists were real men.

Each time I walked into Langan's, I never failed to relish the fact that I too could now recount a news story that I had been on. Okay, so mine were more likely to involve domestic bustups in Queens than foreign coups, but with my pager on my belt and notepad in my bag, I still felt like Lois Lane. But tonight it all suddenly seemed like a poor exchange for a life with someone like Angus. Especially as I was now discovering what other lame specimens were out there.

I'd always been convinced that finding The One would come with thunderbolts, but what if true love was really about appreciating someone when you had them? What if Angus had been The One, and I'd chosen a career instead?

The door swung open. Dina, a friend of Paula's who worked for the PR agency Harrison & Shriftman, walked into the bar, spotted me, and strode over. Jewish Canadian, with fabulous clothes and frizzy dark hair, she was a tour de force on the PR social circuit.

"Hey, so I guess Paula's still working," said Dina, tossing her Gucci coat on a stool next to me and ordering a whiskey and Diet Coke. "Jesus, I need a drink. My mom's been in town from Toronto all week, nagging me about why I'm not settling down yet. I mean, in this town? Gimme a break."

"Tell me about it," I said miserably, lighting up another cigarette.

"You okay?" said Dina.

"Not really. My old boyfriend back in England got a new girlfriend."

"Shit, that always sucks. Better get you wasted tonight. But wait a minute, didn't you break up with this dude ages ago?"

"Yeah," I said. "But I didn't expect him to fall in love with someone else."

"What you need is a good girls' night," said Dina. "We have to look after each other in this city. All guys suck."

But I didn't want a good girls' night. I wanted my boyfriend back. And that was the problem—Angus didn't suck.

Paula clattered over to join us in a pair of six-inch Jimmy Choos.

"Bye, sweetie." She blew a kiss at the guy she'd been talking to, then turned back to us.

"Jeez, that flack. He had enough Botox in his forehead to wipe out a small nation." She hailed barman Joe.

"Get Bridge another drink too. Her ex-boyfriend's got a new girl-friend," said Dina.

"Oh my God, not that guy from England *still?* You dumped him last year, honey," said Paula. "Still, that must grate, especially after those losers you've been dating here."

"Cheers," I said.

"Who's been dating losers?" said a voice behind me. I spun around. Jack had walked in and now stood behind the three of us. I tried to sit straighter on my stool.

"Bridget has. You know all those losers she puts in her column," said Paula. "I mean, who the hell was that guy who said you talked too loudly on the subway? Excuse me, but why were you even *on* the subway?"

"For once, Paulita, I would have to agree with you," said Jack. He smiled at me. He unthreaded his tie and ordered a Makers Mark.

"Cheers, guys," I said, feeling my cheeks go red. "Kick a girl while she's down, why don't you?"

Jack looked confused by my comment.

"Angus, Bridge's old boyfriend in England, got a new girlfriend," explained Dina.

"Oh, sorry to hear that," he said, glancing at me again.

He didn't really look sorry.

The conversation turned to a discussion of whether Paula should address her lack of a man by adopting a Dachshund she passed in the window of a pet shop in Cobble Hill every morning.

"Are you out of your mind? You're so busy you can barely take con-trol of your own life," said Jack. "You couldn't possibly be allowed to take responsibility for another living being."

"Well, clearly you haven't heard of doggy daycare, Jack," she huffed. They passed me another drink.

Paula then admitted that she had her eye on the dog because she fancied the pet shop store manager.

"That guy is so hot, he gives me tingles in my panties, and I don't mean cooties," she said.

"Paulita, *enough*," said Jack.

We were all still in Langan's two hours later, drunk, and the bar had filled up. By now I was veering between the alcohol-fueled delusion that Angus and India wouldn't last, a stomach-wrenching misery that I had blown my one shot at true love, and a strange heady feeling that Jack's presence sort of made everything okay.

I found it impossible not to watch him as he meandered through the groups of reporters, nursing a tumbler of whiskey, cracking jokes, or nodding sagely, depending on who he was talking to. Behind his sarcasm and snarkiness, it seemed he had a genuine fondness for people. But there was also a strange, uptight barrier around him that made it impossible to work out what he was really thinking.

Occasionally, quite often in fact, he would catch my eye, but I couldn't tell if that was accidental. Dina and Paula were meanwhile still plying me with drinks, insisting that sisterhood was the only way to survive in New York.

Eventually Jack reappeared near us at the bar to order another whiskey. Braver now, I went to stand next to him and got out a cigarette.

"So you're pretty cut-up about the ex-boyfriend, huh?" he said.

"I just feel really afraid all of a sudden. What if he was the love of my life and I let him go?"

He lit my cigarette.

"Maybe if you were the loves of each others' lives, you wouldn't have let each other go."

"But do you think it really works like that?"

He looked at me as if to say "Don't you?"

"I think one day you meet someone, and they rock your world, and you know that's it. You can't settle for anything else."

"Really?" I suddenly wondered what would rock Jack's world.

"Bridget, you seem like you're pretty special."

Jack called me special? He barely knew me.

"There's someone out there who would do anything for you, and he's the person you should be with. Angus, your ex, whatever his name is, I'm sure you loved each other. But I didn't see him flying out here fighting to get you back."

"No, I guess not," I said. Actually that was quite a good point.

"And don't forget, you went back to England, and then you still moved here again."

"I know, I know."

"I think you should wait until you find someone who you would cross the world for—and who would cross the world for you," he said.

We stood in silence for a moment, leaning on the bar, our shoulders nearly touching. The rest of Langan's seemed to fade into a blur, but then I was hammered. Suddenly all I wanted was to have his arms around me. I stubbed out my cigarette.

"Um, so in the meantime, before this knight in shining armor comes my way, can I have a hug to cheer me up?" I said. Tonight I could get away with the request.

"Of course you can," he said quietly.

I held my breath and stepped towards him. I put my arms around his waist, pressing my face into the left side of his shirt. He smelled deliciously of fresh sweat, mixed with clean laundry and smoke. He put his arms around my back, a little stiffly at first, then he held me tightly against him and brushed his cheek on my hair. I stood suspended in the sensation of being so close to him. I suddenly felt safe. Then we stepped away from each other quickly. He turned back to the bar, drained his drink then put a twenty-dollar bill down on the bar.

"Anyway, I got to get going," he said, now avoiding my eye. "Feel better, okay?"

I watched him walk away, immediately hoping to catch him alone again. Was there something between us, or was I imagining the whole thing?

Knickers in the knicker drawer

I began to keep a constant eye on Jack at work. He walked around the office, back straight, his right arm bent slightly behind him, like a cricket fast bowler about to take a wicket.

The *Post*'s business pages were the first read on Wall Street, and Jack helped run the section that was constantly full of key exclusives about mergers and takeovers, hirings and firings, stock and share plunges—all utterly baffling to me. But I had always fancied clever, in-control men—the kind who you would want on your team (as I liked to describe it). And even though Jack wasn't exactly handsome—in fact he frequently looked ruddy, skinned, and hungover—I decided he was the sexiest man in New York.

He sat further down the office from my cluttered row, but my desk—which I had been allocated when I became permanent staff—was on the end. If I wasn't out on a story, he'd sometimes flash me a glance or smile when he passed on his way to the morning or afternoon meeting. Often we would end up late in the office at the same time if the second edition of the business section needed updates and I was writing my column. When he got up to leave, I'd watch him putting on his coat out of the corner of my eye, knowing he was about to walk past my desk.

"Hey, fancy going over to Langan's for a drink?" was all I had to say. I formed the words every single time but couldn't get them out. I already felt like I had "I've got a massive office crush" on you emblazoned on my forehead. And surely if he was interested, he would stop and invite me for a drink. He never did.

Meanwhile, outside the office I was beginning to learn that Paula and Dina had a point about women in New York. With no boyfriends or family around, in a manic, exhausting city, having girlfriends to look out for you was as vital to survival as oxygen.

Gradually I was getting to know three English girls: Pom, an industrious slip of a thing with punky clothes and long, frizzy, blonde hair, who had moved to America on impulse one New Year's Day. She'd scraped by on a tourist visa since, trying to make it as a photographer. Sacha, her laid-back, porcelain-skinned cousin, who worked at the United Nations, went to church on Sundays, and liked to show off about how people mistook her for a young Meg Ryan. And Fi, their excitable, clothes-mad mate. She worked at an ad agency, was in with the big Brit party set, and lived off Hershey's Kisses and wasabi peas. They'd all lived in Manhattan for two years—none of them had boyfriends either. But then they were all four years younger than me.

Olly had introduced me to Pom one night in Milanos when I was still on the exchange. But back then she had been a bit hostile to me—the newcomer—and had spent the entire evening throwing her arms around Olly to prove how close they were. But I'd suspected that her abrasive veneer was a front, and once you got to know her she would be okay.

When I'd moved back to New York, I'd called her up and we'd started out by meeting for the odd brunch and a stroll around the flea market that exploded across a parking lot on 26th Street and Sixth Avenue on weekends. Pom had a fantastic eye for junk and helped me pick out a lamp and cushions for my little bedroom in the East Village. But I was careful never to make her feel like she'd get stuck with me. This, I'd worked out, was the key to making friends.

My slow approach paid off. When I needed Pom the most, I discovered that she had as good a knack for making people feel loved as she did for making them feel uncomfortable.

The crunch came one night not long after Angus called to tell me about India—with the slam of my apartment door. I woke up groaning, knowing what was coming next. Seconds later the whole apartment reverberated with the clatter of high heels mixed with drunken shouting in French.

Pierre, Roman, and their Euro posse had come from Centrofly, a club on West 26th Street, which had a happening VIP room on Fridays. Thanks to the club's French doorman, it was one of the few places where the boys could get past the velvet rope.

That night, I'd agreed to go out with them and had spent a couple of fun hours dancing in the long VIP room, which was filled with a multitude of women in arse-tight designer jeans and sporting ironing-board flat stomachs—the type Pierre and Roman adored. Next to us, Tara Reid and a gaggle of look-alikes were stumbling around a table crammed with bottles of Ketel One and carafes of drinks mixers—which made me feel pretty rock 'n' roll.

With Pierre egging me on, I'd started flirting with a DJ friend of his called Lucian who had just flown in from Paris. That was until Lucian had leeringly suggested we nip back to his hotel for an hour.

"C'mon, I wan' it. I know you English girls love to have fun" was his attempt at seduction.

"I'd rather frig myself on the floor of a slaughterhouse than go home with a random punter like you," had been my oh-so-witty reply.

Admittedly I had found him sexy. He had an angular face and pale eyes—and he danced like a Latino. But I knew myself and Cosmos. Having already knocked back three, I feared that if I touched one more, going back to his hotel would suddenly seem like a good idea. And while flirting was one thing, I wasn't in the mood for some random shag. So I left the club.

Now I groaned under my duvet as the opening chords of Daft Punk's "One More Time" came blasting through my bedroom wall one more bloody time. I put a pillow over my head. I was now thirty, I owned a whole house in London. What was I doing all alone in an overpriced shoe box with a herd of Euros discoing ten feet from my head?

There was a knock on my door. It opened before I had time to shout "Bugger off." Lucian stumbled in and careered onto my bed.

"Hey, English," he slurred in a cloud of smoke and alcohol fumes. "Pierre and Roman said you were in this room. Can I lie down here?"

I refrained from pointing out he already had.

"Lucian, I'm almost asleep. You'll have to go somewhere else." I shoved him hard in the side. "What happened to your hotel room?"

He answered me by clumsily wrenching off his T-shirt and throwing a heavy arm over my waist.

"Oy, Frenchie, you can't stay here," I hissed, squirming away from his grip. He lay comatose, face down on the pillow.

Wide awake now, I lay listening to the thudding music in the darkness. So now I had one DJ in my bed and was being tormented by an aspiring one next door. Why the fuck had I moved to lonely, selfish New York? Maybe if I prayed hard enough, I would wake up back in my bedroom in Shepherd's Bush with Angus next to me and my cat at the end of the bed. Then my insides wrenched: Angus and India.

Lucian seemed to come around. He moved onto his side and ran his palm across my tummy. I turned away from him crossly, but he kept his hand on the side of my waist and I didn't throw it off. After a couple of minutes, he slid it under my T-shirt and began to rub my back.

"Oy, stop it. What are you doing?" I whispered. But it did feel quite nice.

His hand moved up and down across my back. I ignored him. Then it crept to my tummy again and slid downwards across my pelvis. My body responded with small, pleasant tingles. I pretended to be asleep. His hand moved in a circling motion and gradually, oh-so-gradually, caught the cotton band of my knickers. I told myself I would throw him out at any minute. Then slowly, his fingers nudged underneath the cotton. It felt kind of sexy under the warm covers.

Sensing victory, he pulled my knickers off altogether. Now I did turn my back on him in protest. "Hey, fuck off, okay?" I said. But he knew I'd let him take them off. He pulled his own pants off and softly nuzzled my neck. Then I felt him reaching for his jeans pocket and heard the unmistakable sound of a condom wrapper.

"Lucian, forget about it!" I was going to say, but I didn't.

He pulled me onto my back again, ripped the wrapper with his teeth, spat it off the bed, and put the condom on with impressive one-handed dexterity. I lay silent while he did it. What the hell was I doing?

I had no idea. Caught somewhere between loneliness and "who gives a shit?" I hoped it might be worth it.

He climbed on top of me and sank his face into the pillow by the side of my right ear. He began to move his body quickly, his breath sharp with stale booze. His thrusts got faster and harder, and he clamped his hand on my left breast—I wasn't sure whether for his sake or mine. Then he came with a big, heavy groan. He dropped his whole weight on top of me as satisfaction flowed over him and he panted into the pillow. Then he rolled away. We still hadn't kissed, spoken a word, or even looked at each other, for that matter.

He sat up, retrieved his pants and T-shirt, and put them on.

"So, I'm gonna go smoke some joints," he said. Then he got up and joined the party in the next room.

The door shut behind him. It was now dawn outside, and a cold glow filtered in through my Venetian blind. Jesus. Had that just happened? I pulled my legs to my chest, feeling sick. Now he would be sitting down with Pierre and Roman, rolling a spliff—and thanking them for my services, no doubt. Oh God.

I wanted to go out to the bathroom and wash, but I couldn't face them. I didn't even care so much about the physical stuff, but more that I had been pathetic, desperate, and weak enough to let it happen. He probably did it all the time, the arrogant DJ wanker.

I turned over and my eye caught the picture Angus had given me of us at his father's house in Gloucestershire when I'd first left England— which I kept on a plastic chest of drawers by my bed. I sat up and picked it up, cradling it in my lap. There I was, so carefree as he held me in his safe arms. It was as if I were looking into another life.

"Wish you were here to hold me now, babe," I said quietly to his smiling face. The first tear I had shed since I moved back to New York fell onto the wooden frame.

I wiped it away. I reminded myself that I had so much to be proud of. I lived in the greatest city in the world, as Jack called it. I was doing the job I had always dreamed of. I had my name in the *New York Post* every day on top of real news stories, and even my own column on a Sunday that ran my photo for all to see.

I crawled over my bed and looked out of my window at the view of Midtown's jumbled building blocks. The sky was now pearly silver, and the low rising sun had turned the right flank of the Empire State Building to salmon. A police siren wailed in the distance, drifting up over the treetops in Tompkins Square Park. All I could think was that I was alone in a place where I was special to precisely no one.

"Right, put your stuff in a taxi. You're moving in here for a week," said Pom. I'd called her a few hours later when I thought she might be up.

At first I had decided not to tell anyone, ever, that I had allowed a total stranger to walk into my room, have sex with me, and then return to his mates to get stoned. But the moment I had heard her voice, it all tumbled out. Her glorious response had been to blame the whole thing on Pierre and Roman.

"I mean, they should never have shown that nasty opportunist your room!" she'd huffed indignantly.

Pierre had looked slightly sheepish when I'd walked past him making coffee in our kitchen and looking hungover as hell.

"You okay?" he'd said gruffly, rubbing his eyes before lighting a Marlboro.

"Fine!" I said gaily.

But we both knew that he knew what had happened. I felt like I could never face them again.

Pom and Sacha lived in a loft at the then-desolate western end of 14th Street in the Meatpacking District. True to its name, the cobbled six-block corner of Manhattan that was lined with warehouses with iron awnings was a working area where at five in the morning the city's supply of fresh meat—huge carcasses—would be loaded from growling trucks into dank, blood-splattered storage rooms. Even during the day the streets were coated in grease, and in the summer the place stank of rotting flesh.

Pom and Sacha's block, between Ninth and Tenth Avenues, would two years later transform unrecognizably into a chic shopping Mecca with a row of glossy boutiques including Stella McCartney, Alexander McQueen, and La Perla. But back then the street was almost all boarded up and plastered with torn bill stickers promoting bands that no one had ever heard of. At the far corner of Tenth Avenue, you had to pick your way through used condoms and broken glass.

Only the grimy supermarket, Western Beef, with its orange awning that looked like it was about to crash down at any moment, was a hive of activity—that being the constant unloading of crates of cheap food, including perishables, that got piled up on the sidewalk every Monday and seemed to take a week to get into the store.

The girls' loft was an abandoned production studio with big windows at both ends. In it Pom had built three small bedrooms. At one end of the room was a sitting area with a battered sofa and futon, a screen print of the Pink Floyd band members, and a view out onto 14th Street. At the other end was a makeshift kitchen with a cooker and shelves—and, best of all, a big glass-topped table. Three floor-to-ceiling cupboards which had once been crammed with electrical equipment lined one side of the loft. Pom and Sacha had stuffed the hardware into boxes and hung their designer clothes up there instead. The bathroom was barely bigger than the shower stall.

When I arrived that Saturday afternoon, Pom had put fresh sheets on the bed in the tiny, windowless third bedroom that had fairy lights strung around it. The room was used by her other cousin, Liberty, a model who was usually away on fashion shoots. She had also fixed the bedside lamp, put a posy of daisies in a glass next to it, and cleared out a drawer for me in a chest of drawers.

"You always feel more at home once you've put your knickers in the knicker drawer," she said.

And I did.

Later that evening Pom, Sacha, Fi—who lived two blocks away on 13th Street—and I sat at the table eating my first ever sushi delivery—delicious miso soup, edamame, spicy tuna rolls, and salmon sashimi. The perfect meal to pick at while girlie gossiping—and so cheap compared to London.

By now we couldn't stop giggling about the already euphemistically branded "Lucian Encounter." Safely in their apartment with a new bed to sleep in, I'd decided the only thing to do was to shrug it off and laugh about it. After all, what girl didn't have a few dubious shags to her name?

"Once we had this boy to stay at my apartment who climbed into my bed every night and tried to mount me while I was asleep," said Sacha. "On the last night he got me so drunk over dinner I gave in, but it was over in three minutes. I felt like screaming at him 'What do you think I am? A wanking machine?'"

"What about this? One guy I was in bed with once kept trying to shove my hand down his boxer shorts and telling me to hold his pet slug. I mean, what was he thinking?" shrieked Pom.

We cried with laughter, and suddenly I felt like I hadn't laughed properly for months.

"Okay, so all head-pushing, hand-guiding, penis-in-face-thrusting, and condom-wrapper-spitting is officially banned from this loft from now on," said Pom. "Not that we actually get any blokes in here to ban."

"Maybe you should write about the Lucian Encounter in your column. Why you should never let a guy pass out drunk on your bed," said Sacha.

I had thought about this.

This week a total stranger walked into my bedroom, pretended to pass out, then had sex with me without talking to me or kissing me—and then left again to join his friends!

Nope. There were some things the people in my office, the rest of the city, and my parents just didn't need to know.

Lights, camera,
the wrong kind of action

I stood in front of the mirror that hung precariously in the kitchen of our loft, tearing outfits on and off faster than a stripper on speed. My mission was Kate Winslet–meets–Carrie Bradshaw, with a touch of Lois Lane of course. But even with a fresh selection of Paula's cast-offs to pick from, the transformation was proving tricky.

That evening I was to do my first ever turn on TV. I was to "have a drink" with an upper East Side matchmaker called Lisa Ronis who was going to set me up on dates so I could write about the experience in my column. We were going to be filmed for a fly-on-the wall documentary called "To Live and Date in New York." I'd been asked to take part in the show as the city's English-still-searching-for-love columnist, and I'd accepted saying it would be great publicity for the Sunday *Post*. Of course it was vanity that had actually made me agree.

Gradually my column was becoming a popular slot in the paper, as—bar the Lucian Encounter—I shamelessly described everything that happened to me as a single person in New York: from sending flirty e-mails to a blind fix-up suggesting we meet in a hotel bar "because we might need to get a room later," only to arrive and discover I'd been communicating by mistake with an acquaintance of Sacha's who was a professor at the U.N., to the evening I tried to pick up guys at a New York Knicks game and ended up coated in beer. I wrote about how Fi and I had spotted Meg Ryan (the real one) at a fashion party and had obsessively followed her all night—only to find ourselves stuck in an almost-empty VIP room, leading off another VIP room which was so closeted we might as well have not been at the party. In another column I worked out that I had drunk twenty-nine cocktails in one week—although my parents, who religiously printed my column out from the Internet—didn't like that one very much.

But my life in New York was transformed three weeks after the Lucian Encounter. Pom called to say Liberty had got engaged to her English boyfriend and didn't need her room, so would I like to move into the 14th loft permanently? Now I had my own little New York family to come home to—except this family hung out at fancy parties and rolled bedtime joints. I stopped quietly wondering if I'd totally fucked up by leaving London.

Now, between juggling my reporting job and column at the *Post*—and nursing my crush on Jack—I was determined to prove that being single in your thirties was the greatest time a girl could have. And I believed it—most of the time. I wrote in one column:

Thanks to *Bridget Jones* and *Sex and the City*, we've all been brainwashed into believing that a single women in her thirties is a serial screw-up. But at what other time in life would a woman have the maturity to know herself—and cash—to do as she pleases? Not to mention being at her sexual peak.

In another:

Truth be told, I love to wail about my litany of failed affairs, just as I love listening to my friends moaning about theirs. My roommates and I can spend hours around our kitchen table, swapping tales of awful guys, excruciating dates, and awkward sexual encounters. But I doubt we'd get through so many cups of tea if every conversation started "You're not going to believe what the baby did today!"

After all, New York was a city where you might not easily find a husband, but you could do anything else if you put your mind to it—even become a TV star!

My cell phone rang while I was still in front of the mirror. Fuck. I snatched it up. It was still only 8:30 A.M. As usual, on the day I wanted a quiet time in the office I was being sent out early. I shoved the phone under my chin as I opened Sacha's wardrobe and began to riffle through her much more exciting array of togs.

"City Desk, hold for Jerry," said a copy kid. I pulled out a fitted cream silk Chanel shirt and held it to my body in front of the mirror. Now that was more TV.

"Morning," said Jerry, the assignment editor who had replaced Marilyn. "We got a four-year-old in the Bronx stabbed to death by two kids with a ballpoint pen. I need you to get up there as soon as you can."

With the shirt still under my arm, I grabbed a pen and the nearest thing on which to write the address—a sushi menu on the kitchen table.

"Two kids, eight and nine, were playing with the four-year-old in a stairwell, then they stabbed him with the pen. The mother came out and found him."

I scribbled down the facts but tried not to visualize them.

"Where are the kids now?"

"The toddler's in the morgue, the other two are in the 44th precinct. We think they're going to be arraigned in Bronx Family Court today. Just get to the scene, meet photo there."

Five minutes later, I was running down 14th Street to the L train subway station on Eighth Avenue in a creased blue crepe skirt, T-shirt, and flip flops, with Sacha's Chanel stuffed into my bag. I'd have to worry about the transformation into Kate Winslet later.

A twenty-minute subway ride transported me from the wide 14th Street sidewalk jostling with suited Manhattanites marching to work to a steamy Bronx high street where ragtag old men and homeboys hung out smoking in front of fried chicken joints. The temperature was already well into the eighties.

Already sweating, I weaved my way through a slow-moving throng of women pushing baby strollers and turned two corners to Sheridan Avenue. At the end of the block was a bodega which had yellowing windows plastered with signs for discount cigarettes and beer. Opposite it a crowd was milling outside a brown brick, U-shaped, six-storey apartment building. One woman was gesticulating angrily at a male reporter, who was scribbling in his notebook. Two TV vans were parked out in front, their long satellite antenna poles extended like periscopes. I spotted two photographers I recognized from other jobs standing chatting and smoking.

I walked up to them, taking out a cigarette.

"Hey there. Bridget—from the *Post*, so what's the deal?"

"The mom's up there, 5A, she's talking. Check out the blood stain on the stairwell."

"Where do the kids who did it live?" I asked, fag in mouth as I scraped my already grimy hair back into a ponytail.

"Good question. Word is they're foster kids, living on the first floor. But those families either ain't opening their doors or they've taken off."

"Ah, Bridge, about time." I looked around. Matt, the *Post*'s photographer, was walking across the street carrying a cup of coffee.

Matt was a handsome, blue-eyed, lumberjack of a guy, and the joke was that Gretchen the picture editor had hired him to cheer up the single female reporters. But I liked Matt because he was good with people and fun company on stakeouts. And I already had my office crush.

"Guess they've been up already," I said, nodding at a pink-skirted Channel 7 reporter who was talking into her cell phone like she was commanding the Starship *Enterprise* to beam her up out of this sweltering Bronx Street.

"In and out," said Mike. "You'll be about third. Not bad for the *Post*."

Matt and I pushed through the collection of residents and into the entrance of the apartment building. Inside, the musty smell of the festering garbage chute hit our nostrils. In front of us the metal elevator door looked like it had been attacked with a battering ram.

"Let's take the stairs," I said.

At the top of the fifth flight, panting in the heat, we stopped. A patch the unmistakable brown of a blood stain had pooled out across the floor of the landing. Next to it the filthy metal lid of the garbage chute hung half open, away from the wall.

"Well, that's grim," I said, trying to sound cheerful.

"Wait up," said Matt. He crouched down and took pictures.

The door of 5A was ajar.

"Fuck, Jerry never told me the family's name," I whispered back to Matt.

"Valentina Manufort is the mom. The kid is—was called Jesus."

I wrote the names on my hand.

We walked down a narrow hallway in the apartment. It opened up to a kitchen which was furnished with a Formica table and four chairs with yellow plastic-covered chairs. Behind it a man and two women, one older, sat on a threadbare brown sofa. They looked West African. The woman in the middle had eyes swollen from crying.

The trio looked up at Matt and me, resigned, as if they had been waiting for us to arrive. A window was open to the muggy air outside, which echoed with the whir of tired air-conditioning machines. Inside, tragedy filled the room.

"Mrs. Manufort?" I said, dropping to a half kneel to offer the woman in the middle my hand. "We're from the *Post*. I'm so sorry about what happened."

"Her baby was killed two steps from his home," said the older woman in an anguished pitch. "How can it be that two young kids can do this terrible, terrible thing?"

The question hung in front of us, one we were not there to answer.

I exchanged glances with Matt, who was standing by the table with his face tensed so as not to show emotion.

"If you could tell me a little about Jesus, about how you are feeling now," I said, hating myself for the banal question.

"Jesus, he was my angel," said Valentina Manufort. "I only sent him and his sister out to throw a diaper in the garbage chute. Then I went out and saw my baby on the floor. I didn't see anything else. . . . "

Fresh tears tumbled down her face. Matt flashed his camera. I wrote her words in my notepad, feeling lines of sweat sliding down my back.

"He was two steps from home!" she wailed.

I struggled to think of something to say to make it all right.

"We want those boys punished," said the man, who had said he was the boy's father. "If you don't stop them today, they are going to go out and do worse tomorrow."

"Ma'am," said Matt back to the mother. "Do you have a photo of your boy we could look at?"

It was the father who responded again, producing a cheap, black plastic frame which they'd obviously had ready. He handed it to me first. Inside it a toddler with big, mournful eyes was wearing a sailor outfit and holding a moon-shaped rattle. The photo desk was going to love that.

I put my notepad on my knees and admired it out of politeness before handing it to Matt. I tried not to imagine the same little boy's confusion as his playmates turned on him in the stairwell. Matt placed the picture on the kitchen table and crouched down to fix it in his camera's view finder.

The sight of her dead son seemed to drain the last ebbs of strength out of the mother. She clutched my arm.

"You get married, you have a child, and you think everything will be what it should be. But it never works out like that. Life don't stop, it just becomes harder," she said flatly. "His father, he works sixteen hours a day in two security jobs. Now my boy is gone."

The door at the end of the corridor suddenly swung open with a commotion. A man wielding a news camera on his shoulder came marching into the kitchen, followed by a stick-thin woman wearing a black, tailored suit and holding a microphone. Behind them, two other camera crews came trooping in.

"Where's the mom?" said the first, swinging his camera around like a rocket launcher. His prey located, he bore down on the sofa, flicking on the light on the top of his camera as the woman stared up at him.

"You, you're the mom of this kid, right?" She blinked into the bright light which illuminated her smooth, brown, tear-streaked face.

"Hey, you," he said to me. "Move over, you're in my shot."

In seconds the TV reporter was at the sofa too. She already had the boy's photo frame in her hand. I was invisible to her.

"Valentina, will you just hold this picture of your son?" she commanded, then switched her voice to a creamy, earnest tone and thrust her microphone into the woman's face.

"Mrs. Manufort, tell us, what are you going to do without your little boy?"

The mother looked down at the picture and then up at the onslaught of strangers who were filling her kitchen. She began to shake her head. Matt was already retreating down the corridor.

"Ma'am, thank you so much for your time," I said, putting my hand on her arm.

"And next time," I snapped to the TV reporter, "I'd appreciate it if you had the courtesy to let me finish my interview before you start yours."

"We're going live in fifteen, we can't wait," she snapped back. The grieving trio looked at us with resignation.

I got up and pushed my way past the TV crews to the front door. In the hallway, a cameraman from the Spanish-language station, Univision, was filming the blood stain.

I found Matt outside on the sidewalk, kicking his foot against the building wall and smoking a cigarette. I pulled out my phone and dialed the office while he scrolled through his pictures in the display on the back of his digital camera.

I wondered if we would ever get used to marching in on people's misery, focused only on what the paper needed before deserting them and their grief. But then I realized we'd got used to it a long time ago.

Lisa Ronis, the matchmaker, had told me to meet her at the Atlantic Grill on Third Avenue and 76th Street at 7 P.M. She sat waiting for me in a pose of groomed perfection at an outside table when I eventually tore up, straight from the Bronx.

On the sidewalk next to the al fresco seating area, the "To Live and Date in New York" crew—a cameraman, sound guy, and trendy young girl with frizzy hair holding a clipboard—were looking impatient.

I introduced myself, out of breath and apologizing. I had sweat patches under my arms, and my hair was pressed to my forehead like a nylon wig. In the fifteen-minute subway journey back from Grand Concourse to the Upper East Side—another world—I had tried to eject the events of the day from my head.

"Ready to go?" said the clipboard girl in an Australian accent.

"I just need to change my top," I said, pulling Sacha's crumpled Chanel from my bag. I might as well have produced a severed head.

"Er, don't worry about that," she said, eyeing it distastefully. "It doesn't matter too much what you look like. We've already got some fabulous-looking girls on tape, so the variety will be good."

So much for my glamorous new career in TV.

"Okay, just walk towards us down the street, and tell us your name and what you're doing in New York," said the cameraman.

I wanted to tell them I'd just spent eight hours fruitlessly running a half-mile stretch of a Bronx street in between Sheridan Avenue and Bronx Family Court trying to find two boys who'd stabbed a four-year-old to death with a pen, but I suspected that wasn't quite what they wanted.

"Uh, I'm Bridget Harrison. I moved to New York from London in 2000, and I work as a reporter and dating columnist for the *New York Post*."

"Wait up!" said the cameraman. "Maybe we could just get a hair brush."

Sitting across the restaurant table from Lisa Ronis, I got out my notepad again. I flipped past the pages that contained the details of Jesus's death and wrote "Matchmaker Dating Tips" at the top of a clean sheet.

Lisa was of an indeterminate age, somewhere between thirty and forty-five, with smooth olive skin, shoulder-length dark hair, and doe-like eyes under finely arched brows. I still looked like something the cat had dragged in and was now feeling a little drunk. The vodka and tonic I'd ordered off the barman and just consumed in one guzzle was shooting to my cheeks. I tried to ignore the fact that a big, fluffy sound boom was bobbing above our heads and there was a cameraman standing at our table pretending not to be there.

Lisa, clearly no novice at TV, started up in an animated flourish.

"I tell ya, Bridget, there's no city tougher in this world than New York."

You're bloody telling me, I wanted to say.

Lisa posed her theory that so many fabulous women were single in New York because all the fabulous men they wanted to date were too busy with their fabulous careers to find them.

"I mean, who wants to date a guy who's got time to schmuck around in bars?" she said with a well-polished shrug for the camera.

I do, I felt like replying.

Lisa described herself as an ex-"turbo-dater" and told me she started her business after she had a run of success at fixing up her friends.

"You've got to treat dating like a business plan. Set up time slots available to you when you can devote yourself to self improvement—haircuts, manicures, waxing. Then set out a sequence of blind dates with guys who match your criteria. Expect him to make the reservations. I school guys on this, by the way. And have a mental set of questions you want to ask a date to find out if they're what you're looking for."

"Doesn't that sound a bit formulaic and unromantic?" I said.

"Honey, there's no point in being desperate for children, then wasting your time with some guy who never wants to be a father. And women your age have to think about that."

Hurray. I was so glad she'd reminded me. I ordered another drink to cope.

Lisa said she had a database of hundreds of eligible men and women who were all waiting for the perfect partner. For the mere sum of $3,000 a year, singles could get matched to eight hopefuls in her book.

"Any fabulous men and women floating around New York, I will hunt them down and get them for my clients first." She banged the table as she said "hunt them down," then leaned towards me conspiratorially. The sound boom swung to follow her.

"I've been behind at least fifteen marriages and more than ten serious relationships through the years. And you could be next. I can think of several men already who would adore you!"

"Really?" I said doubtfully, grabbing my vodka and tonic from the waiter so quickly that it spilled.

Lisa got out her black book and pencil and asked me what I was looking for in a guy.

"Well . . . he has to be clever, funny—and good at things," I said, trying not to slur my words. A vision of Jack striding through the office flashed into my mind. His cool command of the chaos at the paper was still the best aphrodisiac I knew. I made myself promise to invite him out for a drink the next time I saw him late at work.

"Anyone special you have an eye on?" said Lisa as if she'd read my mind. The cameraman closed in. I glanced nervously at the sound boom.

"Er, no, not really," I said, turning crimson. I was pretty sure Jack would be horrified if he found his name being mentioned in a reality TV show about dating.

"And past relationship history?"

"Uh, I had a serious relationship back in England."

"And what happened to that?" she asked, peering at me again.

"I moved to America a year ago and it didn't work out," I said flatly.

If someone had told me a year ago that I'd end up discussing Angus with an Upper East Side matchmaker who was going to fix me up on blind dates, it's likely I would never have left. But then I'd never have met Jack.

Three days later I went with the TV crew to meet another match-maker—a zany, coiffured woman in her fifties called Janis Spindel, who charged $15,000 a year for her services. And, yes, she told me, there were plenty of men who were prepared to pay that kind of sum to find the right woman.

"But that's almost a down payment on a house," I said, incredulous.

"Not for the kind of men I'm dealing with," she sniffed.

As a precaution against looking like a sewer rat this time, I had taken the morning off work and spent ages choosing a groovy, ironic, pink T-shirt that Pom had given me that said "Playboy Playmate of the Year" across my boobs and a classy, floaty Calypso skirt borrowed from Sacha.

Janis greeted me in an expensive Upper East Side coffee shop called AKA in a gold lame blouse—and eyed my T-shirt disparagingly. She told me she could size someone up in a matter of minutes. Clearly she had already decided not to let me loose on her big-paying clients.

To top Lisa, Janis told me she had scored 300 relationships and 100 marriages in her career. She scoured the city, from gyms to parks to charity events, looking for matches for her clients. On any given day an unsuspecting New Yorker might find her literally running at them from down the street, promising them all sorts of romantic adventures in exchange for their card.

Then she told me she had an exciting LA producer who might just go for my "artsy looks," but warned I'd have to have a makeover first.

"Men like women who look after themselves," she said, eyeing my grubby nails and disheveled curls. "Now what would you wear if I sent you on a date with this guy to a SoHo restaurant?"

"Er, tight jeans, a vest . . . And I guess my red Manolo Blahniks." They were actually Sacha's but I reckoned this would sound good on TV.

"Very good!" she proclaimed. "Women should always wear high heels on a date and their hair down. Men love long hair, preferably straight."

As Janis lectured on, it occurred to me that, be it the older professional crowd paying for a dating service or the twentysomething hipsters using bars, the Internet, and speed-dating nights as their hook-up territory, the principle was the same. First impressions were everything. No wonder everyone complained that going on dates felt more like a job interview. It was a miracle that anyone ever got to the second date. And most of us didn't.

Sandy—the producer from LA—called me several days later on Janis's instruction, but he refused point-blank to be filmed for the TV show or written about, saying he'd rather die than turn up in a tabloid dating column. He picked me up at 11 P.M. from the News Corp building in his black Porsche on a sweltering night (he said he couldn't meet me any earlier as he was working late). In his early forties, Sandy looked like a cross between Woody Allen and Ed Harris as the bereted producer from *The Truman Show*. As we drove through the theater traffic in Times Square, he took sidelong glances at me in his passenger seat, as if I were a mutt he'd just rescued from the dog pound who he could take back in the morning.

We order pan-fried sole, fries, and arugula salads at an outside table in a new, chic Italian restaurant called Macelleria that had opened in the Meatpacking District. I struggled through conversation about the movie industry while feeling wracked by guilt that he had forked out $15,000 to a matchmaker—to get me. The only thing that seemed to impress Sandy was that I asked for mayonnaise with my fries.

"So, how do you reconcile your real dating life with all that stuff you put in your column?" he asked a little sneerily.

"Oh, the column. You know, it's just supposed to be a fun read on Sundays about trying to get by as a single girl in the city. It's not my entire life by any means. My main job is as a news reporter."

He clearly wasn't convinced.

"Well, I can't imagine any sane guy would want to have anything to do with you," he said.

I laughed gaily, assuming he was joking. It never occurred to me that he might have a point.

He dropped me off an hour later outside the loft and whizzed off into the hot night. I never heard from him again. (I found out from Janis the following year that he had married a 6-foot Scandinavian beauty who worked for Calvin Klein.)

Sanjay, my second match-made date, was described by Lisa as "wacky and up for anything." He turned out to be an intense twenty-eight-year-old banker who said he only dated blondes and didn't want to settle down for another ten years at least, because he was focusing on his career. So Lisa had been right about the need to find out your date's priorities early on.

I took Sanjay to a record label party for Groove Armada at Windows on the World, the glitzy restaurant at the very top of the World Trade Center, from which you could see the whole city spread out like a glittering blanket of orange lights. (Fiona had secured the invite through work and had sacrificed it to my cause.)

An uncomfortable Sanjay had agreed to be filmed for "To Live and Date in New York," but clearly regretted it when we had a deathly getting-to-know-you drink with the cameras rolling and he suddenly realized he was about to turn up on TV as the kind of guy who would pay to be fixed up.

"Look, I only signed up with Lisa because I'm just too busy to meet people," he said, glancing shiftily out at the twinkling sprawl of New York that stretched out to the horizons, 100 floors below us.

"So what exactly do you do?" I asked.

"I look after distressed debt," he said.

I looked blank.

"It's like if a date is really ugly on the outside but a good person underneath. We do the same with companies."

"Fascinating," I said, still baffled. Was he dropping hints about me?

"And so you write about your sex life for everyone to read?" he said.

I was taken aback. Now he was being sneery too. Surely people didn't actually see it like that?

"No, my column is more about being a single girl in the city," I mumbled

"We'll, I hope you don't write about me," he said.

Now it was my turn to glance nervously at the view below us. We were being filmed for a dating TV show, for Christ's sake. It was a bit late to be shy.

Then, with the cameras still on our backs, we shuffled self-consciously onto the dance floor. But after several more swiftly consumed drinks, Sanjay suddenly seemed to lose all his reservations about being in my column and on TV. He ceremoniously un-did his top shirt button and leaped into manic, zany dancing mode.

"You know what! I'm a pretty impulsive guy when I get going," he shouted in my ear. "Energy, that's all you need!"

And a bottle of vodka.

He grabbed my hips and began to furiously wiggle, bump, and grind me, shouting, "How low can you go?"

The trendy crowd on the dance floor shuffled away from us in horror, and I could see the camera crew laughing at us. But I had no option but to enthusiastically wiggle, bump, and grind back.

The only thing less sexy than bad dancing is embarrassed dancing—God, I hoped this wasn't about to be beamed into people's homes.

"Now that was great TV!" said the crew when we eventually made it back to the bar. I was beginning to regret ever having got involved with "To Live and Date in New York."

I was more regretful after Sanjay offered to drop me home in a taxi. The moment we were alone in the back of the cab, he leaped on me, trying to match our mouths for a make-out session as the car sped up the West Side Highway.

"C'mon, sex columnist, you owe me," he slurred in a haze of vodka fumes, falling onto me as the cab turned onto West 14th Street. I ducked away, wondering if perhaps I did.

As I climbed the four flights of stairs to our loft, I cursed my vain aspirations for fame. If I carried on like this I would be single forever—and deserved to be.

Here come the English brides

If you're a single girl at a wedding, it's almost impossible not to think a combination of the following: (1) What will my own wedding be like? (2) Who would I marry today given the chance? and (3) Now that I'm all dolled up in my Sunday best, who can I kiss?

But I vowed not to be distracted by any of the above as I got out of the car with my old friend Henry at Cherry Hill, Oxfordshire, in a sunset pink dress with my hair in a wispy up-do that took days of practice to perfect. As we walked across a freshly mown lawn towards a white tent, in front of which a mass of guests milled about drinking champagne in the late summer sunshine, I reminded myself that this wedding was simply a great chance to catch up with old friends in England. But my insides were churning. Angus would be among those old friends.

Milly was one of the gang of London friends with whom we'd spent Millennium New Year's Eve in Jamaica, and her wedding was the second one I had flown back for over the summer. The previous one had been in a tiny village in Scotland, and I'd missed my Easy Jet flight from London to Glasgow. I'd sat in a miserable café, cursing that because I was single, I'd had to make the complicated journey to Scotland on my own when everyone else seemed to be blending the trip with a romantic vacation—stopping in country hotels en route with their other halves.

But at Milly's wedding at least I had someone to arrive with. Henry and I made a beeline for a young-looking waitress who was standing by the marquee entrance holding a tray of champagne. We took a flute each and gulped down some of the tingly nectar.

"Ah, that's better," said Henry. "It's so important to start a wedding on the right note."

We went to say our hellos to Luke the groom and his best man Alex, who were standing together looking dashing by the marquee in morning suits.

"Good luck, matey. It's going to be a fantastic day," said Henry, slapping Luke on the back.

"Sooo excited for you," I said hugging him, with one eye scouring the crowd for Angus. Was he here yet? I couldn't ask.

"Thanks so much for coming all the way from New York, Bridge," said Luke.

"So got your speech ready, Al?" said Henry, "We're all expecting you to bring the house down."

"Don't talk about it, mate," said Alex, shrugging nervously at the large crowd of guests. "I'm sweating so much I might have to change my shirt."

I smiled along with the conversation—and then I forgot them completely. Angus was walking across the lawn towards us.

He was alone (I'd checked he wasn't bringing India), wearing a cream linen suit and a pale purple shirt with a white rose in his buttonhole. His face was tanned golden and he'd grown a small blonde beard which made him look like a rugged Norwegian explorer. Damn, damn, damn. Why couldn't he have just lost his hair and put on twenty pounds since we'd been apart?

I pretended not to have seen him and started laughing really loudly at Alex's jokes. Seconds later he was with us.

"Hi, folks, what a fine day! Luke, congratulations, and how is the lovely bride?" he said, shaking hands with Luke. It was typical that he'd been the one to remember to inquire about Milly.

"Good, good," Luke replied. "Upstairs with her mum, as far as I know."

I stood studying my champagne bubbles. Then he finally turned to me.

"Hi, gorgeous," he said brightly. "Did you just get back from New York?"

"Yesterday, actually!" I said even more brightly.

We embraced, and the scent of his Eau Savage blew away the year since I had last seen him. Suddenly I wanted to cling to him for dear life. He on the other hand seemed crushingly unfazed by my presence.

"Great to see you, Bridge," he said as he let me go.

The marquee smelt of warm air, rush matting, and roses when Henry, Angus, and I trailed in at the back of the crowd, having made the most of the champagne. Long benches had been set up for guests, and a simple wooden pulpit wreathed with white roses waited at the front for the happy couple. The three of us gravitated towards an empty bench near the back. I entered the row first while Henry stopped to say hello to someone, so Angus ended up following me.

Stopping at our adjacent seats, we both picked up and studied our service programs. In the list of unhealthy things to do your heart, I was sure that standing next to the ex you had once planned to marry while at someone else's wedding ranked pretty highly. I felt tempted to make a joke about it but had a sneaking feeling Angus would say, "This day isn't about you, Bridge."

Instead I scanned the tent looking for other people I knew and was amazed by how many of my contemporaries now had young children. There were toddlers everywhere, dressed in cute little cotton summer frocks, and mothers cradling babies in posh shawls. The place looked like a kindergarten on a summer outing.

Rosie, an old university acquaintance, and her husband, Mark, squeezed into the row in front of us. She was clutching a newborn in one arm and a pudgy toddler who was happily mushing some kind of melted chocolate thing into her face in the other. No way. It seemed like only yesterday that Rosie and I were taking Ecstasy and dancing on speakers at raves, and now she had *two* kids? Rosie had always been a knockout twenty-four-hour party girl, but today she looked shattered. You could see the foundation smeared on her once-clear skin. Her pink, floppy hat cocked awkwardly to one side while she shifted the baby in her grasp and tried to wipe the melting chocolate off the toddler. She gave us a hassled wave before turning to whisper crossly at Mark, who picked up the older kid.

Watching her, it struck me that women in their thirties seemed to end up in two groups. There were those with young children who looked back wistfully on their single days and wondered how their glamorous, uncomplicated lives could have turned so suddenly into an exhausting battle against nights of getting no sleep and days of wearing food. Then there were the single women who, for all their independence and beauty sleep, spent most of their time panicking that they should be changing diapers instead. Weddings, I supposed, were the brief, joyous interface between the two.

"Milly and Luke, I have had the pleasure of meeting you both over these past two weeks as you have prepared for this happy day, and what strikes me most is that you are best friends. In the future, that wonderful friendship will be the blessed bond that holds you together," said the vicar to Milly and Luke, who stood in front of him. I didn't dare look at Angus.

"Love is not just about passion, but companionship and respect. It is the knowledge that you will stick by each other and grow together, wherever this life will take you."

Unless one of you buggered off to New York, that was.

Then Milly and Luke became the next of my mates to be married, and the day continued in the typical joyous formula of an English country wedding. There were speeches and toasts on the terrace in front of Milly's parents' rose-covered cottage, and we sat down for the roast beef and new potatoes at round tables decorated with jasmine in another, larger tent. By six o'clock, the noise in the tent had raised to a calamitous level, thanks to the copious amounts of English-style boozing. Gradually guests gravitated onto the dance floor. But I couldn't face gigging around alone, trying to look like the girl who just loves to dance while surrounded by couples. So I milled from table to table, sitting on corners of friend's chairs and catching up instead.

"Hear you're quite the Carrie Bradshaw these days," said one.

I thought of Sanjay trying to snog me in the taxi and the dreaded Lucian Encounter.

"Not quite," I replied.

Meanwhile, like all parties where recent exes are lurking, I was constantly aware of where Angus was in the tent. He seemed to be chatting and dancing with everyone except me. So I drank to keep myself cheerful.

An angelic-looking waiter was manning a makeshift bar by the dance floor, and he grinned at me every time I went over. I began to grin back. At least at weddings there was always the catering staff to flirt with, even if they were a bit on the young side these days.

On my fourth trip to the bar, I decided to go in for the kill with Angel Boy.

"So . . . I guess you're working until the end of the night. . . . Any plans after that?" I winked at him.

"Actually, my girlfriend's picking me up and we're going to our college disco," he said.

Oh, mortification. Why couldn't he have ducked the question? Did he have to remind me he was at least ten years younger than me—and that even he was taken? The little twerp.

"Shame, because tomorrow I'm going back to the set of *Sex and the City,* and I was going to invite you to come," I slurred.

He looked confused. "Look, are you sure you want another drink?"

I changed my order to water and staggered out of the tent to try to compose myself.

I looked up at the stars in the inky countryside sky. Was I now destined to be that aging figure of tragedy at a wedding, pretending it was okay to still be single? But it *was* okay to still be single. I knew it was. Why should everyone end up getting married between the ages of twenty-six and thirty-two anyway? Surely it showed they were all just unimaginative slaves to timing. But then, did there come a point when one had to be practical and accept that timing was important? After all, shriveling eggs were waiting to be fertilized and aging parents were waiting to be grandparents. Oh, fuck. Here they were, the same old questions still nagging in my head. I reminded myself that worrying about it all the time wouldn't change anything. Positive, I had to be positive.

"Bridget Harrison. You are only tragic if you think you are," I said out loud to the garden.

"What was that, Bridge?" A small group of people smoking cigarettes on the lawn all turned to look at me.

"Er, nothing, nothing. Just getting some air," I mumbled and hurried past them.

It had grown quite dark in the garden. I spotted a bench made out of logs halfway down the path towards the cottage. I sat down, sipped my water, and took some deep breaths. A sprinkler was running on the flower beds behind me. It pattered soothingly on the shrub leaves. The steamy scent of roses and lavender hung in the air. I began to feel a bit better. I decided that one day I'd have a cottage garden too, even if I would have to tend to it alone.

I heard footsteps on the path. Angus appeared from the direction of the house.

"You alright, Bridge?"

"Just needed some fresh air. Isn't it lovely out here?"

He sat down on the bench next to me.

"So how are you really?" he said quietly.

"I'm fine, fine. Finally adapting to New York life." I paused to make sure my voice would come out in an appropriate tone. "So how's it going with India?"

"It's good, she's good." He paused. "How about you, you seeing anyone?"

I looked out across the lawn and back up at the scatter of stars above us.

"There's this editor at work, but, well, it's early days."

Early days? That was an understatement. But my spirits lifted a little when I thought of Jack. Jack was my hope as I gradually let my past go.

"Well I hope he's a cool bloke," said Angus.

"Yes, he is cool, and really smart. He's the rising star of the paper." I paused. "In fact, he's just been made my boss."

"*Your boss?*"

"Yeah, well, he just got moved from business to news. So when I get back, I'll have to kinda report to him," I said in a light, jaunty tone. I was still trying to get my head around it myself.

The strands of "Isn't She Lovely" by Stevie Wonder echoed out in the night from the marquee.

"Sounds a bit complicated to me," said Angus.

Now *that* was an understatement.

The longest day

The morning of September 11, 2001, I was woken just before 9 A.M. by Pom standing in my bedroom doorway and looking a little alarmed, brandishing our loft phone.

"Your friend Kathryn called from Channel Four in London. She says a plane just flew into the World Trade Center, can you call her back and tell her what's going on."

I had no idea what was going on. I was fast asleep in a box with no windows.

Shit, shit. I must tell the office was my instinctive response. I scrambled out of bed, grabbed the phone off Pom, and dialed work.

"Hi, it's Bridget here. I think a plane just flew into the World Trade Center. Do you need me to go down there?" I said importantly.

Denise Buffa, a reporter who was standing in as the morning assignment editor that day, was already on overdrive.

"We've got eight reporters and photographers down there. There's been a second plane, we think it's a terrorist attack. I need you to get to the office as soon as you can to start writing."

Three minutes later I was standing on 14th Street, searching wildly for a cab and trying to call Kathryn back on my cell phone. All around people who had been on their way to work were staring in amazement down Hudson Street at the twin towers which shot up in the near distance downtown. They were visible from every avenue if you looked south.

The top floors of both skyscrapers were on fire. Orange flames licked out from the distinct vertical grooves of their cladding. Vicious black smoke poured from behind the flames, pluming into the sky. It looked like someone had stuck two giant roman candles on the end of Manhattan.

I thought of my date in Windows on the World with Sanjay just two weeks before. God, I hoped that no one was still up there now. But, no, surely they must have all got out.

Now thinking only of my instructions to get to the office, I spotted a cab and beat three other pedestrians to it. As the taxi drove north up Eighth Avenue towards Midtown, we passed gatherings of people on every corner, all staring southwards at the towers. They looked like extras in a King Kong movie when the giant beast tromped through the city, all milling with their hands to their faces in disbelief at what they were witnessing.

"This is some crazy shit," said the driver.

"I'd say so," I said, wishing I wasn't going north but south, to where the action was.

The office, when I got there at 9:25 A.M., was quickly filling up with reporters, on shift or not, who lived in Manhattan and could get to the office. The hardcore of the rewrite staff—those who could produce copy the fastest and most fluently—were already glued to the wires and TVs, preparing to take notes from reporters already down at the World Trade Center. Today no one was sitting at their desks, but instead crowded in the main editor's arena under the TV monitors. Every news station was showing the slow-motion repeat of United Airlines Flight 175 going into the South Tower. I looked around the office for Jack. He wasn't in yet.

Denise then called out my name and told me to go down to Bellevue Hospital to wait for casualties. At First Avenue and 20th Street, Bellevue was one of the nearer hospitals to the Twin Towers. I checked for my pager and notepad, then hurried down to the street to look for another cab.

Amazingly the traffic was still moving, although slowly, and now people were streaming out of buildings and along Sixth Avenue towards Central Park. Others anxiously gathered outside our building to watch the monitors that beamed Fox News onto the concourse. The image of the burning towers flashed repeatedly on the TV screens. Down Sixth Avenue you could see them burning for real.

My second taxi driver had his radio tuned to 1010Wins News, and as we crawled east through the narrow cross streets past hurrying, scared pedestrians, we listened to an announcement that a plane had also hit the Pentagon. Other planes were feared missing, perhaps near Chicago and LA. The White House's West Wing and Capitol Hill were being evacuated. All planes across the United States had been grounded.

It struck me that I was alone in the back of a cab in a city under attack, as America descended into chaos. But for some reason I wasn't scared. I felt only a strange sense of awe that something huge was happening that was out of anyone's control. And whatever did happen next, I had a job to do for the *Post*.

Less calm was a 1010Wins radio correspondent who was describing the burning towers live on air from a roof in New Jersey. As she watched and we listened, the South Tower fell. She cried out, a strangled anguished wail. "Oh my God, the tower, it just fell! One of the towers just fell!" She sobbed. "Oh my God, oh my God, oh my God." Still I wished I was down there.

The ugly concrete monolith of Bellevue, sandwiched between First Avenue and the FDR—the route that stretches up the east edge of Manhattan—was in a state of apprehensive activity as I got out of the cab and quickly worked out where the first casualties would arrive. On the left side of the building, an area outside the Emergency entrance was filling up with a line of ambulances preparing to be dispatched downtown. As I hurried towards them, a troop of medical students fitted out in green scrubs marched across the parking lot towards the Emergency entrance, their young faces looking pale and determined. I later found out they had been pulled straight from their classrooms to get ready for the flood of casualties.

The main foyer of the hospital, meanwhile, was becoming crowded with grim-faced New Yorkers turning up to donate blood—anything to help out. Hassled staff tried to organize chairs for them and get them into an orderly line as their numbers grew. Regular patients—many wearing hospital gowns, some in wheelchairs or on crutches, others wheeling IV drips—suddenly looked scared, lost, and weak in the mayhem.

TV crews and reporters were descending—we were all there—the *New York Times,* the *Daily News, Newsday,* CNN, Fox, NY1, Channels 4, 7, and 11, 10.10 Wins, and even someone from the BBC. At first we rushed around the hospital freely, trying to get into the emergency wards. Rumors swirled that whole floors had been cleared and that beds were already crammed with the bloodied and dying (the stories all turned out to be untrue). But quickly the security guards rounded us up, and the harangued hospital communications director begged us to stay in one place, promising updates as soon as anything happened. Shortly after, we heard the North Tower had fallen too.

As the surreal morning moved into afternoon, we gathered every hour for a press conference in a foyer at the back of the hospital, each time being told that the number of casualties which had arrived at the hospital remained little more than a dozen. I called the office from a pay phone each time, but I had little to tell them. I spent much of the day sitting outside the south entrance of the hospital that backed onto the FDR, which had been closed, watching a steady stream of wailing emergency vehicles, trucks, fire engines, and ambulances speeding downtown. But none seemed to come back.

I'd quit smoking (again), but today I decided to start (again). A CNN cameraman handed me a Marlboro Red, and we sat on the concrete steps leading up to the hospital double doors, listening to the sirens.

"Not much point in worrying about dying of lung cancer when the world's probably about to end," I joked. A nurse in greens scrubs joined us to get a light.

"What's going on around there? Where are all the injured people? There must have been hundreds of people in the towers," I said to her.

"Honey, your guess is as good as mine. We been waiting all day. They say either people walked away or they didn't make it out at all," she said.

The three of us sat there, smoking in silence trying to get our heads around what she had just said.

A car pulled up. It was caked in thick white dust. The windshield wipers had barely managed to scrape a patch for the driver to see through.

"Fucking hell," I said.

The car belonged to one of the hospital directors, the nurse told us. He had gone down to the Emergency Command Center at the World Trade Center. The director got out of the car, and he was also covered in white dust. As we ran over with our notepads, a gust of wind hit the windshield, flinging the dust up into a cloud which enveloped us all. Suddenly my eyes were stinging and I felt like someone had poured acid into my lungs.

We staggered around coughing, shielding our faces, backing away. The dust smelt acrid and bitter—a distinct, spine-chilling smell that the entire city would soon come to recognize as the stench of Ground Zero.

As I rubbed my streaming eyes, it finally began to dawn on me quite how bad things must be downtown. I hoped our reporters were safe, and I wondered how Jack and the rest of them were doing in the office.

A woman appeared at the entrance, covered in the same dust. She looked lost and disorientated. We surrounded her, but even the pushy TV reporters were subdued today.

She told us her name was Tiffany Keeling and that she had flown in from Albuquerque for a training session in computer systems at Morgan Stanley on the sixty-first floor of the South Tower. It was her first time in New York, and just before 8:45 A.M. the training group had taken a break. Everyone had been standing around, looking out of the windows admiring the view.

"Suddenly there was a bang and everything shook. Then we saw hundreds of papers falling past the windows. We thought there was a tickertape parade," she said.

As we scribbled furiously in our pads, she told us how she had then spotted fire on the street far below, so she and her colleagues had grabbed their bags and started walking down the emergency exit stairwell. But two floors down, the building speaker system had told them they weren't in imminent danger.

"At that point a lot of people went back upstairs again," she said as tears began to fall down her dusty face, leaving shiny lines on her cheeks. "I haven't heard from any of them since."

She had still been trudging down the seemingly neverending stairs when the second plane had hit. "Suddenly there was chaos. The whole building was shaking, cracks were appearing all around us, there was blood all over the stairs. You could smell the fumes of the airplane fuel," she said.

For the first time, I allowed myself to imagine the horrific scene inside the towers—one I would eventually come to know so well after dozens of interviews over the next few months.

Tiffany Keeling told us she only made it down because a stranger had found her on the twenty-fifth floor, collapsed and exhausted, and told her he wasn't leaving the building without her. When they finally made it to the bottom, they stumbled out across the street from the towers and fell to their knees.

"There was just a sea of people in between the buildings and where we were sitting," she said. "Then someone said there was another plane. I looked up and thought I saw a shadow. Next thing I knew, the building was coming at me. It was just coming down. I dropped to the ground and pulled my jacket over my head and I thought, 'I'm going to die today.'

"Then it felt like it was hailing on my back. I couldn't breathe, the air was solid. At that point I thought I was dead. Then I remember someone saying to me, 'You're not dead, you're not dead.' I was led away, but I didn't know how I was walking. Then I looked back, and all the police cars, all the people who had been in front of the building were just gone. They were just gone."

She wept openly now and the group of reporters and camera crews stood silently around her, stunned.

"What happened to the guy who helped you out?" I said.

She looked at me and simply shook her head. I wished I hadn't asked.

Later I saw her standing alone in the car park, the dust still matted in her hair, crying and trying to call a taxi from a pay phone. It hit me that she was alone in New York, unable to leave, with no idea what had happened to her friends and with only nightmares ahead of her. She wandered off towards First Avenue, and as I watched her I suddenly wondered why I hadn't gone to help her. Even today, I was viewing someone's grief as an opportunity to get a quote.

By 11 P.M., most of the media had left the hospital, and the TV crews were preparing to do final live segments for the late news. I called the office once more. I got put through to Steve.

"Can you keep working?" he asked. "We're hearing police units from upstate are gathering on the West Side Highway to go down and help with the rescue."

"Of course," I said. Somehow as long as I was still working I would be safe.

I stopped on First Avenue, bought a packet of cigarettes, and began to walk the eleven avenues across and up Manhattan to the West Side. The city was empty. The ever present din of taxi horns, gridlock traffic, and buses had been extinguished. Instead a horrified hush echoed down the long avenues, broken only by the wail of new sirens. Shops were shut, normally packed restaurants were closed, and the bars were empty. As I walked alone in the darkness, able to hear my steps on the sidewalk, it felt as if the whole city was under siege.

I passed a few dazed people also wandering along, and every face carried the same look of stunned disbelief. "It seems the city's a dark place tonight," said one man standing on 40th Street as I headed west from Fifth Avenue. "This world will never be the same again."

As I turned to pass Bryant Park, the posters and tents erected for New York Fashion Week fluttered eerily in the wind, looking strange and out of place. Glossy ads on bus stops for H+M, Swatch, and Nokia phones suddenly looked meaningless. Times Square was devoid of its crowds, and the bright lights shed a hollow neon glow onto the empty pavement. A few tourists walked around looking lost as if they'd been woken up too early and were not quite sure where they were.

In this part of town a few bars were open, and small pockets of people stood around TV sets as if they were watching a Yankees game. Instead every station was playing over and over again the moments when the South Tower and then the North Tower disintegrated in a cloud of dust.

I got to the West Side at midnight, and as Steve had predicted, lines of county police cars from upstate New York, Pennsylvania, and Connecticut had gathered on the closed highway. The uniformed volunteer operation was being organized from a small trailer in front of the Javits Convention Center. But you could tell no one really knew what to expect or what was going on.

Solemn groups of uniformed policemen stood around in the darkness next to their cars, talking quietly. I got out my notepad again and approached one officer leaning against his car. He told me his name was Sergeant Glenn Carlson and that he was from the Mount Pleasant Police in Westchester County in upstate New York.

"They've been pulling in all day," he said quietly, nodding to the dozens of police cars lined up behind his own. "We came down at 3 P.M. this afternoon, and we're standing by to do whatever is required. We'll do anything, anything to help. We'll direct traffic, help with the crowds, pull bodies out. Whatever they need us to do."

A few vehicles down, Officer Timothy Mahoney from Dobbs Ferry, Westchester County, sat smoking a cigarette in his car and staring downtown.

"There are men buried down there, maybe some still alive. We'll work until they tell us to go home," he said.

I called the office again. This time Jack answered the phone himself. His voice sounded hollow and exhausted. Since coming back from the wedding in England, I had begun to dream that we might get together, despite his promotion to the City Desk. Now the idea seemed ludicrous, frivolous, irrelevant.

"So wassup?" he said.

I told him I'd interviewed the volunteer cops as Steve had requested, and he told me to dump my notes to one of several reporters still doing rewrite in the office, and then to go home and get some sleep.

"We need you ready and rested for tomorrow," he said.

"Is everyone alright?"

"Yeah, the reporters and photographers down there, they all got through it. Some are still there now."

His voice dropped.

"Are you okay?"

"Yeah," I said.

There was nothing else to say.

Anthrax this

· ·

"Hello my name is Bridget Harrison. I'm a reporter with the *New York Post*. I know this must be a very difficult time for you, but I'm writing a story about the first people to have applied for death certificates for their loved ones after the World Trade Center attacks, and I gather that you took the step of applying for one for your wife. Um. I was just wondering if you have received it yet."

"Hi, it's Bridget Harrison, the reporter with the *Post*. We spoke yesterday. Just wondering if anything arrived in the mail today?"

"Hi, it's Bridget from the *Post*. Any news? Oh right, it came. I'm so sorry. So would you mind if we sent a photographer to take a picture of you—and it?"

It was three weeks after September 11, the whole city was mired in bereavement, and I was cringing at myself. Few tasks were worse than trying to coerce a grieving person into making an appearance in your newspaper. And it felt like this had now become my one and only job.

The global headline-grabbing events of the actual attacks on the World Trade Center had now turned into thousands of human stories of lost loved ones. The traders and secretaries who'd worked on the upper floors of the two towers; the managers who'd gone for breakfast meetings at Windows on the World; the carpenters and steelworkers who'd been carrying out repairs; the on- and off-duty firefighters, cops, and paramedics who'd rushed to Lower Manhattan after the planes had hit.

All around Manhattan, photocopied pictures of missing husbands, wives, sons, daughters, and fiancés in holiday snaps, graduation pictures, and wedding portraits fluttered on every bus stop and lamp post. They were plastered next to ticket booths at subway stations, at Penn Station and Grand Central, and on the wall of the Armory on Lexington Avenue, which had turned into a victims' help center. In the days after the attacks, families had flooded there, hoping a missing loved one might still turn up unidentified in a hospital. In the office we called it "The Wailing Wall."

Each day reporters were dispatched to the Armory, to Ground Zero, to memorial services, and now gradually to the first funerals for fire-fighters—epic occasions attended by 3,000 of New York's Bravest in ceremonial uniform, lining the street as a fire truck and coffin slowly passed, accompanied by the mournful sound of the NYPD Pipes & Drums. At each one, a huge American flag flew from a fire rig, the Stars and Stripes glowing brilliantly in the bright fall sunshine. On those occasions, I understood American's patriotic pride—and felt it myself. I would never forget the resolute grief of those families who'd lost good men who were too young to die.

The editor-in-chief—Col Allan—who had replaced Xana five months previously—decreed that we would be the paper of the city's heroes. We covered every single funeral over the following months, and over the next three years, as remains were gradually identified.

Meantime, when city officials announced they would issue fast-track death certificates for September 11 victims, I was assigned the task of approaching the first batch of seventy families who had applied for them. Col was determined that we would run the first historic photo of a 9/11 death certificate, which meant I had to call the families every day to make sure we got the photo the very morning the certificates arrived in the mail.

It was bad enough having to call and ask someone just once if they'd received their death certificate for their loved one, let alone doing so four days in a row. But however much I dreaded picking up the phone, I was more afraid of being beaten by one of the other papers—and then having to explain why.

On my desk I kept a pile of papers with each family's name and phone number, tracked down through computer records by our library staff. I took a deep breath before dialing every number, never knowing what to expect at the other end—stoic helpfulness, a lonely need to talk, difficulty in stringing a sentence together, and, mostly, phone-slamming fury at my request.

On October 5, 2001, the first 9/11 death certificates landed on doormats. The following day the *New York Post* front page showed the death certificate of a thirty-nine-year-old Cantor Fitzgerald, bond broker who'd worked on the ninety-first floor of the North Tower. His wife told me she knew the moment she watched the attacks on the TV that her four children would not see their father again. The death certificate didn't bring closure, she said. That came when she saw the towers fall.

"Right, I see," I'd said, my phone receiver jammed under my chin as I typed her words onto my computer. For the umpteenth time in the past three weeks, I couldn't think of anything adequate to say.

But at least work at the *Post* was all-consuming that extraordinary fall. While the entire city lived in anxiety that Al-Qaeda wasn't done with us yet, the *Post* became a comforting community. Anne Aquilina arranged for pizzas to be delivered to the office, because we had no time to run for lunch and we stayed late most nights. Langan's was doing a roaring trade, as we were all drinking heavily.

But for many New York singles, their much-championed independence turned into a jumpy dread of nights alone. Often people were woken by wailing sirens or the sudden roar of F–16s patrolling the sky, petrified a bigger attack was underway and there was no one to turn to.

Pom, Sacha, and I now slept with our bedroom doors open in the loft, and I noticed we'd started to call "good night" to each other from our beds like we were doing an impression of *The Waltons*. Fi, whose own roommate had rekindled with his recent ex-girlfriend and had fled to the Hamptons, came over most nights and ended up sleeping in Sacha's bed.

I, too, wondered what I would do if a dirty bomb exploded in the city and we suddenly had to flee chemical fumes. Who would I turn to for help with no family in New York? Would it be weird to call Jack? I fantasized that he would battle through mass panic in Manhattan to find me and whisk me to some cozy upstate farmhouse. Then I reminded myself that even if a dirty bomb went off, we'd be covering it. Jack would be too busy in the office to come rescue me.

But although there was apprehension and grief in New York, there was also defiance. It was amazing how quickly the city got used to the previously inconceivable idea that Lower Manhattan was now a dusty ghost town leading to a vast, smoldering pile of twisted metal and concrete which had been the awesome Twin Towers. Now if you looked downtown, dirty brown smoke filled the gap in the horizon where they had stood.

At night—as encouraged by the mayor—Fi and I often went to Lower Manhattan restaurants that were now desperate for customers. Beyond Liberty Street, the sky was eerily bright from massive white spotlights that beamed down on Ground Zero to illuminate the 24/7 rescue effort, and the acrid stench that I had first smelled outside Bellevue Hospital filled the air. Each time it made you say prayers for the rescue workers still toiling there.

Two weeks after the attacks, I wrote a column about how a city that had no time for anyone had suddenly become a caring place. I'd noticed how people had started to smile at each other on the street and to help women with strollers on the subway. At the F train stop on 14th Street, someone started to leave five-dollar bills for a sleeping beggar who was usually lucky to get a couple of quarters in his cup. The most self-centered city in the world was looking out for its own.

There were also endless jokes about September 11 sex—with guys claiming it had never been so easy to hook up, as no one wanted to sleep alone. I had found myself spending the odd night with my old flame, vague Tom. We'd bumped into each other on the street and gone for a catch-up drink, and I'd suddenly found myself pawing at him, desperate for affection.

Ironically, I now got to spend more time than ever with Jack. He came into Langan's most nights, looking exhausted and red-eyed, and we often swapped glances in the bar. But despite my dirty-bomb rescue fantasy, I told myself that romance was now out of the question. Instead I was happy to make do with knowing that he and I—and everyone at the tabloid—were at least in these strange new circumstances together. And we were.

Shortly after I had written the death certificate story, I was working late on a new column about my encounter with Tom, titled INTO THE

ARMS OF STRANGERS, when Jack and the editor-in-chief reappeared in the office. They gathered all the staff together and announced that the *Post* had been hit by anthrax.

An envelope addressed simply "Editor" had arrived in our office some time over the past three weeks and ended up in the editorial department. It was eventually opened by a writer, Johanna Huden, who was now suffering a black lesion on her right middle finger. Envelopes laced with anthrax addressed in a similar hand had already been sent to NBC news anchor Tom Brokaw, ABC News and CBS News, and Senators Tom Daschle and Patrick Leahy. All had been sent through the main post office in Trenton, New Jersey. (In all, five people eventually died from the anthrax, including a photo editor in at the Florida-based tabloid the *Sun* and two employees of a Washington, D.C., mail facility—in addition to a Vietnamese immigrant from New York and a ninety-four-year-old woman from Connecticut who cops believe touched cross-contaminated letters.)

Everyone in the office looked solemn during the announcement. Then we all went to Langan's and made jokes about the fact that, thanks to our chaotic dump of an office, an anthrax-laden envelope had sat around for a week unnoticed and unopened.

Two days later, the *Post* ran a front page with a picture of Johanna sticking her bandaged middle finger up at Osama Bin Laden and whomever else might be responsible for sending out the lethal letters. The headline over her birdie was ANTHRAX THIS.

Over the next week, men in white spacesuits tromped through the office to carry out tests—while we all still sat at our computers in our normal clothes. The area of the office where the envelope had been found was cordoned off and covered with plastic sheets and "toxic danger" signs. We stuck balloons and paper stars on the plastic to make it look more cheerful. Because we were the *New York Post*, we had the city's grief to document and its lost heroes to champion.

And of course we were all secretly proud that someone had bothered to send *us* anthrax rather than the *Daily News*.

My big foreign assignment: rainy village, UK
....

"Tabloid news reporting is not in any shape or form glamorous," my friend Sarah at the *Times* had always said. "You live at the mercy of a desk full of news editors who can send you anywhere, day or night, whether you like it not. You are the person someone least wants to see when they're in a situation they least want to be in. You have to force people to give you information when odds are it will shaft them. And it's unrelenting, because no matter what you do, the paper will always want more."

"But, come on, isn't it amazing to be dispatched across the world to where the action is at a moment's notice?" I'd always said back. Sarah had worked as a reporter for a UK tabloid for many years before moving to the *Times*.

"Yeah, it's amazing to be woken up at 2 A.M., told to get out of your warm bed and drive to some miserable village in central France where the mistress of some second-rate TV host has suddenly turned up— arriving at dawn to find the whole place shuttered up and having to sleep in your car."

Now as I stood in the rain banging on the door of a pub called the Slaughtered Lamb in a drab little hamlet near Guildford in southeast England, straight off an overnight flight from New York, I wondered if she'd had a point. I would rather have been anywhere right now than freezing to death in this godforsaken place with no idea when I'd be able to leave again.

"Hello, is anyone there? Do you have any free rooms?" I called through the pub door letter box, sounding like a one-woman Nativity play.

"Sorry, we're not open for another fifty-seven minutes," came a voice from inside.

"Could you make an exception? It's chucking it down out here."

"Rules is rules." Oh, glorious England. It was so good to be back.

I retreated across a soggy triangle of grass which constituted the village green of Peaslake, got back into my hired Fiat Punto, and put my head on the steering wheel. The backs of my eyeballs stung with lack of sleep. It was only 10 A.M.

Less than twelve hours before, in New York, Jack had rushed up to my desk and told me to get on a plane to the UK as fast as I could. Generosa Ammon, whose wealthy Wall Street husband, Ted Ammon, had been mysteriously bludgeoned to death in the Hamptons, had just married her shady electrician boyfriend. The pair had suddenly materialized in Peaslake, Surrey.

Ted Ammon had had a country home in the village, ten miles from Guildford, and Generosa was now apparently using it for her honeymoon.

The scandalous Ammon saga had been enthralling New Yorkers since Ted had been killed in October, a month after the World Trade Center attacks, providing a little salacious, gossipy relief in a paper still full of September 11 stories.

Ted Ammon had been whacked over the head as he lay sleeping in bed, right in the middle of a bitter custody battle over the pair's adopted twins and his $50 million fortune. With Ted dead before divorce papers were signed, Generosa had bagged the lot, and everyone suspected that the electrician, Danny Pelosi, had killed Ted. (Pelosi was to be convicted of the murder two years later.)

I was the obvious choice to go on an assignment to the UK, but I was still proud that Jack had asked me. Making the paper great had become Jack's all-consuming passion. I wanted to prove it was mine too.

I had grabbed my phone and snagged the last seat on a packed flight to London, rushed home to throw some clothes in a bag, and then cabbed it to JFK. I'd landed at Heathrow seven sleepless hours later, rushed straight to a Budget car rental office, and driven for two hours in the rain with a map between my knees.

And now the fucking pub was closed for another "fifty-seven minutes." Stuck in the Punto, I gave up on my plan of showering and called Geoff, a photographer from a Southeast England news agency, which had tipped us off that Generosa and Danny were in the village. Geoff gave me directions to a nearby lane and told me to look for a long, narrow drive barred with gates that said "Coverwood House, Private Property."

I was already there when his old, battered, white Land Rover pulled up. We got out of our cars and shook hands like spies in a John le Carre novel.

"So what's the plan? Do we just steam up there?" I asked.

"Not likely, can't you read the sign? I can't afford to get arrested," said Geoff. "You'll have to ring them."

He told me he had followed the couple out of the lane the night before and cornered them in Guildford. Remarkably, Danny had slipped him his cell phone number, which he now handed to me. I dialed it, not entirely sure what I was going to say.

"Yeah?" snapped a Long Island accent after several rings.

"Hi, Danny? It's Bridget Harrison here. Do you have a couple of minutes for a chat?"

"Chat? Do I know you?"

"Er, not exactly. But if you come meet me, I'll explain. I'm, er, I'm standing at the end of your drive."

"My drive? Who are you?"

"I'm a reporter from the *New York Post.*"

"Jesus Christ, you fuckin' people. Can't you just leave us alone?" He slammed down the phone.

I dialed his number again. He answered immediately.

"What do you want from us?"

"I was just wondering how you and Generosa were doing—on your honeymoon." I looked desperately at Geoff, who offered some advice.

"Tell him you're not budging until they come down and talk to you," he said.

"Danny, I'm sticking by your gates until I get to meet you in person," I said.

"Knock yourself out. If you set foot on my property, I'll have you thrown in jail." The phone went dead again.

I turned to Geoff. "He wasn't enormously receptive."

"Don't worry, he'll come down. She's not happy we're here, but he just can't resist the attention."

Geoff was a solid character in a beige anorak. He'd been covering the South East for twenty years, and I felt emboldened by his presence. But suddenly he announced he had to go and pick up his wife from Safeway. "I've got my picture, anyway," he said cheerfully. "Best of luck."

Now alone in the dripping lane, I stamped my feet to keep warm, anxiously staring up the driveway for signs of life. What if Jack had sent me all this way and I got nothing?

Beginning to panic, I approached the gates and tried to push them open, but they were locked. I wondered if I should start clambering through the bushes towards the house. What would Lois Lane do? Then suddenly I heard the sound of a car.

A green Jaguar came crawling down the driveway, twigs snapping under its tires. The gates clunked, then slowly opened. Danny Pelosi was at the wheel.

Quickly I stepped out to block the car's path, praying that the speculation that Pelosi was a psychopath who'd whacked Ted Ammon over the head in cold blood was wrong.

He saw me, but the car kept up its pace, its low hood heading straight for me. I stood rooted to the spot, thinking of Jack. If I died on an assignment, would he tell people at my funeral that he had loved me all along? Would getting his attention be worth a broken bone or two? Pelosi screeched to a halt within a foot of my knees. He leaned over and opened his passenger door.

"If you wanna talk, get in," he said.

Close up, Danny was sallow-faced with darting, ratty little eyes. His jet black hair was combed back, thinning over his temples. But he had an elegant Roman nose, and I could see why a desperate, unhappily married woman like Generosa might have fallen for him while he toiled on her fixtures and fittings.

He turned to me in the car and flashed a charming smile.

"Look," he said, "me and Generosa, we're just here trying to settle the kids in school. Can't you leave us alone? The twins have been through a lot. People have been saying Ted might have been gay."

Not that old chestnut.

I asked him what he and Generosa had been doing since they arrived.

"You know, the usual stuff. We're just trying to live like a normal English couple. Relaxing, not answering the telephone, not speaking with lawyers. We've had dinner in Guildford, we walked to some old churches."

The idea of anyone visiting churches in the south of England in January was so improbable I laughed.

He flashed me a hard stare but kept the sugar in his voice.

"You know, once all this is out of the way, I see a very good life for me and her here in England. England is like upstate New York. I always intended to move here eventually."

He glanced out of the window shiftily. I could tell he was lying.

"And what about Ted's death?" I said.

He turned back to eyeball me. His dark eyes had turned cold.

"The cops are wasting their time if they think that had anything to do with me or Generosa. She nor I had nothing to do with it. You got that?" he growled.

I nodded, taken aback by the sudden venom in his voice.

"And I'm tellin' you, if you come on my property again, I'll have you arrested. Now get the hell out of my car."

He leaned over to open my door, and for one moment I thought he was going to elbow me in the face. I scrambled out of the passenger's seat, and he reversed back up the drive through the gates, his tires spraying me with freezing mud.

Shit. I had Pelosi and now he was gone again. I should have refused to get out of his car until he told me something I didn't already know. But now instead of having a scoop I was, well, just soaked. There was no option but to return to the pub.

The Slaughtered Lamb was a pub which had clearly not seen a makeover for years. It had a small saloon with drab, tobacco-stained walls and red velvet stools set around shiny, dark wooden tables. In one corner two men in battered tweeds who looked like they kept pet weasels in their pockets sat in front of two pints of bitter and two packets of Rothman cigarettes. The stink of stale smoke and industrial cleaner hung in the air.

A wiry barman who looked like he'd never seen the sun was unloading glasses from a dishwasher. I asked him if there were any free rooms.

"All of them," he said, not looking up from the dishwasher.

When he'd finished with the glasses, he led me out the back door to a low prefab building that looked like it had been spirited in from the movie *Psyhco*. There were five shabby doors with numbers on them, each next to a window covered in lace curtain. He opened No. 1. to a musty room containing twin beds covered in faded green eiderdowns to match the wall paint. An ancient TV and fridge stood in one corner on a Formica dressing table. There was a bathroom at the back with a plastic shower squeezed in one corner.

"Do you have Internet access, by any chance?" I asked cheerfully, feeling like banging my head on the wall at the misery of it all.

"There's a phone line. Can't you plug into that? Now if you're settled, I've got to get back to the bar."

"Oh, before you go . . . Just wondering, you don't know anything about that house on the hill, do you? Coverwood? Or anyone who might?"

"Nope."

"It's just I'm a reporter from New York and I've got to do a story on it. There's an American couple there who—"

"Sorry, can't help you." And with that he was gone.

I sat down on the saggy bed, defeated. But at least I had spoken to Pelosi. I dialed the office to tell them.

Steve came on the phone. He sounded rushed and disinterested as I relayed my news.

"They had dinner in Guildford? Was it pizza? Find out if they left a tip. Do people know them in the village? Find out if they have any staff you can talk to. Where are the kids going to school? I'll need you to file no later than 5 P.M. There's a lot going on today." Then he was gone.

I put my head in my hands. Maybe I just wasn't cut out to be a reporter. I couldn't have cared less if Danny and Generosa had eaten pizza in Guildford and left a tip. And where the hell was I going to find their staff? There was nothing else for it but to knock on every door in the village. I picked up my notepad and headed back out into the rain.

Peaslake was a collection of old cottages and postwar bungalows strung along three roads in a dip in a valley, with the pub and green at the bottom. Perhaps I could find a cleaning lady who worked at Coverwood House? But this wasn't an episode of Miss Marple.

"Tabloid newspaper? You're asking about someone's private life. I can't help you, I'm afraid"—followed by a door slammed in my face. That was the response at every house. I might as well have been canvassing as the new Guildford candidate for the Nazis.

I wondered what Sarah would have done in her tabloid days. She would have had the balls to march up to Coverwood House and demand to speak to Generosa in person, private property or not. I decided to drive back up the hill. I parked the car a quarter of a mile from the drive entrance, ignored the hollow tiredness in my stomach, and headed into the bushes.

A thick wooded area sloped upwards to where I guessed the house would be. I clambered though it, my jeans and shoes immediately soaking up the rainwater clinging to the branches and brambles. I was freezing and alone in a dark wood. But at least I wasn't having doors slammed in my face.

Eventually I spotted the mansion through the trees. It was a large, gray, stone Tudor affair topped by big, ugly chimneys. All the lights were on, bright in the winter afternoon darkness. The Jag sat out front in a gravel driveway.

I tried to work out what to do next—other than stand behind a tree with my heart pounding in my mouth. Did I even have the balls to crawl up and peer through the windows, let alone bang on the front door?

Then suddenly I heard a car door slam, followed by the rev of an engine. The bright white beam of headlights swung through the trees.

Terrified, I launched myself onto the soggy ground like a crazed marine. Tires crunched down the wet driveway, disappearing towards the road. Then it hit me. What the hell was I doing sprawling in this stupid wood? I should have been staking out the lane, waiting to follow them. Fuck. Fuck. Fuck.

On a story like this, there always seemed to be so many ways to proceed. Why did I always pick the wrong one? It was now nearly 6 P.M., three hours before deadline in New York, and all I had was the brief interview with Pelosi. Stumped again, I had no option but to go back and work the pub.

The Slaughtered Lamb had filled up when I walked back into the saloon. Now at least eight more elderly men were stationed in front of pints and ashtrays. A younger couple sat in the window, sipping gin and tonics. The barman was pulling a pint of Guinness for a middle-aged man wearing walking boots who was standing at the bar holding a £5 note. I sidled up to him.

"Hi there," I said cheerily.

The man looked around at me like I'd just spat in his pint.

"Evening."

"Just wondering, actually . . . if you knew anything about that house over on the hill, Coverwood."

No response.

"Um, I hear there's an American couple staying there. . . . Wondering if anyone had seen them recently?"

"The place is empty most of the year, that's all I know," said the man.

"You want to ask that table there. They're the locals," said the barman. What? Was he actually being helpful.

I took my tenth deep breath of the day and walked over to the table of old men.

"Hello there, guys, um, I hear you're the locals. I was just wondering if anyone knew Coverwood House?"

A hostile silence descended.

"Why are you askin'?"

"Er, well, I'm a writer for an American newspaper, and I'm trying to contact the people who live there." After my reception in the village, I hoped "writer" might sound a bit classier than "reporter." But no. One of the men thumped down his pint so hard his bitter slopped over the top of its rim.

"I've heard about you. You were snooping around earlier, weren't you? Knocking on doors in the village. Disturbing people."

It felt like the whole pub had gone quiet.

"Er."

"Well, no one knows anything about that house, and if they did they wouldn't tell you, anyway. That's residents' private business. There's no place in this village for people snooping from the media."

Every eye in the place was now definitely on me.

"Heard you're staying here in this pub 'n'all," another man said accusingly.

I think you mean Bate's Motel, I felt like replying.

"Yes, I am. Would anyone like a drink?" I said instead

"We'll get our own, thanks."

I retreated. The barman shrugged. I ordered a large vodka and tonic for myself, then returned to my damp room and plugged in my laptop. I would have to make do with the few notes I had.

Merry widow Generosa Ammon and her electrician boyfriend-turned-husband Danny Pelosi have hotfooted it to England, where they claim to be yearning for a quiet time on honeymoon . . .

It took me an hour to write my—admittedly somewhat lame—story and another to work out how to get online to send it. Then I realized I hadn't eaten since I'd left New York. I decided to brave the saloon again. So what if I was the local leper? I could at least treat myself to a hot meal before bed.

"Sorry, we stopped serving food at nine o'clock," said the barman when I asked for a menu. It was now eight minutes past.

"Is there any way you could make an exception? I literally haven't eaten all day."

Apparently not. I had a dinner of salt-and-vinegar potato chips.

Then I returned to my room, lay down on my bed, and stared at the ceiling in misery. Did some people actually enjoy this kind of work? All those years I had dreamed of being a reporter—to end up stuck in a grim village alone eating potato chips for dinner in a pub full of people who hated me. Yes, Sarah had been right all along. News reporting was the most miserable job in the universe. And I wasn't even any good at it.

The creeping fear washed over me again. What if I had totally fucked up my life? If it hadn't been for my stupid Lois Lane fantasy, I might have stayed in the UK and been married by now. Right at this moment I would have been coming home from a healthy evening of yoga and about to cook dinner for Angus. Okay, so yoga was boring and I couldn't cook, but I would have learned by now.

Instead I was stuck in some hellhole pub with no boyfriend at all and with another lame story in a paper which would be garbage-truck fodder by this time tomorrow. Okay, so I had my column. But for how much longer could I go on making jokes about my pathetic love life? And maybe Sandy, the producer who matchmaker Janis Spindel had set me up with, had been right. What if it was actually putting guys off?

I thought back to three weeks earlier, when I'd flown home for another uneventful Christmas at home in Ealing with my mother and father, older brother Andrew, also unmarried, and my younger sister Jacqui, a painter who lived alone on a canal barge. Like every other year, it had just been the five of us.

On Christmas Eve my mother and I had been in the garden putting nuts in her new bird feeder, and she'd pointed to a scrappy fir tree planted by our falling-down, neglected wooden playhouse.

"The Austrian Tourist Board gave me that tree when it was tiny. I planted it thinking we'd bring it in the first Christmas we have a grandchild," said my mum.

The tree was already eight feet tall.

"Hmm, I doubt you'd get it through the back door now," I'd cracked as we stood looking at it. But I'd felt bad.

Now I closed my eyes, trying to blot out the depressing green paint in the room. Maybe it was time to face the fact that I was crap at my job and come home, even if my friends were all now onto their second kids . . .

My cell phone blasted into my sleep. Fuck, it would be Steve calling to complain about my story.

I reached for it and mumbled a hello.

"Bridget, it's Jack."

I sat up, suddenly wide awake.

"So how are you doing out there in the motherland? It must be quite late by now."

"Hi, fine, great. No, it's not yet midnight." I paused. "Sorry, I think my story was pretty weak. I've been really trying, but . . . "

"I read it, it's okay. I know you're doing your best. The quotes from that scumbag Pelosi were great. He talks such shit."

"He told me they were settling the kids into school. I'm pretty sure there's a super-expensive boarding school not far from here called Cranleigh. I thought I'd go check it out tomorrow and find out if the twins are there."

"Yeah, that would make a good follow. No staff in the village, right?"

I felt close to tears.

"Jack, everyone hates me in this village."

He began to laugh. "Not you—Bridget Harrison, the sexy *New York Post* columnist."

"No, they do. They really, *really* hate me." I laughed too. *Did he actually just call me sexy?*

"Maybe you didn't ply them with enough drinks."

"I offered. Thought they might be up for a couple of rounds courtesy of the *Post*, but they weren't having any of it. Said they'd buy their own, thank-you-very-much. Guess the English accent doesn't work so well over here."

We were both giggling now, and suddenly I didn't mind that I was alone in a damp hotel at the wrong end of the universe.

"Just to warn you, by the way," I said. "I'm staying in the Bates Motel, so I might be dead by the morning. You'll have to send someone out to replace me."

"No one can replace you, Bridge."

I went hot all over. *He actually said that?*

"Anyway, I've gotta go. But keep going, okay? Get as much as you can on that school."

I pressed my phone to my chest. May be I wasn't ready to leave New York just yet.

Single white columnist

···

"Hey, you're Bridget Harrison, that columnist from the *Post*, right?" said a guy in a black vest standing next to me at the bar in the Hog Pit as he ordered a round of tequila shots.

"Yeah, that's me!" God, at this rate I'd be giving autographs soon.

"Then I got a question." I reached in my bag for a pen. "We all want to know when you're gonna get laid!" He nodded across the smoky room to a table of guys who raised their bottles of Bud at me, sniggering.

"Oh, um, soon," I stammered before scuttling to the back room where the girls and I were playing pool.

The Hog Pit, a divey cowboy bar on the corner of 13th Street and Ninth Avenue, was a two-minute walk from our loft and a beacon in the still up-and-coming Meatpacking District. Often Fi, Pom, Sacha, and I would hang out in the bar's back room playing pool.

When I returned from the bar, Fi was parading around wearing her customary skin-tight jeans which skimmed her fake-tanned belly, working out her shot. I plonked the Coronas down on our table.

"There are some guys next door who just asked me why I never get laid in my column."

"Well, did you tell them you were in love with the one person in the whole city you can't write about?" said Fi, her spaghetti-strap top falling forward so you could see a flash of her pert boobs in an expensive lacy bra as she leaned over the pool table.

"As it happens, I didn't," I huffed as Pom handed me the cue.

It was late spring and the city was finally feeling normal again. The wail of fire truck sirens still made people glance around nervously in the street, and when the wind blew northwards the acrid whiff of Ground Zero would come from nowhere, sending a chill down your spine. But busy, striving New Yorkers had better things to do than be cowed by Osama bin Laden indefinitely.

Thanks to my brief appearance on "To Live and Date in New York," my column was now more popular than ever. But while readers enjoyed relating to my trials of being single in New York, they, like I, wanted romance.

Dear Bridget, My roommates and I have been reading your column religiously since we discovered it a few months ago. I've even turned my gay male friends on to it! Your column is like a transcript of various episodes in my life. Unsuccessful setups by otherwise well-meaning people, friends all around rushing to get married and have kids, other bizarre New York dating scenarios. Please find a nice guy soon so we know there's hope for us all.

Dear Bridget, I have been following your adventures over a year now, and it amazes me you still don't have a boyfriend. From your writing and your picture, you seem like a relatively intelligent, normal girl, even if your looks are quite plain. If you can't do it, who can?

Dear Bridget, Let's not fight this any longer. I'm desperate for a younger woman and you are just desperate. I have been married for forty-five years, and my wife does not use my services as she once did. I told her of your lousy love life, and she felt bad for you. We have discussed it and she agreed that I should offer my body for you to use.

Dear Bridget, I can't believe that there are not some great eligible fellows working at the *New York Post* who would be delighted to go out with you. I feel sad sometimes when I read your column, and it would give me great joy if you met a really wonderful fellow who would appreciate you and want to marry you.

Yes, some readers sounded just like my mother.

Agonizingly, writing about having an office crush or not being able to tell a guy you're madly in love with him would have made an ideal topic for my column, but I couldn't do it. After my trip to Guildford I'd worked doubly hard at the *Post* to impress Jack, but it was clear he was stressed out. There was still a constant stream of World Trade Center–related stories to cover, U.S. troops were now embroiled in Afghanistan, and a fresh spate of violence had kicked off in the Middle East. And, I reminded myself, he was my direct boss. Even without my column in the mix, telling him I'd completely fallen for him now seemed impossible.

It was only on Sunday evenings after a boozy brunch with Fi that I'd crack and nag her to call him to see if he wanted to pop out for a drink. I was too timid to do it myself.

And boozy brunches were becoming alarmingly regular for us. Although New York now felt like home, I still hated waking up alone each weekend with no plans. These days I'd even begun to miss having to get up for Sunday lunches in Ealing with my parents.

Fi and I had started having brunch at a rowdy Brazilian bistro on West Broadway called Felix, which by afternoon turned into a disco frenzy with everyone dancing on the tables. And after a couple of stiff Bloody Marys, I'd suddenly think it was a great idea to get Fiona to do that drunk-dialing. She'd met Jack in Langan's one evening when I'd dragged her there to inspect him, and she'd approved. But disappointingly, he clearly thought it less of a great idea to meet two paralytic English chicks on a Sunday night—the eve of another brutal week at the *Post*—and he usually politely declined. And poor Fiona was convinced Jack thought it was she who was in love with him, not me.

Meanwhile I tried to look for other guys to fancy. And salvation finally came a few weeks after my encounter in the Hog Pit—or so I thought.

One Sunday afternoon I spotted a guy standing squashed into a corner in Felix. He looked endearingly out of place amongst the European crowd, in cords and a baggy sweater.

He had appealing reddish hair and dark freckles, so I wandered over to say a casual "hi." It turned out he was a Yale graduate called Christian who now taught English at Columbia despite being just thirty-one. In my shallow lust for clever men, I was won over on the spot.

He told me he was in Felix waiting for a French friend. I cranked up my English accent and tried to impress him with my love of Shakespeare—waxing lyrical about *The Tempest* and *Macbeth*. Astonishingly, he took my number. The following week he invited me to a piano recital at the famously literary Algonquin Hotel.

Truth be told, listening to a piano recital was not at the top of my list of great dates, but compared with many I'd been on, the evening went like a dream. Christian was attentive and quite funny when he got going. As I sneaked looks at his earnest face in the dark during the recital, I persuaded myself I was perfectly happy to be sitting there with him and not with Jack.

At the end of our date, Christian walked me back to the subway at Times Square.

"Okay, well, bye then. Thanks for a great evening," I said lingering, hoping I might get a kiss.

"I'll call," he'd said instead.

Disappointed, I returned home to Pom and Sacha, who were excitedly waiting to hear how things had gone. When I relayed the absence of a snog, they reminded me it was normal in New York to date a couple of times before anything physical happened.

And to my joy, a flurry of articulate, flirty e-mails from Christian followed, so I boldly asked him if he would take me for a neighborhood dinner in Carroll Gardens, where he lived.

He picked a cozy bistro called Patois on Smith Street, and there I impressed him all night with my knowledge of the latest developments in Israel. (I'd been reading up on the international wires all day.) When he ordered a second bottle of excellent wine, I began to imagine myself curling up with him on Sundays and making intellectual banter over the *New York Times*.

When we emerged onto Smith Street, I hoped things would develop, but I tried not to look too eager.

"So I guess I should think about getting a taxi," I offered.

"You can call one from my place, if you like."

Yes!

He lived in a cluttered one-bedroom apartment with piles of books everywhere. But despite my hopes for a hot night of intellectual loving, he sat down on the sofa and started flipping through the Yellow Pages. I sat next to him and shed my denim jacket.

He took out his phone and called a taxi number. We sat side by side waiting for it like patients in a doctor's office.

"So have you got an early start tomorrow?" he asked eventually.

"Ten-ish, not too early." Could it be any more obvious that I was angling to stay?

But the taxi arrived in minutes—as they always do when you don't want them to. And he gave me a peck on the cheek good-bye. When I got home, Sacha and Pom were getting ready for bed and were shocked to see me.

"Well, I suppose it's good to let the tension build," said Sacha doubtfully from the bathroom doorway.

Good? What was good about constant pacing, tossing, and turning in bed and glaring constantly at my phone?

"So, come on, what do you reckon? Should I call him and tell him we're going to the Hog Pit?" I said for the third evening in a row, sitting at our kitchen table after work.

"I don't know, Bridge," said Pom cautiously. "You only met up with him four days ago."

"But I can *tell* we like each other, so why should we act like cat and mouse?"

"Because he hasn't called," said Pom.

"But I guess there is a theory that if you want to ring someone then you just should," said Sacha.

I decided Sacha knew best after all. I dialed his number, but he didn't pick up. I left a message. I left a couple of breezy messages the days after that too.

Meanwhile I wrote a column about the torture of going on a date and waiting to be kissed. I changed Christian's name to Alex, his job from English teacher to wildlife photographer (as I'd always fancied going out with one). After my experiences with Sandy and Sanjay, I had decided not to tell Christian that I wrote about my love life in the paper. I knew he fancied himself far too much of an intellectual to sully his hands with the *Post* anyway. Brad, my editor, titled the column THE LIP-LOCK LIMBO OF A GREAT FIRST DATE. E-mails poured in with advice.

Dear Bridget, It looks to me like this gentleman is afraid of failure, like so many in New York are. I've had more dates than you can imagine. In my experience this gent needs to be really, really kissed like dynamite to ignite him, and you'll have to make the first move.

Dear Bridget, My sense is that this guy is either a) too shy, b) too juvenile, c) has a little sugar in his tank, if you know what I mean. As a guy who sees the dating rituals unfold over and over again, it's my opinion that this guy isn't worth the time and energy. Move on!

Dear Bridget, With respect, I have read your column for the past year and it might seem to an untrained eye that you are making a complete pig's breakfast out of this business of assimilating yourself into New York ways. Residents of this city like to feel they have something special. DO NOT present yourself on a plate.

I stopped calling Christian every time I made a plan to step outside the loft, but the following week fate delivered me a friend's housewarming two blocks from his apartment. So I'd e-mailed him with an invite, saying the party would be full of "fun English girls," and this time he responded. And when we got to the party, he was so charming and chatty—mainly to the other guests—that I could barely contain myself from proudly nudging Sacha and Fi every time his back was turned.

"So who's Jack again?" I whispered smugly.

When we finally left after midnight, the girls quickly jumped in a cab back to Manhattan, and I suggested to Christian we grab a drink. We found a place around the corner from his apartment and found a space at the bar. I nestled my legs between his. He seemed comfortable, but the moment he finished his first drink, he stifled a yawn.

I drained mine too, and we sat studying our empty glasses on the bar. So, mate, this is the bit when you ask me if I want to come back and stay, I wanted to say. But he was silent.

Reminding myself I was a confident, liberated woman, I rehearsed in my head a bold "So are you going to take me home now?" But I only managed a "So?"

"So I had a great evening. Your British friends were really cool," he said.

Yeah, forget them. What about me?

I leaned over and lay my head suggestively onto his knees. He patted my back.

"Same again?" said the barman, picking up our empties.

"No, thanks," said Christian. I gave up.

"Well, I suppose I should be getting back to the city," I said pointedly.

"Sure, let's go," he replied.

On the street I saw a cab with its light on crawling down the block and reluctantly stuck my hand out. Then suddenly Christian pulled me to him.

"Thanks so much for a great party," he said, wrapping his arms around my back.

I looked up at him and, thinking of the "dynamite kiss" advice from a reader, I shamelessly clamped my lips onto his mouth. He took my head in his hands and—finally!—we were making out.

"God," I stammered when we paused to catch our breaths. "For someone so reserved, you're pretty sensual when you get going."

"Sensual." "*Sensual*"? Fuck, had I actually said that hideously cheesy word?

Christian stepped away from me, looking around embarrassed.

"Shit, I can't believe I'm making out in the street like a student," he mumbled.

"Well, we don't have to," I whispered, trying to recover my composure.

"Look, I'd better get you home," he said and hailed the next cab.

I cursed all the way back over the Brooklyn Bridge.

That week Christian's e-mails dried up. His phone rang and rang when I called—a couple of times to casually suggest drinks. I was mystified. Surely the "sensual" clanger hadn't been that bad? Five days later, he finally e-mailed.

"Bridget, hey, sorry it took so long to get back to you. Thanks for the drink invites this week. Was in Chicago and then ended up in a prolonged celebration of my birthday. Hope you're having a good week. Best, and talk with you soon."

"Best"? "_Best_"? When I read the word, I knew it was over. The fact that I hadn't been invited to his birthday was also a fairly big clue.

"Talk with you soon" might as well have read, "Fuck off, you're dumped."

At first I was confused. Then I realized I probably had never handled a guy so badly. My frequent calls and desperate come-ons were the equivalent of dating suicide in New York. In two weeks of knowing Christian, I had been on his case almost every day—against all Paula's rules. And even if I knew it for myself, readers kindly rammed the point home too.

Dear Bridget, Here's some advice. Never, ever leave a stream of calls on a guy's answering machine. Let him do the chasing. That is, if you don't want to be branded as a stalker.

Dear Bridget, Finally you get a date and you're all over this guy like a cheap suit. DUH!

Dear Bridget, Sorry to say it, but you've been the victim of the Third Date Syndrome. This guy was probably excited to meet a new chick, but he became alarmed at where things would go. No offense, but if you had made it to the fourth date, this guy would be worrying he'd get stuck with you as a couple, especially as it was clear how into him you were. He probably didn't want a girlfriend.

And of course what guy could possibly want that?

My next attempt at romance came not from a Brazilian brunch spot but in a field in Argentina. At the end of May, Sacha was invited on vacation by an Italian lawyer friend of hers called Palu, whose family had a ranch in the flat, arid Argentine cattle country, Las Pampas.

When Sacha mentioned the trip would involve four days of hanging out, drinking wine, and riding horses, I demanded to come. True, the only riding I'd ever done was on donkeys on the beach in Western Super Mare where my grandparents had had a mobile home. But to gallop across a field like a cowgirl was a fantasy I'd had all my life.

It was short notice to beg days off from the *Post*, but the next day I went into work and cornered Jack in his office.

"Jack, I know I shouldn't ask, but could I have three days off? I've been invited to Argentina to go horse riding." I was so excited I forgot to be shy of him. I was practically jumping up and down in his doorway.

Jack cocked his head to one side and smiled at me from behind his desk.

"Calm down, you look like one of the Muppets," he said. "I assume you haven't used up all your vacation days, so go. And have a good time."

"Jack, I love you," I said without thinking, then ran.

The moment Sacha and I arrived at Palu's ranch, it was as if we had stepped into a fairy tale. The house was a low, whitewashed villa with cool, polished flag stones. Our bedroom had shutters that opened out onto cool, lush gardens. But it wasn't just the accommodations that pleased me. Palu had invited a gang of Argentine friends who lived in Buenos Aires, including Caco, a quiet, dark-haired lawyer who was investigating the banks' role in Argentina's economic crash.

The next day, those of us who wanted to ride set off on horseback up a shady lane from the villa towards the fields where Palu's family's cattle were grazing. As the group novice, I had been given the oldest and slowest nag, but as we rode through meadows of wildflowers under a sapphire blue sky, gently bobbing on our mounts, I decided that I was a natural equestrian.

That was until Palu suddenly kicked his horse into a gallop and the pack followed, including my old nag, which began to peg it across the field like he was the favorite to win the Kentucky Derby. Alarmed, I wobbled around precariously on my saddle. My horse already knew I had no clue how to stop him. And as the others broke away, he put his head down to keep up. I fell forward, clinging onto his neck for dear life, my mother's words ringing in my ears.

"Horses are very dangerous animals. Make sure you wear a hat and get extra insurance." Oh, come on, I was a busy reporter and columnist. Oh, shit.

Then suddenly Caco pulled up his big black horse alongside mine. He must have spotted my near-death situation.

"Don't worry, I'm next to you, okay?" he called. "I'll grab the reins if you need me to."

And that was it for me.

By dinner time I couldn't take my eyes from Caco. He was the quietest in the group and claimed his English wasn't very good. While the rest of us made merry, he sat smiling at our jokes and smoking cigarettes. In the day he wore crisp white shirts and jodhpurs, which only fueled my crush.

The following day Sacha and I sat on our horses, drooling whilst he rounded up the wild ponies in one of Palu's fields. He was crouched over his horse at full gallop, his white shirt pressed to his chest by the breeze.

"Oh my God, Bridge, he's like Mr. Darcy from *Pride and Prejudice*," cracked Sacha. Yes, we were living a fantasy.

True to the Darcy character, Caco was friendly but remained shy and a little aloof despite my obvious mooning. But then on the last day, Palu suggested a sunset ride and mentioned that Caco had offered to take someone on his horse, because this evening everyone wanted to come and we were one horse short.

"I'll go!" I said before anyone else could get in first.

That evening we rode out to the fields again under the crimson Pampas sky, and this time I sat in the black horse's saddle while Caco effortlessly straddled its bare back behind me. He gave me the reins and held onto my hips. I let the horse splash into a lagoon where wild flamingos had gathered in the evening light.

"*Oh my God!*" I mouthed to Sacha when she led her horse into the water next to ours.

"You two look like you're in a condom advert," she giggled. I was glad Caco couldn't see the pathetic smirk on my face.

Then as we all headed home to the villa, he asked me if I wanted to gallop.

"Yes, please," I squeaked. I would have shagged him in the saddle if he'd asked.

He reached one strong, tanned arm in front of me to hold the reins and put the other around my waist.

"Ready?" he said. Then he kicked the horse and we shot off across the field. The flamingos took flight as we thundered past the lagoon, the sun dipping behind the horizon as we sped towards it. It occurred to me that I was literally galloping into the sunset with my life in Caco's hands.

When we got back to the stables, he helped me off the horse. My legs were shaking with exhilaration.

"Are you okay, Princess?" he said.

I was lost for words—and this time for the right reasons.

That last night I noticed Caco glancing shyly at me after supper, and when he went to lie in a hammock on the villa's veranda, I boldly clambered into it next to him. It was a clear night and the sky was sheer black. We lay back together looking upwards, and he pointed out the Southern Cross. Then after everyone else went to bed, he kissed me.

The following day, Sacha and I had to return to New York—and reality. But if my column readers had wanted romance—surely it didn't get any better than this.

Caco and I had swapped e-mails, and he'd told me to come back any time to see him. Back at my desk at the *Post* and smirking at the thought that I had found my own personal Mr. Darcy, I boldly began my column:

VACATION ROMANCE OR SOMETHING MORE?

Does it ever work to keep a holiday romance going—or should it be left as a great memory? Every day, I now turn on my computer hoping for an e-mail from a guy I only met for a few days who is now 5,000 miles away.

Instead e-mails of advice from readers came flooding in.

Dear Bridget, I just read your column and I DEFINITELY think you should get in touch with this guy. I recently went to Thailand and met a guy from Israel. We only spent twenty-four hours together. But since I got back, I plucked up the courage to call. Since then we have talked every single day and now he's coming to visit!!!

Dear Bridget, I want to offer my opinion of your recent article. Please relegate this hunky Argentinean lawyer/gaucho to the confines of oh-sweet-memory and move on. Otherwise you'll make an ass of yourself. Although it wouldn't be the first time.

Dear Bridget, There are thousands of children, animals, elderly, and the disabled in New York who suffer daily from lack of love and care. There are programs for them, and I suggest you put some time in, and I guarantee you will be cured of your compulsion to find ridiculous romance whenever you leave your apartment.

The week after my column about Caco went in the Sunday *Post,* I was sitting in the office waiting to be assigned when Jack rang my phone extension and asked me if I wanted to go and grab some lunch. Taken aback, I agreed, ramming the sandwich I'd already bought in a drawer. I went down the elevators to find him smoking by his pillar. He suggested we walk down Sixth Avenue to a deli that made great tossed salads.

We weaved through the lunchtime Midtown throng, and I felt the same nervous excitement at being alone with him. So how come you've asked me to lunch? You never ask me to lunch, I wanted to ask.

"So how's it going at your end of the office?" I said instead.

"Hectic as ever," he said.

We turned into Café Europa and joined a queue of suited office workers who like us had rushed out to fetch lunches to take back to their desks.

Jack handed me a bowl of mixed greens.

"So evidently you had a great vacation then," he said, suddenly looking shifty.

"Yeah, it was pretty amazing. Thanks again for giving me the time off."

"I read your column. That Argentine guy, the lawyer or whoever he was. You seem pretty smitten."

I was stunned that he was even interested.

"Oh, Mr. Darcy. Well, you know, the horse riding, the manly heroics. I'm a total sucker for all that kind of stuff."

Jack looked at his feet.

"So are you going to go back to Argentina to see him again?"

Had he gone ever-so-slightly red? My own cheeks were about to break out.

"Well, he lives on the other side of the world, so I doubt it," I said quietly.

Then he looked directly into my eyes with his steady, pale-blue gaze. And in that salad queue, I knew that for all my crushes, dates, and romantic adventures, he was still the only guy I really wanted. The one I couldn't have.

I need a hero—
and only one will do

··

When it comes to love—okay, a long-term crush—there's got to be a moment when you decide to blow the consequences and take action. Mine came as I stood caught in the middle of West Broadway watching a taxi hurtle towards me in the rain.

"Oh, fuck," was all I managed before its wing mirror smashed into my wrist, its passenger door whacked my knees, and I flew back onto the road. I heard screeching brakes and saw rain drops, and then black blotches clouded my vision and I gave myself over to fate—and, I hoped, Heaven.

I came around to see Fi's eyes, round as saucers, staring into mine. She was bent over me. The traffic was honking angrily around us— which probably meant I wasn't in Heaven.

"Oh my God, Bridget are you alright? Can you hear me? You so nearly died just then, I can't tell you. Is your head okay, can you move?"

I wanted to crack a joke, but I couldn't quite form one. My head swam, my knees burned, my back ached on the hard, wet road.

"Urg." I tried to sit up. I felt like I had aged a hundred years.

"Is she okay?" called a pedestrian.

"Lady, get out of the frikin' road," shouted a less sympathetic man leaning out of a delivery truck.

"Why don't you just fuck off?" shouted Fi as I clutched her arm and she helped me stagger to the far curb of West Broadway.

"Sorry, sorry, everyone," I said in a very English manner, suggesting to the drivers and small crowd of onlookers gathered on the sidewalk that it was "my fault entirely." And it was.

I had a bad habit of dashing across streets in front of oncoming cars, always timing it so I got past them at the last second. And it usually worked in Manhattan, where most streets were one-way. This evening I'd rushed out in front of a truck on West Broadway to go to the ATM, but I'd forgotten that West Broadway was two-way.

Now the taxi driver, who'd been coming up the other side, was swearing on the sidewalk. He was so shaken up he'd locked his keys in his running cab. A cop appeared—as they always do in Manhattan two seconds after something happens—and asked me if I wanted to file a complaint against the taxi driver. I said no.

Fi took over, bundling me into a new taxi to take me home. I inspected my arm and realized that by unbelievable luck, the chunky silver bracelet I was wearing had taken the full impact of the taxi's wing mirror. It now had a large dent in it, but my wrist was intact.

Sacha and Pom were away in London, so back at the loft, Fi filled the kettle for a cup of tea while I sat on the sofa holding ice to my bruises. Then she put me to bed.

I woke up late the next day, turned over, and groaned. My bruised knees were throbbing and swollen. My whole body felt like it had a toothache. I pulled the covers up and tried to go back to sleep. Instead I found myself staring at the brick wall in my tiny room. The empty loft was silent. Misery washed over me.

I prided myself on the tough, can-get-through-anything attitude I'd adopted in New York, but now I realized how easy it was to become fallible and frail. More annoying still, now that I actually had an excuse to play the wilting flower, there was no one to be my hero. No one was rushing to my bedside, thankful that I had not died. After two years in New York, I was still special to absolutely no one.

I turned over again, wincing as my knees caught the covers. Then I noticed my dented silver bracelet which I'd left on my bedside table. Angus had given it to me one Christmas when we were still together. I heaved myself out of bed and retrieved my phone from my bag. I hadn't spoken to him for over six months, but I still knew his number by heart.

As Angus's phone rang, I eagerly got ready to tell him how his bracelet had miraculously saved me. But the phone clicked through to voice mail. My heart heaved a little on hearing the familiar old greeting.

"Angus, it's Bridget here, in New York. I'm just calling to say I got hit by a taxi last night. Well, my arm did anyway. I'm okay and everything, but thought you'd like to know that your bracelet saved me. How amazing is that?" I had adopted a strange, chirpy voice. "So, anyway, um, hope you're doing okay. How's India? Things are great here. Well, I'm not dead at least. Ha, ha. I guess that's it, really. Speak to you soon."

I dropped my phone on the bed. What the hell was I doing? Did I think he'd jump on the next plane to see me? Feeling tears welling, I realized I had to pull myself together. I grabbed the phone again and called Fi and demanded we go for an "I'm alive!" celebration. She sounded doubtful, but I insisted all I needed was a drink and some company.

We met in Pastis, the bustling French bistro on Ninth Avenue, which naturally meant peach Bellinis and French toast. Several hours—and peach Bellinis later—the inevitable request came up.

"Fi, phone Jack and tell him I got run over by a taxi."

"Oh God, not again. I swear that boy thinks I'm in love with him."

"*Please*, Fi. For me."

As the afternoon had gone on, I had realized that the only thing in the world I wanted was for Jack to know that I had been hurt and to care. The idea of even one word of concern from him was worth more to me than a whole spate of calls from anyone else—not that anyone else was calling.

Then it hit me. If I had been two seconds faster across West Broadway, I would have been under the wheels of the taxi. Instead I was sitting in Pastis sipping champagne cocktails. Why the hell was I wasting my fragile life—and boring my friends to death—endlessly yearning for Jack from afar?

I snatched Fi's phone up from our table and dialed his number myself.

Shit. He was on voice mail too.

"Jack, it's Bridget. Just calling to say I got hit by a taxi last night. I'm fine and I'll be okay to work tomorrow, but, well, I just felt like hearing your voice, actually."

I slammed down the phone and we both stared at it on the table.

"About bloody time," said Fi.

For the second time in twenty-four hours I felt like I'd given myself over to fate.

The phone rang two minutes later. We both jumped. She picked it up, then smiled.

"Hi, Jack." She handed the phone to me.

"Hey, I just listened to your message. Are you okay? Where did you get hit? Do you need to see a doctor?"

Jack sounded genuinely worried, which was very pleasing.

"No, I'm fine, just shaken up. I sort of wanted cheering up, that's all. I'll tell you the gory details when I see you at work." I already felt enveloped by a warm, happy glow—and slightly embarrassed I'd been so overdramatic.

"Where are you now?"

"Fi and I are having an 'I'm alive' celebration in Pastis. We're going to continue it over the road in the Hog Pit."

"I'm coming by," he said

Half an hour later I was on a bar stool in the Hog Pit, anxiously inspecting my yellow knees when Jack came through the door. I hoped they'd look suitably impressive. He was wearing a blue tennis shirt and canvas pants, and his hair was messy and weekend-like. He looked more endearing than ever.

Now quite drunk, I threw my arms around him before I could stop myself. He pried me off him, looking me up and down in concern.

"Are you sure you are alright? Did you hit your head? You know the symptoms of concussion, right? Have you felt at all dizzy?"

Only when I see you, I nearly said, but for once my mental cheese detector stepped in first.

The three of us spent the evening at the bar and, now having his attention on me, I was hyperactive with happiness. At the end of the night, he walked me home and I played up my limp so I could hold onto his arm. As we crossed 14th Street, I was again amazed by the power that people could have over each other. Simply by showing up for a couple of beers in the Hog Pit, he had turned one of my blackest mornings in the city into one of my favorite evenings. Whatever the consequences, I now had to tell him how I felt.

Girl takes action to get action

How do you tell a guy who is known for his reserved, inscrutable nature that you have been in love with him for two years? How do you break it to your increasingly high-powered boss that you'd quite like him to be your boyfriend too?

It would be tough. *But then so was moving to New York,* I told myself. Then I wrote out a threepronged plan of Jack-attack in my reporters' notepad.

1. Flirt with him and see if he flirts back.
2. Broach the physical barrier between us so that touching him no longer feels like trying to leap the Grand Canyon.
3. Engineer alone time together and see how long he sticks around.

Not so hard. And this, I reckoned, would tell me once and for all if Jack did quite like me too—or if the whole thing was a sorry figment of my imagination.

So a week after the Taxi Encounter, with the Jack-attack plan in my pocket, I found myself strategically propped up at the bar in Langan's next to Paula, with one beady eye on the door.

By this time Paula had begun dating a burly Australian at the *Post* called Paul, who had been brought over to oversee the production side of the paper. The pair were chalk and cheese, he a soft-spoken, beer-drinking, darts-playing Aussie, quite different to her motor-mouth, glamour chick persona. But Paul brought out the homey side of Paula that lay under the designer clothes and outrageous one-liners, and they could often be seen trotting out to get coffees together, Paul smiling quietly while Paula ranted about some crazy party she'd had to attend.

And watching her office relationship blossom now gave me hope that one could both work and date without causing the world to explode. Paul and Paula were in fact one of seven couples at the *Post*. We all spent so much time at the place it was inevitable that people would hook up. So why couldn't Jack and I?

"Y'know," said Paula dreamily, interrupting my thoughts, "I just don't know if I can face the Hamptons this year. All I wanna do is go upstate and barbecue with Paul."

She had bought a tiny house in the Catskills, a wooded, mountainous region three hours north of the city where you could still nab a farmhouse for less than $150,000. A bargain when a studio in Manhattan could cost you half a million.

"You should come up one weekend," continued Paula. "You, Jeane, Dina . . . maybe Jack . . . "

I looked shiftily into my drink, wondering if she had guessed. I felt tempted to confess to her, but I reminded myself that, however good a friend Paula was, her line of work was still gossip.

Then, right on cue, Jack walked through the door and headed towards us. I activated the The Plan.

"Hello, sexy, how was your day?" I said boldly. No look of horror at the "sexy." So far so good.

"Over at least. How are your taxi wounds?"

I pulled up my sleeve to show off my still gory grazes.

"Ech, maybe I didn't need to see them." He turned to the bar and ordered himself a Maker's Mark.

"We were just talking about going upstate to Paula's new pad one weekend," I chanced next.

"I'd come," shrugged Jack. Wow. The Plan had legs.

"Guys, it'll be so great. Paul does this Aussie thing where he puts a beer can up a chicken's ass and cooks it under a bucket," said Paula, looking dreamy again.

"Paulita, you're so in love it's creeping me out. Has Paul hypnotized you?" said Jack.

"Jack, you wouldn't know love if it was staring you in the face," she retorted.

I nearly choked on my straw. I glanced at them furtively, but neither seemed to have noticed.

After one drink, Jack announced he was going downtown, so I offered to catch a cab with him. In the bar the atmosphere had been jovial, but as we climbed into a taxi, Jack became noticeably quieter. *Stay cool. Stick to The Plan,* I told myself as we clanked down Seventh Avenue.

Jack checked his phone messages, then he threw his head back on the seat, frowning.

"Are you okay, babe?" I said trying not to blush at the "babe." "Sometimes you look so tense, I worry you might explode."

"Do I?" He turned to me. His frown vanished into a rueful smile. "God, what happened to me? At what point did I become the bad, uptight guy in a suit?"

I laughed.

"Well, you're not that bad. You smoke and drink too much to be a real suit."

"No, I've got to face it, I'm a total loser. Sometimes I even get up in the middle of the night and pace. I actually pace around my bed with anxiety. I really do care that everyone is happy, but there's always something, people complaining about their salaries, their schedules, their assignments."

"Oh, you can't worry about them. Reporters live to complain. Gossiping and moaning is part of their psyche."

He turned to me again with a look of despair.

"Does everyone hate me at work?"

"Jack, you're mad as a fish. They don't hate you. You're a fantastic editor. You're fair. You take shit from the boss and don't pass it on to everyone else. People like working for you."

Out of the window, the streets were descending quickly towards 14th Street, where I'd have to leave him. It was time for the next step.

"So are you calling it a night then?" I said as we neared the orange awning of Western Beef on the end of my block.

"Not sure. I have no plans . . . "

"Do you fancy coming up for a cup of tea?" I felt as if I'd asked him to strip me naked on the back seat of the cab.

His phone rang. He cursed and snatched it up again. He began listening intently. It was obviously the office.

"Look, just don't run anything until the lawyers have been over it again with a fine-tooth comb, and whatever they say goes, okay? Run the headlines and captions past them too."

I put my hand on the car door handle, not sure whether to wait for him. He was listening and looking out of his window. He seemed to have forgotten I was there.

"Yeah, I know what the boss thinks, but he's going to change his mind pretty quickly if we get sued," he said impatiently. "In fact, you'd better let me know what the lawyer says. Who's on tonight?"

He nodded again. "Very good." And hung up.

He turned back to me and his face suddenly looked haggard and tired—much older than his twenty-nine years.

"Actually, I'm pretty beat," he said.

Damn. Damn. I cursed as I trudged up the steps to my apartment alone. But tonight I'd been offered a side of Jack that I hadn't seen before. His sudden flash of vulnerability made him even more endearing.

Determined now, I engineered to share another cab home with him from Langan's a week later. This time it was a Friday night, and we'd both had a few drinks—and I knew Pom and Sacha were out of town.

"Okay, tonight you're coming up for tea, no excuses. You've never even seen our swanky loft, have you?" I said.

"You're right, I've been dying to check out the Brit girl lair," he said as he followed me out of the cab. As we walked up the stairs, I tried to keep a lid on my nerves. At the top, I ushered him to our kitchen table, went to the stove, and filled the kettle.

"Wow, you girls really landed on your feet with this place," he said, sitting down on our wide, cushioned bench which Pom had recently covered with a furry cattle-print fabric. "I take it you didn't do the sewing," he said, picking up a cushion.

"No, it was Pom. She's very good like that." Then I gabbled on about how Pom had found the loft originally and how they'd rescued me from two nightmare French bankers (omitting the small detail about shagging Lucian).

I walked to the other end of the room to put on a CD. I chose Macy Gray and noticed my hand was quivering as I took it from the box.

As I walked back towards him, I weighed my options. I could sit on a chair at the end of the table like an old mate, or I could plonk myself oh-so-obviously on the furry bench.

Broach the physical barrier! said The Plan. So I flopped down next to him and put my head on his right knee. I felt his leg tense. He rested his hand gingerly on my arm.

"Ah, that's better," I lied. I had never been in such an uncomfortable position in my life.

The chorus of "I Try" drifted towards us from the stereo.

Shit, there she was warbling about how two people should be to-gether when they're not—too apt, *way* too cheesy. I hoped he wasn't listening too hard.

Then in my mind I tried to compose my speech. How I'd thought about him since that time I'd talked to him by the pillar after the decapi-tation in Erminia, how he'd saved me from despair in darkest Guildford. How after all our encounters I was sure there was something between us and how after my near-death taxi experience I just had to tell him how I felt.

"Jack," I began. "I need to ask you something . . . "

"Go on," he replied.

I took a deep breath. This was it.

"Well, sometimes I wonder . . . "

A key rattled in the front door. No! Jack quickly withdrew his hand. I scrambled to sit up.

Whether there's something more between us than friendship, I didn't say.

The door opened. It was Sam, a long-ago ex-boyfriend from London who was over in New York for a stag weekend and was staying on our sofa. I had been so wrapped up in my plan of Jack-attack, I had actually forgotten he was staying.

"Alright, how's it going?" said Sam. He weaved towards us, beam-ing. He'd obviously had a few drinks. "Ah, lovely, the kettle's on."

"Sam, this is Jack, my friend from work. Jack, Sam—my ex from university," I said.

Bugger, what did they say? Never mention an ex in front of a potential new man.

They shook hands across the table.

"Hey, man," said Jack.

"So, you two having a snaky after-hours tryst, then?" cracked Sam.

"Don't be ridiculous," I snapped.

Sam began rummaging in the freezer for bread to make toast. I put a cup of tea in front of Jack hoping to catch his eye, but he suddenly looked incredibly uncomfortable. I considered inviting him into my bedroom but vetoed that idea as my room was made up entirely of my bed.

Sam's toast popped and he settled himself at the table with a plate, a pat of butter, and a pot of Marmite. Jack finished his cigarette, took two sips of his tea, then announced he should probably get home. Battling my disappointment, I walked him to the door.

"Thanks for the tea. See you Monday," he said, giving me a swift hug. He retreated down the stairs. I slammed the door and turned on Sam in a fury.

"Sam, I can't believe you just said that!"

"Sorry, I couldn't help it. You both looked guilty as sin. Are you trying to shag some married bloke at your work?"

"He's not married!" I said.

As a columnist at the _Post_ my name had gradually found its way into PR's contacts books, and these days I was invited to an array of events. But unlike the Page Six gang—Richard Johnson, Paula, and Chris—I rarely made the cut for A-list parties. My invitations were more likely titled "Sushi Making for Singles," "Cocktail launch for _The Hook-up Handbook_," and "Girls' night: all you need to know about vibrators." But if I needed an excuse to go out, my e-mail inbox could usually oblige.

Now I scrawled through it daily, looking for events it would seem feasible to invite Jack to, and one day I saw an e-mail entitled "New

York KNICKS birthday party at The Park, Champagne with special guests from the team." Jack—an avid Yankee fan—was into sports. It was worth a shot.

"Wanna come as my date? Might get to meet the team!!!" I wrote.

"Sure, let's check it out," he wrote back.

Suddenly I wondered why I'd never had the guts to ask him out before.

We arranged to meet at Langan's after work, and as usual I got there before him. Steve Dunleavy was hunched over a drink at the far end. At the other end, Adam, a young designer from Australia who was on the work exchange from the *Post*'s sister paper in Sydney, was nursing a bottle of Heineken.

Adam spotted me and waved me over.

"Hey, mate, how you doing? Up to anything later?" he said.

"Actually, I'm going to a party with Jack." I thrilled at the sound of the sentence.

"I've got a party in the East Village. We should join forces," he said. *No!*

"Ours is on the West Side, can't get out of it," I said, hoping Adam hadn't noticed how small Manhattan was yet.

Jack arrived looking frazzled. Maybe he felt as tense about our first-ever date as I did. He ordered a double Maker's Mark. At least he was planning to get drunk.

"C'mon, let's get out of here," he said after downing his drink as if it were a shot. "I can't face this place tonight."

"Great, we going downtown then?" said Adam.

As it was still early, we caught a cab to the Hog Pit for want of any better suggestions. Adam asked Jack to play a game of pool and they racked up the balls. Jack didn't look like he even cared that our date had been crashed. But then it was perfectly possible he didn't realize we were on one. To get rid of Adam, I suggested we go for some food.

"Great idea, I'm starving," said Adam.

So the three of us had dinner in a large, wood-interiored restaurant called Markt—another early addition to the Meatpacking District. Jack was still knocking back drinks as if they were water. And so was I.

"So let's go to the Park," said Adam. "Gotta tell the folks back home I've been out with the New York Knicks!"

"Sure!" I said through gritted teeth. Perhaps Jack and I simply were not destined to be.

The Park—part restaurant, part cocktail lounge—on Tenth Avenue and 19th Street, was packed with slender women in backless tops and guys in shirts, slacks, and flip-flops. New York summer was approaching. We pushed our way to its back bar where the Knicks party was being held. The place was crammed, and true to the e-mail's promise, several famous players were sitting at a low table nursing a Moët & Chandon champagne bucket. A crush of women hovered next to them, pretending to be chatting. Jack looked like he'd rather be anywhere else on the planet, but gallantly offered to go to the bar. The moment he was gone, I turned on Adam.

"Look, Ad, it's been great hanging out with you—all evening—but there's something I really need to talk to Jack about, um, something to do with work. Is there any chance you could give us a bit of time alone?"

Adam looked taken aback.

"Sure, mate, no probs."

The moment Jack returned with our drinks, Adam announced he had to take off.

"What got into him?" said Jack, surprised.

I told him to fuck off so I could confess undying love for you, I thought.

But now we were finally alone, awkwardness descended. We sipped our drinks and Jack gave me a quick glance and a smile. We were both swaying from all the alcohol we'd consumed. Suddenly this seemed the wrong place to bring anything about "us" up.

"Guess we're done with this party too," he said eventually.

"Guess so," I said.

We walked out back along Tenth Avenue.

"So do you feel like going to another bar?" he asked with zero enthusiasm. It was clear neither of us needed more to drink.

"Sure, why not," I said despondently.

We turned back into the Meatpacking District and walked straight into the first bar we saw—Rhone, a swanky, low-lit place with a central bar constructed from gray concrete ringed by metal stools that looked like camera tripods. A DJ was stationed behind a table in one corner playing deafening techno. We heaved ourselves onto two uncomfortable stools, and I put my forehead down on the cold concrete of the bar to clear my brain. Jack ordered another whiskey and I asked for a Cosmo. My Plan had been such a failure it was almost comical.

We sat nursing our drinks in the half-light with the techno banging in the background. My knee was touching his on the stool, but now I hardly noticed. Maybe the concept of Jack and I was simply a disaster. He seemed as defeated as me.

"Well, at least you got me out tonight," he said, struggling to talk over the noise.

"Anytime," I mumbled.

He continued.

"God, work, it's so busy all the time. I've been living a deeply tragic existence lately. I'm at the office before 10 A.M., stuck there until late. I feel like all I do these days is pass out on my couch watching DVDs, pining for girls."

"Pine for girls? You? I've never even seen you with a girl. Tell me, what girls do you pine for? Do I know any of them? Maybe I could set you up," I slurred.

Jack dropped his head and looked down into his whiskey. I braced myself for the name he would come up with. Then I heard the words that I never believed might come out of his mouth.

"If you must know, Bridget, I pine for you." His shoulders slumped as if he'd finally given up a fight. Then he lifted his head up again and turned his gaze to meet my wide-open eyes.

"Bridge, I pine for you every day, and I have since the moment I first saw you in the office."

Was this actually happening? I fumbled for words. From nowhere I was having one of those perfect moments that you remember all your life.

"I can't believe you just said that. I mean, you do know how I feel about you, don't you? You know I've had a crush on you for months—obviously you must?"

He shrugged. "I was never sure."

We were silent, suddenly not quite knowing how to proceed.

"It's funny, I've planned this moment in my head so many times. Somehow I'd hoped it would be a bit more romantic," he said.

"Oh my God, it is romantic to me. Nothing could be more romantic," I exclaimed. I slid off my stool and put my arms around him.

He turned, put his arms around me, and pulled me into him, and I put my face into his neck, smelling his scent of laundry and cigarettes. I felt my heart beating hard against his shirt. Then I turned to his mouth and kissed him on the lips. We hesitated for a second, both thrown off by the sudden intimacy. Then he cupped his hand on my jaw. The blaring music disappeared, and so did the rest of the bar. Finally after all the months of wondering, waiting, and hoping, I was frantically kissing Jack.

Did we have a plan?

We stood looking at each other at the bar, smiling stupidly. Then a wave of self-consciousness hit him over the head.

"C'mon, we have got to get out of this awful place," he said.

He took my hand, and we weaved back out of the bar like a pair of thieves leaving the scene of a crime. On the street we continued walking—past other late-night drinkers stumbling around looking for taxis and garbage trucks that had already started up their grinding. The Meatpacking District's ever-present waft hung in the warm air. If Jack hadn't planned his big romantic moment to be in an ear-splitting techno bar, mine definitely hadn't involved the stink of rotting meat.

My apartment was a block away from Rhone, and we automatically headed towards it in a kind of stunned silence. But our hands gripped together tightly as if to reassure each other in our sudden change in circumstances. I realized I hadn't had an action point in The Plan for what was going to happen next.

At my front door he stopped, took my other hand, and looked at me. He at least seemed to have composed himself.

"So what would you like to do?" he said.

I had no idea. Did I want to go upstairs and shag his brains out after all the months of longing? Or would that be too weird and awkward in an already overwhelming night? I wasn't sure if I wanted my first experience of sex with Jack to be some mal-coordinated drunken tumble. But I couldn't bear to let him go. And what did *he* want, anyway?

"I think we both need a cup of tea," I said.

Again I led him up the metal flight of stairs to my loft. As I turned on the first flight landing, he reached out and touched the back of my bare leg.

"Do you know how many times I've wanted to do this?" he said.

I smiled. "What, touch my calf?"

"Yeah, touch Bridget Harrison's calf. Is there anything so wrong with that?"

At my landing I paused to get out my keys. He turned me to face him again, and then we kissed once more. The bright neon of the hallway strip light beamed down on us, but it didn't matter. Leaning against the door in his arms, I decided a mad drunken night of shagging wouldn't be such a bad idea.

"C'mon, let go inside," I whispered, one hand still rummaging in my bag for my key.

We stopped kissing, I rummaged some more. He shuffled a little and looked down at his feet. The neon light was quite bright.

"Shit."

"What's up?"

"I've lost my keys."

I really had, it wasn't a ploy. I hoped he didn't think it was. I hammered on the door, but Pom and Sacha slept through it.

"Well, come back to mine then. We'll get a cab."

We hurried back down to the street again, he hailed a cab and opened the door for me, and we slid across its leather seats. To keep up the momentum, I leaned across and kissed him again, but my teeth banged his mouth as the cab clunked over the pot holes on Gansevoort Street.

"Bloody cabs," I said, going crimson.

"Well known to be a nightmare to make out in," he said. He took my hand and held it tightly again.

The doorman in Jack's building said good night as we passed. I linked arms with Jack and hoped I didn't look like some drunk one-night stand.

Jack opened his front door with his key—produced instantly—and held it for me to walk inside. His apartment was not large, but it was airy, consisting of a long, high-ceilinged room with a small, smartly outfitted kitchen and counter at one end, and a sitting room and window at the other. Along one wall, book shelves were neatly stacked with history books, a large TV, and a vast CD collection. There was a big leather sofa and green glass coffee table with a overhanging '60s vintage globe light. Apart from a full ashtray on the coffee table, the place was spotless.

Jack went to the kitchen and took out two tall glasses, filled them with ice from his fridge, and then filled them up with water from the tap.

I lingered awkwardly in the hallway with my bag still on my shoulder.

"Sorry about the keys. Can't believe I'm so incompetent. You're sure you don't mind me coming back?"

"There is nothing I could be more glad about," he said. "C'mon, let's go to bed."

His bedroom was immaculate, with a big, low bed covered in expensive-looking cream sheets, next to a row of fitted closets. I had been to Jack's place once before when a group of Posties had gone there after a massive night in Langan's. I'd sneaked a peek into his bedroom, wondering if I'd ever get to sleep in there. I still couldn't believe that now I would.

Jack showed me the bathroom.

"I don't have a spare toothbrush, but you can borrow mine if you like," he said.

Phew, he wasn't quite as anal as I'd feared.

"Er, could I have a T-shirt too?" I said to be on the safe side.

I closed the bathroom door and went to splash water on my face to make sure I wasn't dreaming. I looked at my reflection in the mirror over his sink. My eyes were bloodshot, but my cheeks had a strange, rosy glow.

"Wow, I'm brushing my teeth in Jack's bathroom," I said to myself in the mirror.

I sat down to pee, still wondering if were going to have sex. Then I got so anxious about it that I froze. The idea of all that energy and dealing with condoms felt beyond me. I ran the tap. Jack probably thought I'd passed out by now, or that I was too scared to come out.

When I finally emerged, Jack was in his boxers and a T-shirt, setting the alarm on his pager. I shed my clothes in front of him and pulled on a freshly washed, faded yellow T-shirt he'd got out for me.

He went to the bathroom and I got into his bed. His sheets were soft and smooth. I took off my knickers and threw them onto my pile of clothes. Then I leaped up, retrieved them, and put them on again in case he thought I was being too forward.

He came out of the bathroom a few minutes later and sat on the bed, looking down at me with a wide smile. Suddenly he looked like a different person, open and relaxed and boyishly endearing. He pushed a strand of hair back from my forehead.

"Hiya, sexy," he said. "I can't quite believe that you are here."

"Bloody hell, what a night," I said

He got into bed and pulled me to him, and our limbs entangled together for the first time. His skin was soft, and I pressed my face into his neck and breathed in his lovely smell. Suddenly I felt like I could sleep for a thousand years.

"You okay?" he said, stroking my hair.

"Perfect," I replied. And promptly fell asleep.

I woke next morning to the sound of rattling hangers and the swish of dry-cleaning plastic. I opened one eye. Jack was at his wardrobe, already showered, shaved, and dressed in a suit and shirt, riffling through his ties. I turned over, bleary under the warm covers. Now he was back in the bathroom tying his tie in the mirror while reading the *Wall Street Journal,* which he had balanced on the sink.

I tried to sit up. My head ached. My mouth was doing an impression of the Kalahari Desert.

"Urg, what time is it?" I mumbled.

He came over to the bed, sat down, and kissed the top of my head.

"It's 9:30. I've got to get going. But stay here, sleep some more. You don't have to be in for couple of hours, right?"

"Okay," I said uncertainly.

"See you in the office." He got up and hurried down the stairs. I heard the door slam.

I slumped back again. Okay, so that was a bit brief. But he definitely wasn't rushing away from me, just rushing—I hoped. And here I was. In Jack's bed. In Jack's apartment. I was actually here.

I stretched out again under his covers, replaying in my mind how his head had dropped to stare into his whiskey glass in Rhone. That glorious, perfect moment when he'd said he pined for me. Jack seemed so stiff and contained, and then suddenly from nowhere come moments of emotion that made him vulnerable and utterly gorgeous.

He was so different to the many fast-talking, vain men I had met in New York. Jack may not have been the easiest to get to know, but I knew he was an entirely decent person. He could mask his feelings— and bloody well, considering last night's revelations—but I knew he would never lie.

I tingled with happiness. Yes, I really was Lois Lane, and now I'd found my Clark Kent.

I pushed through the frosted glass on the tenth floor of 1211 Avenue of Americas at 11 on the dot. The first thing I saw was the back of Jack's head. He was sitting at his desk, immersed in e-mails, websites, and the wires, checking the morning news list for morning conference. If we had been beaten on stories—if another paper had a picture or quotes we hadn't got or if we'd missed a story altogether—the boss would want to know why.

I walked past the editors' arena with my head down, trying not to smirk. There he was, with so many people relying on him, demanding his attention. But a few hours before, I had had him to myself, his arms around me, wearing his T-shirt, in his bed.

Now I was dressed in a low-cut white shirt with a sexy aquamarine skirt chosen by Pom and Sacha after a slightly hysterical celebratory breakfast, during which I'd recounted the previous evening blow by blow. Normally I wore flat pumps to the office in case I got sent out on a story where I would have to walk a long way, but today I had on my designer Hollywould tan kitten heels. I settled at my desk, a safe distance from his, wondering if he might e-mail me or come by. Perhaps today he would assign me my story in person.

But after the morning meeting it was Michelle, his deputy, who came marching down the office towards me with the news list.

A Long Islander with iron-straight blonde hair and glasses, Michelle was a demon copy editor with a cutting sense of humor. Age thirty, she had risen up the ranks of the *Post* quickly, and we had always had a worky-girly friendship. She loved to joke and complain about Jack's tortured uptightness, and I loved to talk about Jack, period.

"You," she said in her faint Long Island drawl, pointing her pen at me and studying her list. "You're on 'Hero kid.'"

I picked up my notepad and pen.

"A woman in Queens comes home from a party last night. Her drunk estranged boyfriend is pissed that she's been out, so he beats down the door, busts into her bedroom, and starts hitting her with a baseball bat. Nice, right? Then her eight-year-old daughter who's asleep in the other room wakes up, sees Mommy getting battered, goes to the kitchen, gets a twelve-inch bread knife, comes back, and plunges it in the boyfriend's back."

I wrote as she talked.

"The Shack is on it, Dan's at the scene, you're doing rewrite."

"And the boyfriend?" I asked.

"Oh, he's dead," said Michelle in her typical deadpan "humanity sucks" tone. She peered at me. Despite my efforts to look like the office hot chick, my hangover was still in full force.

"What happened to you last night? You look like hell," she said.

The smirk rushed back to my mouth. I was desperate to tell her about Jack, but I knew I couldn't risk it. At the *Post*, a juicy piece of office gossip could beat you to the other end of the room.

"Oh, just had few late drinks," I said.

"Yeah, so did someone up there," she said, nodding to the editor's arena. "Jack's in such a bouncy mood today, I wouldn't be surprised if he was still drunk."

I feigned disinterest. My heart soared. Bouncy mood? Because of me?

Michelle marched off again and I set to work on the story, calling the reporters at the Shack for the details of the little girl's knife attack and checking in with Dan, who was trying to get an interview with her. Jack stayed at his end of the office, but I constantly checked my e-mail, hoping for a message.

It occurred to me now that we hadn't really discussed what had happened. Although presumably he hadn't imagined last night to be a one-off. Oh God, I hoped not.

By the end of the day I was getting anxious. I'd seen Jack from afar several times, but the novelty of his busyness was wearing off. Where was my e-mail? Or quick smile in passing? Oh God, please tell me he was as excited about this as me.

Then, just as I was giving up hope and concentrating on my rewrite, Jack appeared by the row of filing cabinets that divided my desk from the walkway. I looked up, blushing.

"So have you filed 'hero kid'?" he said in his officious work tone while he took out a pen and scribbled on one of the pieces of paper strewn on the filing cabinet.

He let it drop on to my desk.

"You look beautiful today," it said in his spidery handwriting. I snatched it up as my face broke into a huge smile.

He too had gone red, and his eyes were twinkling.

"You'll have it in five minutes," I said.

At 6:30 P.M., with my story cleared by Michelle, I e-mailed Jack to tell him I was going to Langan's with Paula and skipped over to 47th Street to pass the agonizing wait for him to finish. He appeared shortly before 8 P.M., but he was with the editor-in-chief, who I knew liked to drink quietly at the bar just with Jack. They stood together, deep in conversation, and it was impossible to catch Jack's eye.

It was only when the editor-in-chief finally left that Jack walked over to join us. But with Paula—who had the sharpest nose in the city for scandal—standing between us, we were left to make small talk. Then Jack announced he was exhausted.

"You know what, I think I'm going to make my way downtown," he said.

What? I had been desperate to be with him all day, and now he was going home? Or was that a secret message? Did "downtown," not mean home? But he could see I couldn't leave with him. Paula had just bought me a drink. He kissed us both on the cheek.

"Okay, see you then," I said in a strangled voice and watched his back disappear through the door. I felt a flood of rage towards him, fired by my disappointment. Paula kept chatting on obliviously, but I struggled to concentrate.

Shit. Maybe he had just thought we'd had a one-night stand—not that we even had. First he'd rushed off this morning, and now again.

"Bridge, are you alright? You look like someone told you your dog just got run over," said Paula.

"Actually, I just have to make a call," I said. I ran outside and, now shaking with fury, I dialed his number.

"Hallo?" He was in a cab.

"Jack, it's me. I can't believe you just left."

"Sorry, I thought you were having an evening with Paula."

"What? I've been waiting to see you all day."

For fuck's sake. How could a guy who was so smart also be such an idiot? I tried again.

"So are you going home then?"

"Well, I was going to . . . unless you want to meet up now."

My heart leapt.

"Wait for me in the Hog Pit. I'll be there as soon as I can," I said.

Half an hour later I ran into our local bar. He was sitting on a lone stool, reading a set of proofs from the day's paper. I rushed up to him, then stopped.

"Well, hi then." I looked at my feet.

"Hey, come here." He took me his in arms. "God, you have no idea how many times in the office today I just wanted to come up and grab you."

"I don't understand you, Jack," I said, my chin resting on his shoulder. "How can you stroll off like you don't give a toss, and then be like this with me ten minutes later?"

"Years of practice," he said. "I swore I wouldn't have an office relationship or let myself fall for you. It's a pretty difficult situation. Tonight I genuinely thought you might have just wanted to go home."

"I want to go home with you," I said.

That night, back in his big, comfy bed again, we had sex for the first time. In the glow of his small side-table light, he looked into my eyes dreamily and lovingly. This was the glorious moment when I had his undivided attention. When every fiber of his being was engrossed in me and only me. When all of the rest of the city and the *Post* was left behind.

Secret fishing off company pier

It was mid-August, a classic sweltering New York summer, and I was standing drowning in sweat on the Times Square subway platform wielding an electronic thermometer.

"Quick, take the shot, *take it now*, it's 100 degrees!" I shouted at my photographer Luis as I tried to stick the contraption on the wall with a piece of tape.

But another subway car came rattling into the station. The doors opened, a waft of chilly, air-conditioned air rushed out, and the thermometer fell off the wall.

"Bugger," I cursed as the digits dropped back to 98. "Did you get it when it said 100?" Luis looked into his digital camera viewfinder.

"Your hand is in the way," he said. "We'll have to take it again."

"Fuck." I'd always liked measuring things on geography field trips, but this was going too far. Even my knickers were soaked with sweat.

That morning Steve Marsh had appeared at my desk with a massive smirk on his face—always a worrying sign. In the morning meeting, someone had come up with the hilarious idea that the *Post* should find subway stations where the temperature was over 100 degrees. (Although subway cars have air-conditioning, New York stations notoriously do not.)

"Call it SUBWAY SAUNA!" said Steve. "TUNNELS OF TORTURE!"

I'd grabbed the thermometer in a fury. This had better not have been Jack's idea. I'd only just recovered from the previous week when I'd had to stand in Times Square with a sound level meter (and a hangover), measuring whether the screeching of taxi brakes was louder than the growl of buses.

And that was tabloid newspaper reporting for you. One week you had were working on a front-page exclusive, the next you were on a kindergarten science project. Except my front page exclusives were pretty few and far between.

Three hours later, I walked back into work looking like I'd entered a wet T-shirt contest, clutching a soggy notepad filled with world-changing quotes from overheated commuters: "Wow, they've gotta get some AC down here," "I'm dying in this!" "This heat is way too much!" My phone rang. Jack's name flashed up on the display. I snatched it, ready to give him an earful about my failing career, but he didn't give me a chance.

"Can you meet me outside in five minutes?" he said curtly before slamming down the phone.

Suddenly anxious, I picked up my ID tags and headed towards the elevators, glancing at the editors' arena as I passed. Jack was fiddling at his desk, putting his cigarettes in his pocket.

Down on the concourse and back in the sweltering heat, I waited for him by his pillar. He strode past me towards 47th Street and I followed. There was a narrow walkway through the buildings to 46th Street, and he stopped there. As I reached him, he grabbed my waist.

"What the?" I said as his mouth touched my lips and he pressed me against the wall of the walkway.

"Jesus, I thought I was going to get fired just then," I said, forgiving him everything. "What the fuck's got into you?"

"Nothing, absolutely nothing." He pushed my hair back from my face and held it there as if he wanted to get a better look at me.

"I came out of the afternoon meeting, saw you walking down the corridor looking all sweaty, and I just knew I had to kiss you."

"Yeah, and were you in the morning meeting too when they decided to send me to the Subway Sauna?"

"I swear that wasn't my idea."

I put my arms around him again. "I don't believe you for a second."

"At least you're out on the streets," he said, now reaching for a cigarette and lighting it in one well-practiced move. "We've just spent half
an hour debating how much of Britney's left buttock we could get
away with showing on page three. They're still arguing about it now."

I laughed.

"You know we work with crazy people, don't you? Cray-zeee!" He
mock-banged his temple with his cigarette-holding hand. "Tell me
who you know up there who isn't."

"Me?"

"You're the worst of the lot."

Now I kissed him again. This was the Jack that only I saw—and not
that often—the giddy, silly Jack that made my heart wrench with how
much I loved him.

"Shit, better get back. Get me your story early, will you?" he said.

I helped him finish his cigarette and we headed back separately towards our building.

Jack and I had now been dating in secret for three months, and it appeared no one had guessed at work. Our past paranoia about having an
office relationship now seemed like an overreaction. True, he was ultimately my boss, but there were three other news editors that I also had
to answer to. People already knew that Jack and I were friendly, so we
reckoned no one had noticed that things had slightly changed. And if
both of us did our jobs well at the paper, who could criticize us, anyway?

Meanwhile, outside work we were already in a quiet routine. We'd
sneak downtown separately, either have dinner in a restaurant or,
more often, sprawl out on his sofa and order in. Jack was obsessively
tidy, but I loved the fact that I could mess up his apartment and he
didn't care. After I'd been over, his coffee table would be piled with
ashtrays, takeout wrappers, and whiskey glasses that we amassed late
into the night. My clothes—and his borrowed T-shirts and socks—
would be constantly strewn over his bedroom floor.

"Bridge, you are an anal person's nightmare," he would scold,
shaking his head at my trail of destruction. "No, just change that to
nightmare."

I'd retaliate by throwing my knickers at him.

For so long I had been tongue-tied with Jack, but now I couldn't talk to him fast enough. To me he was smarter than anyone I had ever met and always had an answer to whatever madcap question I asked. No sooner would a thought jump into my mind, I'd want to blabber it out for his opinion. He always got what I wanted to say, often before I did—although I suspected he sometimes only listened to half of what came out of my mouth.

At night in bed, I would lie in his arms still chatting away until we had sex, and then he could shut me up and I could revel once again in his undivided attention. In the mornings, I got used to losing him quickly to thoughts of the office. But he'd always scoop me out from under the covers for a kiss before slamming the door behind him, his focus immediately wired into the day.

With his quirky looks and nerdy habits, Jack wasn't as dashing, artsy, or suave as Angus, but I knew already I couldn't spend three months away from him. I could hardly bear to be away from him for three hours.

But dating Jack was not always easy. He was different from the boyfriends I'd had before. They had all been open with their emotions. Not Jack. Angus had cried in movies more often than I did, and we could have easily spent an hour on the phone working through some insecurity about family or work. For Jack, phone calls were for making arrangements—well, they were when I called him anyway.

In fact, Jack didn't like to talk about his emotions much at all—except in sudden flashes of exuberance and anxiety. And he didn't always recognize that need in others. And it was something I needed—a lot.

At the exact time that Jack and I finally told each other how we felt, Pom, Sacha, and Fi also made a big decision—to move back to the UK. They were getting homesick—and fed up with not having boyfriends.

All three had come to New York for an adventure, and now as they neared the age of thirty they were anxious to establish careers—and hopefully families—back home. I decided not to ponder the small detail that they were going back to London to settle down at just the age when I had left.

Pom was the last to go. She was making plans to set up her own boutique underwear company, called Sexy Panties and Naughty Knickers, a dream she said she would never have had the confidence to try without having got through the tough knocks of moving to New York.

Her flight was booked for a Thursday, the week after my subway sauna story. I sneaked out of work early, and we sat in the loft having a final cup of tea and reminiscing about all the nights we'd giggled together there over sushi. I though of Sacha strutting around in her silk boxer shorts; or Fi storming in clutching a bag of wasabi peas, demanding we all drop everything for half an hour of "Fi-Fi Time!"; or the time we'd found a sofa on the street in the East Village and had sat on it drinking Bloody Marys before persuading two guys in the street to carry it back to the loft.

I helped Pom carry her bags down to the cobbles on 14th Street. We stood hugging in the hot air as the sky turned crimson behind the iron bridge of the Highline down the street on Tenth Avenue.

"Pom, you know I couldn't have survived here without you," I said, my voice cracking.

"In New York, you have to have your girls," she said in her pixie-like, high-pitched voice. "And hopefully even in London we'll stay New York girls at heart."

She looked up at the dusty windows to her beloved loft full of her artistic flourishes and DIY endeavors.

"I can't believe this is it. But you know what they say, there never seems to be a good time to leave New York, but when you do, you know you've done the right thing."

She kept waving through the window as her cab clanked off and crossed Ninth Avenue. Then as her hand disappeared, I felt like I'd been stranded alone again in an alien city. When was I going home? My own four months in New York had already turned into two years. My friends had now left. My family was still on the other side of the Atlantic. My job frequently bordered on the ludicrous, and I was no nearer to starting my own family.

The rotting waft of the Meatpacking District in the hot sunset made me feel homesick for the damp, grassy smell of summer evenings in my parents' garden in Ealing. I walked back up the stairs to our empty loft and burst into tears.

Sobbing on the sofa, I grabbed my phone and called Jack's mobile. It was near deadline and a tough time to catch him, but I hoped he'd pick up.

"Jack, I'm so sad. Pom just left. That's it, all the girls have all gone home." I could barely get the words out.

"Jesus, I thought something really terrible had happened," he replied.

"It *is* terrible."

"But you're going to see them again, right?" he said matter-of-factly.

I was suddenly sobered by his tone.

"You're absolutely right. I am going to see them again. Sorry," I said.

"Okay, speak to you later."

The phone clicked off.

Fuck him, fuck him, I raged. When Jack turned his attention on you, it was like being bathed in glorious sunlight. Other times, his inability to understand made me want to throttle the life out of him.

Later that evening, Jack called me from a friend's apartment on the Upper West Side and seemed to have completely forgotten my distress from earlier. He told me a couple of his school mates had just come back from traveling the world, and he was desperate for me to meet them.

Don't you care that mine have all just left? I wanted to shout. I was about to say I couldn't make it just to spite him. But I suspected that if I stayed home, I'd be more miserable than him.

So half an hour later, I was buzzed into a fancy apartment on Central Park West overlooking Central Park. Jack had attended a smart New York school, and many of his friends had wealthy parents. This friend, Jason, had piecing blue eyes and a reddish traveler's tan fresh from Thailand. I flounced in, by now wearing a specially chosen Earl denim skirt and low-cut T-shirt.

"Great to meet you," Jason said. "Finally Jack has someone to make an honest man out of him. The guy can be such a loner, we were beginning to worry he was gay."

Jack was on a sofa in his usual pose, cigarette in one hand, glass of whiskey in the other. His eyes were bloodshot from work and drinking, but his shoulders were relaxed and he beamed at me across the room. I tried to glare at him.

"See this girl," he said. "She is the most awesome woman in the world. I am totally and utterly in love with her."

"I'm only shagging him because I want to get a promotion," I said, my cheeks going red with happiness. What was the point in being annoyed?

Later that evening, I leaned out of one of the apartment's vast windows to breathe in the hot city air. Across the steaming dark expanse of the park, the elegant Upper East Side apartment buildings of Fifth Avenue rose up like the painted backdrop of a Woody Allen movie. Tiny, glowing, square windows, behind which were some of the most expensive apartments on the planet. To the south, Midtown's postcard panorama of office blocks and hotels lit the sky orange-purple. The ever-present honk of taxi horns echoed up into the night.

Behind me I could hear Jack talking to his two friends about the *Post* and how we were closing the circulation gap between our sales and those of the *Daily News*.

"This is the last great newspaper circulation war, and we're going to win it," he said passionately.

I looked back out across Manhattan. I worked for the greatest newspaper in the world, in the greatest city in the world. I had even seen its most historic day. Now I was in love with a native New Yorker who prized that same newspaper and city—and me—more than anything. I glanced back at Jack with pride. The girls might have left for England, half my friends might be married in London. I might be a school science correspondent. But I had New York.

Mr. Right, what do I write?

I stared at the blank document in the computer screen in front of me. I had already stared at it for half the day.

"Isn't New York a wonderful place when you find a gorgeous, clever, successful boyfriend and you don't have to go on any depressing blind dates any more?"

No! Smug coupledom? Who wanted to read that?

It was column day again and I was stuck. No, in fact I was having a total nightmare. I was secretly dating my boss (a headache enough for most) while simultaneously writing about my love life in the newspaper we both worked at. Worse, the point to my column was to laugh at all the things that went wrong with dating in the city. But while it was fine to make jokes at my own expense—I could hardly make jokes about Jack as well.

Up until now I had avoided the thorny problem by that tried and tested method of ignoring it altogether. I now had two new roommates, Alice and Claire, who had moved to New York four years before. Alice was the younger sister of the glamorous Sykes twins who I'd once been so afraid of. Alice was a more down-to-earth, chaotic version but she was still treated like royalty in New York. Both she and Claire had high-powered jobs in PR and were regular fixtures on the social scene, causing our loft to become a treasure trove of free makeup, hair products, and trinkets courtesy of PR party goodie bags. But the girly angst was the same.

Claire was dating a New Yorker called Chris, who wouldn't move in with her although she was desperate to set up her own home. Alice was single—and desperate for a boyfriend. I wrote about their dramas instead of mine.

I also wrote about other topics: the obsession New Yorkers had with British accents, making even the most discerning people wrongly assume you had integrity and class; the morning I'd borrowed a room in trendy downtown hotel 60 Thompson and posed nude for my photographer friend Circe to see what the experience was like (the *Post* office had smirked about that for weeks whilst Jack sat in quiet horror); my irritation with New York's newly implemented smoking ban because it went against the city's famed "anything goes" attitude—and because Langan's was suddenly empty.

But I knew there was a limit to the amount of time I could pretend to be single when I wasn't.

Just give it up! I told myself. After all what was more important—Jack, who I had longed for for two years, or a having a 700-word column in a Sunday tabloid with my name and a cheesy picture of me simpering at the top of it?

But vanity always won the day. Not only was I a reporter, but I had a column—*a column!*—in a real newspaper. New Yorkers wrote to me. Sometimes I got recognized in the street. Jack had his big job at the paper that made him happy, so why shouldn't I have mine?

That night as we lay on his sofa, Jack on his back with his shirt half-open and devoid of its tie, my head on his chest, I broached the subject with him for the first time.

"Babe, I can't go on pretending to be single in my column forever when I have a serious boyfriend."

Jack's body tensed underneath me.

"What's wrong with sticking to other topics?" he said, reaching his arm out for his packet of Camels Lights on the coffee table.

"You know it's supposed to be about my dating life."

Jack groaned. "Why, oh, why was I the one stupid enough to end up with the dating columnist?"

"Oy!" I shoved him between the ribs. "Do you have any idea how many guys write to me asking me out? I have a very nice convicted killer who sends me colored-in drawings and poems every week from Sing-Sing prison. You should think yourself bloody lucky to be with me."

"I do." He sighed uneasily. "And you know I would never stop you from doing anything you wanted to do."

"So if I wrote about having a boyfriend but no one knew that it was you, that would be okay then?"

Jack was stuck and we both knew it. He was too generous in nature to tell me to give up the column. But the idea of his personal life turning up in his own newspaper every week gave him nightmares.

He lit his cigarette and breathed out heavily.

"I guess I'll just have to trust you," he said. I hoped I trusted myself.

The following day I went into work at 6 A.M. and wrote about the dilemma of falling in love with a friend. I wrote about a TV news producer called Aaron whom I had fancied for a long time from afar but didn't know how or whether I should tell him. Over the next few weeks, I described everything as it had happened, from the night Sam had walked in on us to our final epic night in Rhone to the challenge of suddenly trying to be a girlfriend to someone you already knew. I hoped to God it was only the titles that would make Jack cringe.

WHILE HE'S NOT LOOKING, I'M LUSTING AFTER HIM.

HE TOUCHED MY CALF. . . . SHOULD IT END THERE?

SLEEPOVER JITTERS, BATHROOM BLUES.

HEY PAL—WHERE'S MY HAPPILY EVER AFTER?

Because *Post* readers responded in droves.

Dear Bridget, I first saw you on that show "To Live and Date in New York." Boy, did you have some bad dates. So glad you made a move with Aaron. And wahoo! Seems he really likes you too. I had a similar experience with a gentleman I met in my Tai Chi class. In the end honesty is always better than leaving things unsaid.

Dear Bridget, Finally!!! We cheered over brunch today. You go, girl. That scene when your ex turned up to eat toast. HILARIOUS! Hang on to this one, he might be a keeper.

Dear Bridget, Phew, Aaron—though I bet that's not his real name. The waiting, the longing, and now finally it's worked out! It's about time we read a happy New York dating story. BTW I live in Florida with my ninety-two-year-old mom, she's addicted to your column. We can't wait to hear what's going to happen next. . . .

I wished I knew myself.

I sent Jack the e-mails, and he pretended to find them amusing. But I knew he was worried sick over what he had got himself into. The only thing that kept him calm was that no one knew who Aaron was. Or so we thought.

The anniversary of September 11 came around so fast it was hard to believe a whole twelve months had passed since that extraordinary day. The city was preparing for a great day of remembrance—not that anyone had forgotten—and all the New York newspapers were putting together special "One Year On" supplements. Ours was being masterminded by Dave Boyle, our crack picture editor brought in from the *Sun* in London, who had helped revolutionize the look of the *Post*. For six weeks over the end of the summer, Jack assigned me to help write for the supplement—mainly I suspect to fix the tricky situation of my having to answer to him every day. My assignments had included finding babies which had been born on September 11, which we were to gather together for a moving photo shoot with their parents. I called every hospital and midwife's office in the city and tracked down ten mothers, some who'd been in labor exactly at the time that the towers had burned. The husband of one woman had watched the second plane hit the South Tower from the labor ward in St. Vincent's Hospital just thirteen blocks away. He told me how terrified he had felt to bring a child into the world just as it looked like the world might end. But a year on he saw his young son as a symbol of hope—that some good had happened on that awful Tuesday.

I also interviewed the only fireman to be snapped trudging up the stairwell in the North Tower as civilians were filing down. He turned out to be a shy, freckled, twenty-nine-year-old called Mike Kehoe, who was still struggling to deal with having been made the poster boy of September 11. Like many of the firemen, he was uncomfortable with the attention when so many of his comrades had died. On Dave Boyle's order, I made several visits to Mike Kehoe's quiet street in Staten Island before he agreed to give me his only U.S. interview. Life in the firehouse could get difficult if he was seen to be looking for glory, he said. Later as I sat on his sofa with my notepad, he showed me boxloads of letters he'd received from people around the world filled with their gratitude for his heroism. Many of them had the same message: "Dear Mr. Fireman, Thank you for saving all those lives."

He leafed through them, still overwhelmed.

"There were hundreds of other guys doing exactly the same as me that day. If that photo had been taken a couple of seconds earlier or later, you'd be talking to someone else," he said quietly. "We went into the tower, made it up twenty-eight floors, then came down again when we got the orders to evacuate on the radios." The North Tower had fallen minutes later.

"How can you call me a hero? What about the guys who didn't come back that day?" he said quietly.

By now the seeming insurmountable pile of wreckage at Ground Zero had been cleared, and there was a square, concrete-sided expanse in its place—where the memorial service was to be held on the anniversary. The families had been invited to gather at the site to read out loud the names of the dead and then to walk down a ramp to lay roses in a patch of ashes and dirt, which was all that remained of the original foundations of the towers. Church bells were to toll at 8:46 A.M., when the first plane struck, and at 10:29 A.M., the time when the second tower fell.

Through the night pipe-and-drum bands from five city agencies including the New York Police and Fire Departments were to lead processions from the five boroughs of New York to converge at Ground Zero. I had spoken to so many families directly affected by the attacks by then that I offered to cover the procession from Manhattan along with Jeane, one of my favorite reporters on the paper, and then phone in families' stories from the memorial afterwards. I wanted to be there for them.

That day I left Jack sleeping in bed at 4 A.M. and took a taxi uptown to 74th Street to meet Jeane. It was still dark when I spotted her blonde hair and wiry frame standing in the empty street, cigarette in one hand, notepad and phone in the other.

"Cigarette?" said Jeane as I approached. She handed me her packet. We peered up Fifth Avenue. It was deserted. Traffic lights changed from green to red to green again with no cars to keep at bay.

I shivered although it wasn't cold.

"You don't think we've missed them, do you?"

Jeane looked at her watch.

"Nah. They left Broadway and 220th Street at 2 A.M. They can't be here yet."

Jeane, one of the best operators on the street, had started her career on Page Six many years before. She had left the *Post* to get married in Chicago but had returned to the paper over the summer. Even before I'd met her and seen the amazing knack she had of getting people to tell her things, I had liked the sound of her. She had been the one to come back from the News Corp exchange program in Australia pregnant, allegedly after shagging a brilliant but wild reporter on a pool table in Sydney. She vehemently denied that those had been the circumstances of her daughter's conception, but her story reminded me of my first day at the *Post* when Anne Aquilina had talked about "Little Kate" and I hadn't had a clue what she was on about. Now I loved working on assignments with Jeane. She never gave up or gave in.

With still no sign of the pipers, we went to sit on a bench in the darkness.

"You went to meet Jack last night, didn't you?" she suddenly said.

I looked around at her, caught by surprise.

The night before we'd all been in Langans after putting the finishing touches on the supplement. Then Jack and I had sneaked off within ten minutes of each other to have dinner.

I took a drag of my cigarette.

"C'mon, don't deny it. I saw you both exchange glances in the bar. And you both left so quickly. Are you and Jack dating?"

I knew I should flat-out deny it, but Jeane had this conspiratorial way of making you think it would be really exciting to tell her everything.

"Bridge, you know I adore Jack. I won't tell anyone."

And there, sitting in the dark waiting for the pipe-and-drum band, my and Jack's little secret suddenly seemed trivial.

"Jack and I have been seeing each other for several months. No one in the office knows."

Jeane whooped.

"I knew it. I *knew* it! I thought I'd never seen Jack so happy."

"Really?" Jack so happy? Because of me!

"Ah, I hear something," said Jeane. Our conversation died as slowly the moaning strains of bag pipes came filtering through the dawn, accompanied by the low thud-thud of drums.

Slowly it grew louder and I shivered again. It was the sound of sadness, of firemen's funerals.

The FDNY Fife and Drum Corp came into view in the half-light. Behind the pipers, hundreds of people were already walking. Some held American flags and candles. Others carried banners saying "We will never forget."

Jeane and I watched them approach in silence, then filtered in amongst the crowd with our notepads. Yes, there were many more important things in New York than my column and my relationship with Jack.

Our little secret—not anymore

I stared at my computer screen. Could I write about what it was like to go on vacation and lust after your sailing instructor, age thirty-two, in front of your parents? Or would that be mean to Jack?

I had just returned from a family holiday in Turkey, where I had spent every waking hour on the beach watching a tall, athletic guy from Surrey called Mark rigging up dinghies and carrying wind-surfers into the sea. From behind my book and sunglasses I had become obsessed by his lean, golden-tanned, muscular back as he lifted and hauled various bits of nautical equipment across the sand. It was pure lust. Compared to Jack, he was dull as ditch water to talk to. But hey, fancying someone was the fun part of a holiday. I wouldn't have begrudged Jack a crush on a beach babe—not that he ever got time off to go to the beach.

So every morning I had sidled up to Mark in my pink bikini to ask him about the wind for my intermediate windsurfing skills. Mark seemed to be encouragingly taken with me—that was until I asked him to take me out sailing and my mother decided to come too.

The next minute my father had appeared by the side of our dinghy in a canoe, wielding a video camera.

"Bridgie, look this way!" he called while my mother waved happily at the camera. Mark sniggered at the tiller, and I went the color of my bikini.

I had arrived back from Turkey in the middle of the night after an eighteen-hour journey and crept into my room feeling hollow with tiredness. Then I saw a package waiting for me on my pillow. I threw

my bags down and ripped it open. Inside was a beautiful necklace—
a square orange amber embedded in silver.

"Welcome home. Missed you so much. Love you, J" read the note
with it. I had sat staring at it, overwhelmed, Mark now a distant memory. It was too late to ring him, so I went to sleep with the necklace
around my neck.

The phone had woken me at 8:30 the next morning.

"Babe, let me in. I'm outside your apartment." It was Jack.

I'd run out in my T-shirt and opened the door to see him standing
on our landing under the strip light in his work suit. I jumped on him.

"I just couldn't stand the torture of seeing you in the office all day
without being able to say hello properly." Then he'd carried me back
to my little room, throwing off his clothes.

But all the same, I thought as I now sat in front of my computer, my
silly vacation lust for Mark would make for an amusing column—and
I was sure I wasn't the only thirtysomething to still get crushes on the
beach. Jack would understand.

When the column came out it was titled: LOOKING FOR HOLIDAY
ROMANCE—ALONG WITH MOM AND DAD.

When he saw it, Jack raised his eyebrows and laughed it off. But I
could tell he was hurt.

"I see you missed the bit about your coming home," he said.

"I don't want to reveal private things about us," I replied, feeling
guilty.

"It's a bit late for that," said Jack.

Three weeks later we had Paula's long planned weekend in upstate
New York. At 2 A.M. I snuck carefully across the Catskills Hunter
Motel courtyard with my sneakers over my bare feet and my Puffa
jacket over my pajamas. The night now had an autumnal chill, but all
was quiet in the two floors of rooms that ran in a square around the
motel courtyard. I hoped everyone was passed out drunk or asleep.

"Going to your boyfriend's room?"

Bugger. Oh, phew. It was only Jeane.

I looked up to see my friend leaning over a balcony, smoking a cigarette in the shadows. No wonder Jeane always got the biggest scoops for

the paper. She could sniff out nefarious activities a mile away. I pulled my jacket around me and crept up the motel steps to her landing.

"Give us one then," I whispered and she passed me a cigarette.

"God, I thought I'd been rumbled."

Jeane sighed. She flared up her lighter for me.

"Bridge, I have to warn you. Everyone knows you and Jack are dating."

I looked at her, horrified.

"But you were the only—"

"I didn't tell anyone, I swear."

"So how do they know?"

"Because you both act like a pair of lovesick teenagers."

"What? Has it been that obvious?"

"Yup. Paula and Michelle are now claiming they saw it coming the moment you arrived from London and they don't know why it took you both so long. But don't worry. The big joke around the office is that Jack's never been in such a good mood."

I couldn't help breaking into a smile.

This late October weekend, as long promised by newly domesticated Paula, a group of us from the *Post* had all gone up to the Catskills to celebrate Paul's birthday. Jack and I had driven up together, but the moment we'd arrived we'd relegated ourselves to separate rooms and had been studiously ignoring each other. But then perhaps it didn't matter now that people knew.

"Jeane, I know it sounds mad, but I think this might be it for me."

"Uh-oh," she said mischievously.

"No, really. I was pathetically in love with the guy for two years, and now we're together I can't bear to be away from him. He's utterly amazing. I crave his attention all the time. Even at parties he's the only one I want to talk to. It's totally weird."

"Well, you could do worse. Jack's a sweetheart, even if he is a snippy nightmare in the office sometimes. I've never seen a girl make him so happy before."

I felt the warm glow again. And here we were away with all our friends from the newspaper. Why should we hide anymore?

Jeane continued smiling.

"And of course the best thing about it is that the whole office gets to read all about him in your column."

What? My stomach lurched.

"Fuck, no. Is that what people have been saying?"

She leaned over the balcony next to me.

"Bridget, we work at a tabloid newspaper. Our specialty is scandal and gossip. You've been dishing the dirt on your dating life in the city for two years. What do you think people have been doing?"

A sickly wave rippled through my body. It was that feeling you get when you've been agonizing over being caught—and then you are.

"I mean, that was pretty funny when he told you he'd pined for you all that time—who knew! Oh my God, and when you said it was hard getting together with a friend because he told you he had to go home and tend to his dead plant instead of having a romantic night with you. I mean, people did laugh at that—but only in a nice way. That was vintage Jack."

I felt sicker still. Now I could imagine the reporters passing it around, giggling and sniggering at whatever I wrote about Jack. He would die if he found out.

"So how did he take the fact that you wanted to screw that sailing instructor dude, poor him?" she continued.

But I didn't want to talk about that.

"Jeane, what do you think I should do? Should I give my column up?" She flicked her cigarette butt over the balcony.

"I don't know, Bridge. Since you came to New York you've been putting yourself out there. It's a hard thing to do, but I imagine a column's tough to give up. I guess you'll have to hope Jack can keep on taking it. But he's a better man than most if he can."

"But it was one thing when people didn't know it was about him. But if everyone is reading it in the office . . . "

"Maybe you should talk to him about it."

"What, and freak him out more than he already is?"

"Yeah, no, don't freak Jack out or we'll all suffer," she said.

His motel room door was not locked, and he had left the light on in the bathroom so I could see when I came in. He was in bed, one arm thrown over the top of the covers as if he were in the middle of an expressive dream. His eyes were closed and his breathing was deep. I stood looking at him in the half-light. His familiar ruddy cheeks and wild hair looked so sweet I felt overwhelmed by love for him, followed by an enormous sense of having betrayed him.

What had he done to deserve this? Absolutely nothing. I threw off my jacket, kicked off my sneakers, and sat on the edge of the bed. He stirred, automatically putting his arm out to find my waist.

"Baby, where have you been? I thought you'd got the wrong room," he murmured, pulling me under the covers and into his warm body.

"Just making sure everyone was asleep so no one saw me."

I nuzzled my face into his neck and our limbs entwined. Soon he was asleep again and we shifted positions. I found myself on my back, staring upwards with my arm around his shoulders. The bad feeling at the pit of my stomach was now stronger than ever.

When you know,
you know—or do you?

It's stupid, really. When you're single and desperate for a boyfriend, you imagine all your problems will be over when you find one. No more waiting for strangers in bars who may dump you because you don't like dogs or haven't got long hair. No more scouring two sentences in an e-mail for cryptic signs of how much someone likes you. No more inventing a thousand totally rational reasons for why a guy hasn't called.

Then, oh joy, when you finally get a boyfriend—all you do is worry about a whole different set of things instead. Is he The One—and if I'm asking this, does it mean he's not? Why does he seem to get more excited by his guys' poker game than dinner with me?

Yes, your Sunday mornings may be sorted, and you no longer have to waste your sexual prowess on guys who are struggling to simultaneously get off and remember your name. But now you have a more permanent subject on which to unleash your insecurities instead.

And there was a fine example of this playing out in our loft on 14th Street the winter of 2002. Alice, the only single member of the household, found herself lurching each week from one disastrous male encounter to another. There was a lawyer she dated for three weeks who suddenly canceled a date with an hour to spare because—he bluntly told her later—he'd met someone else with whom he'd clicked in a "once-in-a-lifetime way." Then there was a pretentious writer who would lie on our cow-print bench listening to Alice talk, purely so he could hone his transatlantic accent; to be followed by the forty-one-year-old art director who had to lock himself in his bedroom to stop himself from going out and taking ten grams of cocaine. When at home and in despair, Alice got drunk and staggered around the loft headbanging to the Flaming Lips, convinced that she was destined to be alone forever.

Meanwhile Claire would be crashing pots and pans around in the kitchen, cursing because Chris—after two long years—still hadn't asked her to move in. Chris, thirty-five, had made a $40,000 bet with his brother Cromwell that he wouldn't get married until he was forty. Was this the reason he wouldn't commit—or was it just something about *her*? And surely he should screw the bet anyway!

And you could have lit the fairy lights in my little cell-room with the frenetic brain power that came from all the worrying in my head. Not long after we'd returned from the Catskills, Jack had met me in Langan's after work, looking red in the face and humiliated.

"I just went in to see the editor about our wood, and he started laughing his head off asking if he should call me Aaron from now on."

My blood ran cold.

"He said his wife loves your column," said Jack.

"Wow, Col's wife, she really likes it?" I said, vanity instantly taking over.

Jack had put his head in his hands, torn between fury, pride, and resignation. "You're lucky I'm crazy about you," he said.

I grabbed him and kissed him, for once not caring who saw in the bar. But underneath, my anxiety grew.

A dull column or my relationship up for grabs? My and Jack's life kept secret or our tensions paraded for all to see? It was that age-old question—what came first, your personal life or your career?

Other things were beginning to nag too. Jack was American. If I married him, would I have to stay in New York forever? How would my parents take it if their grandchildren ended up living on another continent? Not that Jack had said he wanted to have my children or anything. He was two years younger than me. He wasn't even thinking about it.

But as my angst about my future grew, so did my feelings of insecurity—and naturally I began to take them out on Jack. The pride
that I had felt in watching him being so capable in the office turned
to annoyance over his success. I had to share him with the *Post*—
and the *Post* was still his great love. If I did make the sacrifice to
move away from home permanently, would I always play second
fiddle to his career? Was the *Post* more important to him than I
was? And the problem with an office romance was that you got to
see your love all day—including the times when their attention
couldn't be on you.

Jack by nature was hot and cold. It was only after a fight that he told
me how much he loved me. So naturally I picked fights with him. I became apoplectic every week over his boys-only poker night, or if he
was too tired to come over for dinner with Alice and Claire, or if he
was short with me on the phone.

Jack couldn't understand what was wrong with me. He loved me
more than anyone—and I knew that—so what was the issue? He even
suffered the humiliation of my column to make me happy. Why
couldn't we just get on with life and be happy? But then he wasn't a
girl—who was feeling that same old pressure.

My phone rang one midday in the office. It was Kathryn, my former housemate in London.

"Bridge, how's it going? I'm sorry I haven't spoken to you in ages.
Guess what? I've got some really exciting news."

My mind raced with hasty calculations. No, I was sure of it.
Kathryn had definitely been single the last time we'd spoken a month
ago. Surely she couldn't be engaged or having a baby already.

"I met a guy two weeks ago. I know this is it!" she said.

Know? How did she know?

"I went to this party on Friday at the Royal Academy, and I walked
in and—don't laugh—but I saw him standing under a shaft of light."

Not a thunderbolt?

"Well, it might have been daylight coming in through the glass ceiling. But, Bridge, he was bathed in this surreal glow, and I just knew I
had to go over and talk to him. He's an actor called Ben. We went

home together that night, and I've spent every night with him since. He's totally amazing."

I tried not to sound dubious. Of all my friends, Kathryn—like our other housemate, Tilly—definitely wasn't the kind of girl who ranted on about falling in love every time she met a new bloke.

"Bridge." She had turned surprisingly serious. "You know how we used to think everyone was fucking annoying and smug—and deluded, frankly—when they said, 'When you know, you know.' But I think it might be true. When you meet the right person, it's the most amazing feeling. Everything suddenly just feels so easy."

I put down the phone and felt an irrational wave of fury. Not another bloody love lecture. "When you know, you know." "Everything feels so easy."

So where did that leave Jack and me? Nothing, not even a day at the office, felt easy for us.

One day soon after Kathryn had called, Jack suggested we go home and make dinner together, something we never did. In fact, I had never actually cooked a meal since I'd arrived in New York. Pierre and Roman had got me hooked on the city's takeout habit right from the start—and Claire did the cooking in our loft.

I walked into the office with a lighter step than usual, and I clock-watched all day, desperate for the moment we could go to the supermarket and fill up a basket like a smug, cohabiting West Village couple. But at 6:30 P.M. I got the inevitable call.

"Baby, I'm so sorry. I'm going to have to stay through for the second-edition meeting."

The first edition of the paper had to be off stone (on its way to the presses) by 8:30 P.M., after which the night staff took over. In the second-edition meeting, they would discuss what changes needed to be made to the paper for the next edition around 11 P.M.

If Jack had to stay, it meant a big story was breaking that would significantly change the order of the paper next time around. I knew he had no choice.

"Hon, don't worry. I'll meet Alice and Claire instead and see you afterwards," I said lightly, trying to quell my disappointment. "I doubt you want to let me loose on your nice, clean kitchen without supervision."

I secretly hoped he might say "yes," but instead he was rushing to get off the phone.

"Okay, I'll call you when I get out," he said.

He called again at 10:30 P.M. to tell me he was still at work. I told him I would let myself into his apartment and wait for him in bed. At 1 A.M. I was still alone, naked under the sheets and fuming. Fuck him, fuck him, fuck him. Where was he? Why was I dating a workaholic who put his job before me?

His door finally slammed at 1:46 A.M., and I heard him hurry up the stairs. I quickly turned over, pretending to be asleep, though I knew things must have been bad if he'd had to stay so late.

He tore his clothes off and got into bed. Then I smelled the whiskey on his breath.

"Baby, are you awake? I'm so sorry. God, I've been stuck in Langan's."

What? So I had been waiting at home while he'd been out drinking with the guys?

"Fuck off," I grumped.

He threaded his arms around my bare waist.

"Wake up, baby. God, all I've thought about all night is getting home to you. But it was one of those situations I couldn't get out of. Everyone from the office wanted to go over for a drink after second edition. I had to go."

Don't worry, I understand. I'm glad to see you, I could have said—because I did understand.

"You should have just fucking stayed there," I spat instead.

Jack recoiled. I could sense him staring at the ceiling in despair—or was it exasperation?

In the morning he tried to apologize again. I refused to talk to him. Then just as he was stepping out of the door, I ran out of bed and grabbed him. Now I was apologizing.

Visibly relieved, he came back upstairs with me, pulled off his clothes, and got back into bed, telling me how much he loved me. He was half an hour late for work that morning. I saw that as a rare victory.

The next day, appeased, I began cautiously to write about a subject I'd been mulling on for a while. The idea that because everyone works such long hours in New York, it was not only almost impossible to find time to date, but once you had a boyfriend, it was impossible to spend quality time with him.

I described how Aaron and I were constantly working late and passing out in bed, exhausted. How at weekends all we did was get drunk because we were too shattered to have the energy to make the most of the city. I didn't care that people at the *Post* knew I was writing about Jack and me—they all knew it was true for them too.

> It seems like this entire city if full of people who work way too hard. While people who visit New York go for champagne at the River Café and spend hours wandering around the Met, the rest of us who spend ten hours a day in the office might as well be living in a small, provincial town.
>
> Sometimes I feel like Aaron and I spent half our time drunk and the rest of it hungover. My roommate Claire's favorite lament is that her sex life revolves around morning breath and a headache.

That Sunday I left my loft in the early evening to go around to Jack's apartment to watch *The Sopranos*. When we had first got together, Sunday nights had been Jack's sacred alone time, before the onslaught of the week began again. But recently I'd started to share Sunday nights with him.

I rang his bell and let myself into his apartment. He was sitting on the sofa, staring straight ahead. The Sunday *Post* was next to him. His looked so angry, I thought he might explode.

I approached cautiously.

"Are you okay, babe?"

He cast the paper onto his coffee table. It was open to my column. The title was NO SEX AND THE CITY.

Shit. I had somehow deluded myself into hoping he wouldn't see the headline. Truth be told, I'd cringed at it myself.

"Oh, come on, it's not that bad," I said, sounding utterly insincere.

"Bad? Bridge, you have no idea, do you? Everyone in our office reads your column. My family reads it." He looked at me, and for a

moment his blue eyes were sad and pleading as if he couldn't understand why I didn't understand. I felt a vicious wave of guilt.

"Every week there is some humiliating detail about me in the paper.
When I come in on Monday mornings, people snigger behind my
back and call me 'Aaron.'"

"Look, you have never said you minded me writing my column,"
I said weakly.

"Just because I don't object doesn't mean I have to like it." He sat
down on the sofa with his head in his hands.

"Baby, sometimes I just wish you could get another job," he said
more kindly.

"You get another fucking job!" I shouted back. The great thing about
guilt and insecurity is the way it makes you angry and defensive.

"Just because you're the hotshot editor and I'm a lowly reporter, why
should I be the one who has to get a new job? Is what I do at the paper
not as important as what you do? Am I completely dispensable?"

"No, no, of course not." He shook his head, knowing he was in a
hole with someone who was not showing reason.

"Have you any idea what I gave up to move to the U.S.?" I fumed.

"Er, I don't see your life in New York as having been that tough.
Most people would give their right arm to have had the opportunities
you've had," snapped Jack in his annoying way of telling it like it is.

"Who are you now, my dad?" I retorted.

Jack lit a cigarette.

"You know what, I'm going back home to the girls," I said.

I stood rooted to the spot, glaring at him. Any second now he
would get up and hug me, apologize, and beg me not to leave.

He leaned back on the sofa, looking exhausted. Not the right
response.

"Okay, well, I'm off then." I paused a moment longer, giving him a
last chance to react, then stormed back towards the door.

Still no response. I stomped into his building corridor with tears in
my eyes. Pride willed me to march off towards the elevators. But I
knew I couldn't face a night of misery back in the loft waiting for him
to call. Or not call.

I stomped back in again. He was still on the sofa smoking, looking haggard. He glanced up at me as if he didn't care if I was back or not. Suddenly that scared me.

I went to sit next to him and put my arms around his shoulders.

"Babe, I'm sorry. I know it's a nightmare for you, and I honestly appreciate it so much that you put up with it for me."

"Let's forget about it. I don't care, it's not important," he said flatly.

We had fought. I had his attention again. But we both knew my column was still sitting there like a third person in the room.

Hot dogs and solitaire

....

"He won't be in. Surely not today of all days, after what happened," I said to *Post* photographer Robert Kalfus as I pushed the bell at 206th Street and we stood listening to its muffled shrill sounding somewhere deep inside the ground floor of the brick, suburban house.

"You just never know," said Robert with a shrug, shifting his camera on his shoulder and stamping his feet to keep warm. Robert, as he told me every time we went on a job together, had been one of the three rogue snappers who'd broken into Son of Sam's Brooklyn apartment back on August 10, 1977, and had taken world-famous shots of the serial killer's creepy apartment. Little surprised him.

I pushed the bell again. It was 10:15 A.M.. Five hours ahead, at home in Ealing, my family would be just sitting down to Christmas lunch in the dining room. My brother Andrew and my sister Jacqui would be pulling crackers while my mum plugged in the electric carving knife and my father double-checked the video to make sure he was recording the Queen's speech.

In Queens it was minus four and dirty snow covered the ground. I shivered, about to call the desk to say there was nothing doing. Then a shadow moved in the corridor behind the door's frosted glass. Robert and I exchanged glances. I tried to think up a convincing opening line.

A key clinked, followed by a fumbling with the chain, and then an elderly man with a thin frame and sagging oval face slowly opened the door.

"Mr. Russo?"

"Yes?" he said, holding onto the door frame to steady himself.

"Hello, sir, we're from the *New York Post*."

He looked back blankly with eyes that had gone opaque with age.

"Um. We've come about the accident. I was wondering if you had a couple of minutes to spare."

He pulled his burgundy cardigan around him as the chilly Christmas air seeped into his hallway.

"I guess you'd better come in," he said flatly and shuffled back down the hallway. We trudged in after him. Robert closed the door behind us.

Night editor Mike Hechtman was covering for the holiday. He had handed me the assignment when I'd called in at 9:30 that morning, still reveling in the weirdness that this was the first Christmas Day I'd ever woken up without the crunchy weight of an old pair of tights stuffed with presents from Father Christmas waiting on the end of my bed.

"Need you to go to Queens. An old couple, married thirty-nine years. She went out last night to pick up a pizza for their Christmas Eve dinner and got hit by a car on Francis Lewis Boulevard. Straight over the hood, dead. Hit and run."

"That's full of holiday cheer," I replied. "What's the address?"

"206th Street, but Robert's driving from the office. Hey, find out what the old guy's going to do with his wife's presents, okay?"

The Russos' small sitting room was dim, and the wintry light battled to get through old lace curtains, but the place was merrily festooned for Christmas. In one corner, a little tree was bright with gold tinsel. Christmas cards threaded on cotton hung like bunting along one wall, and silver paper chains had been looped from picture frame to picture frame around the room. On top of an old TV, the Mary, Joseph, sheep, and cows of a Nativity set were gathered around a manger, and the room was crammed with cuddly Christmas figures. Rudolf the Red-Nosed Reindeer sat in the middle of the sofa, next to him three elves wearing bright green britches and red hats with bells. A furry Santa reclined under the tree while another perched on top of a bookshelf.

"It took Martha a whole day to do this last week," said Mr. Russo as we stood in the middle of the room taking it all in. Then he went silent and looked confused.

"I'd better sit down," he said.

We went to a table in the room's adjoining breakfast area. Robert plonked his camera on a tattered tablecloth, and I sat down and fished around in my bag for my notebook.

"Er, we're very sorry about what happened to your wife," I said. "We were just wondering how you're doing."

"When she was gone for an hour, I said to myself, 'Something has happened to her.' Then the police came around. They brought me her handbag with her credit cards and all her things still in it."

I began to scribble.

"She only went out to get a pizza. She didn't like to ask them to deliver when she could drive herself. She was the one who organized our meals," he said.

I stared hard at my page. Where was this guy's family? Surely there was someone who should have been dealing with this.

"We were going to go to Martha's cousin on Long Island today," he said as if I'd said the words out loud. "But with the snow, they said driving over to get me was too tough."

Silence descended. Mr. Russo looked like he didn't know what to say next. Nor did I.

"So what are you going to do for Christmas dinner?" I said.

"Oh, I don't know." He glanced back at the kitchen door. "There's some frankfurters in the fridge. I suppose when I'm hungry I'll heat one up and play solitaire."

No. I blinked my eyes. I couldn't cry here. I couldn't let myself imagine Mr. Russo in the still, quiet house after we'd gone, shuffling into the kitchen and back again with a hot dog on a plate and eating alone, surrounded by his Christmas toys.

"I asked her to marry me ten times, and she said, 'no.' On the eleventh time she said, 'yes.'" His voice sounded cheery again.

I nodded, my throat tight with sadness.

"This you and your wife?" said Robert, picking up a black-and-white picture of a couple that was sitting on a wooden dresser next to a pot of holly sprayed with fake snow. In the picture was a young Mr. Russo—in uniform—with his arm around a fresh-faced woman with curled hair. She was staring up at him. They looked like a classic 50s couple.

"We met at a party in Valley Stream forty years ago. She loved to dance to Frank Sinatra records," he said, smiling. "Doobie-do-be-do, doobie-do."

"Mind if I take a picture of you with it?" said Robert.

He handed Mr. Russo the picture, and the old man stared at it as if trying to comprehend its contents.

"I was in an airborne division in World War II. We loved to dance. Doobie-do . . ." He trailed off, looking up at Robert.

The flash of the camera went, again and again. Mr. Russo blinked in its brightness. Then he got up and walked to the sofa and picked up the toy reindeer.

"Meet Rudolf. He's my friend. Martha brought him home for me."

Mr. Russo squeezed Rudolf's middle and a loud electronic rendition of "Jingle Bells" filled the two small rooms. Mr. Russo nodded along in time with the music, his face like a child's upon hearing a song for the first time. Until the ditty ended and silence descended again.

"She loved to dance," said Mr. Russo quietly.

"Sir, how about a picture of you next to Rudolf on the sofa?" said Robert.

The old man sat down and huddled Rudolf and the elves in a row next to him as if all five of them were about to watch a Christmas special on TV. Robert knelt on the floor in front of them and snapped away. Mr. Russo suddenly looked exhausted. It now seemed to dawn on him that he had two strangers in his living room.

"Will there be anything else?" he said.

I stood up at the table. We had what we needed. I told myself that perhaps our uninvited company was worse to him than no company at all. Or was I just making myself feel better about leaving him? Once we departed we would never have to return. He would be left in his loneliness. And I would be enjoying a late, cozy Christmas swigging wine, opening Jack's presents.

"Sir, thank you so much for your time. Really, we are very sorry about everything," I said, wishing I sounded like I meant it as much as I did. We edged nearer the living room door.

"We'll see ourselves out," said Robert. "Thank you for your time, really. And if there's anything you need . . . "

Mr. Russo remained on the sofa with Rudolf and the elves.

"Merry Christmas," I said without thinking.

Back outside icy rain was falling. I got into the passenger seat of Robert's car and slammed the door. I bowed my head, clutching my notepad in my lap. Tears welled in my eyes, and I pushed my fingers and thumb into my eye sockets to stem them.

Robert got in the other side and slung his camera on the back seat and went to start the car. He looked over at me and took his hand off the ignition key.

"You okay?" he said.

I nodded, my face scrunching and red. Robert would think I was a new reporter who wasn't used to it all. I wanted to tell him I'd never broken down on a story before.

"I'm sorry. I didn't even cry when I was covering all that stuff for September 11. That was just . . . fuck, that was just so sad."

Robert opened his glove compartment and pulled out a plastic bag filled with cookies.

"Want one? I made them this morning." he said, holding the bag open next to me.

I took a biscuit, smiling for a moment—God, photographers kept weird things in their cars. I put a piece in my mouth. It tasted eggy and sweet.

"I've got some fish cakes in the back if you're really hungry," he said. "I made them too."

"No, no, I'm fine," I replied, wiping my sodden face with the back of my sleeve. "I'm fine now, sorry. I'd better call the desk. Where are we going next?"

We got back to the office in the early afternoon, and I paused at the editors' arena to check how much I was required to write. Mike was sitting on one side of the section. Jack was on the other, reading copy on his computer.

"Great, so you got the old guy. What about her presents—did he open them?" Mike began to cackle. "Bet he'll never order a pizza again!" Mike had been at the paper for over thirty years. He could make a joke about anything.

"I didn't ask about the presents," I said in a low, strangled voice. Jack spun around in his chair, looking at me, concerned. I wanted to run into his arms, but instead I pretended to barely register him.

"Mike, it was really, really sad," I mumbled.

"Give us a page lead," said Jack before Mike could crack any more jokes.

I rushed down the office—which was almost empty today—and sat at my computer without turning it on. I reminded myself that this was just another job. A page lead meant 500 words to go with a picture that would be the main feature on the page. It would be easy. I had done it hundreds of times before. Once I had only dreamed of being a news reporter, and now I was one.

My phone rang, it was Jack. Often he went into the privacy of his office to call me—although he was only ten yards away.

"Baby, are you okay?"

"Sorry, I don't know why this story got to me so much. Maybe it's Christmas, being away from home, knowing that old man is going to be all alone for the rest of his life."

"It's a pretty sad story, even for this city."

"Jack, I'm just not sure if I can do it anymore."

"Baby, you know the time to worry is when you don't feel it, not when you do."

"Most of the time I don't feel it."

"That's just not true," he said quietly. "Jesus, I wish the next five hours would evaporate so we could go home to our Christmas together. Wonder what Tilly's kiddies are up to?"

"Me too," I said, smiling again. Tilly and her boyfriend, Andrew, had come for a stay, along with their twins, Odessa and Ruby, who were now two and a half. And now that I had a serious boyfriend of my own, it didn't freak me out that Tilly had a family. In fact, it was exciting to play with children. I rarely saw them in New York. Jack and I had even baby-sat one night, wrapping presents by the

Christmas tree in the loft, listening to an Elvis CD. That peaceful night as he'd sat on the sofa, shaking his head at my terrible wrapping skills while the little girls slept, I'd hoped that this was a premonition of our future.

I put the phone down. All those times I'd whined about being on my own, and there were people like Mr. Russo who were really on their own. It was time to appreciate what I had now—because as Mr. Russo was cruelly coming to realize, tomorrow it could be gone.

Later than night after we'd had dinner with Tilly and Andrew, Jack and I walked together through the West Village to his apartment. The temperature had been dropping all day, and the morning's freezing rain had turned to snow again. Now the streets were silent except for the crunch of our footsteps on the sparkly ground.

As we crossed Washington Street, I stopped Jack and put my gloved hands around his coat and pressed my face to his cheek. Our eyes had been watering from the cold and the tears from my eyes mingled into wet lines on his face. I held him like that, listening to the sound of his breath in the crisp, wintery stillness.

"Jack, I know I'm a pain in the arse, but I really do love you," I said.

"Baby, I know you are. And I love you too."

War and no peace

....

Jack and I sat giggling uncontrollably in Voyage, a cozy little restaurant near his apartment where we often went for dinner on Monday nights.

At the table next to us, a West Village gay couple was arguing about Weapons of Mass Destruction in Iraq. One guy was waving his fork which had a piece of sausage on the end of it—and suddenly the piece of sausage shot across the table and landed in the other man's lap.

"Saddam Hussein hasn't got anything in those palaces but a bunch of hookers and gold-plated bath tubs," he said as the offending morsel went airborne. Splat. His partner leaped up in annoyance, throwing down his napkin.

"Don't you throw pork products at me. You know we can't risk that madman being able to launch a nuke at us in under forty-two minutes!"

Jack and I dissolved into hysterics.

It was mid-March, President George W. Bush was making his case for military intervention in Iraq, and it seemed like the whole city was riled up about whether we should go to war. You couldn't get through an evening without the thorny topic rearing its head. And in September 11–scarred New York, there was no middle ground. Either you thought that Bush was a warmongering maniac about to alienate all the good will of the rest of the world we'd been showered with since the terrorist attacks—or that it was high time the U.S. started kicking butt.

Jack—who was quietly for the "intervention"—and I—who was overly opinionated against it—had had many rows about it ourselves. Of course at the *Post* we'd all known the war was going to happen for months. But it grated me that the paper I worked for was so pro–military action.

"We're patriotic, the paper of heroes, what do you expect?" Jack always said. "Everyone is always so down on America, but they forget we have done more to help the world than any other nation."

"Yeah, right," I'd huff. Whatever I believed, if I got into it with Jack he would always be able to argue me into the ground.

The topic was so hot I'd written several columns about how friends and lovers were feuding over the war, including myself and Aaron. The most recent was titled: THE DINNER PARTY FROM HELL.

There's nothing in life like bad timing.

Not only am I in a terse standoff about the war with my boyfriend—my parents are coming to town to meet him for the first time. The night is a disaster waiting to happen.

My mum and dad are typical Brits who are against the war. Aaron is pro-military and a bit of a closet Republican.

Nothing annoys Aaron more than people who make sweeping generalizations about the U.S.'s arrogant conduct towards other countries. It's my mother's favorite subject.

Of course I had exaggerated slightly. True my parents had called to say they wanted to spend a weekend in New York—because wasn't it about time they met Jack? Even if he did live on the wrong side of the Atlantic, they knew by now he wasn't a passing phase.

And in reality I was desperately proud of Jack and knew he would charm the pants off my parents. Of course my mum would probably go on about how disgraceful the war was, but Jack would diplomatically keep the discussion focused on the views of the paper—not his own. And anyway, even if my mum was outspoken, I suspected he'd think it was amusing that she was just like me. Plus, my mother looked great for her age, so hopefully he'd think I would too—for when we got that far.

"*Pork products*?" Tears still cascaded down Jack's cheeks as we walked hand in hand back to his apartment building from Voyage later that night. "Tell me he didn't actually say 'pork products.'"

"Yeah, well, I thought he had a good point about the palaces," I said.

Jack squeezed my hand.

"Baby. Don't start."

"Okay." I jumped up to kiss his cheek. "But just keep your Yankee fightin' talk to yourself when my parents are here or *you* might get some pork in your face too."

"I will, I will," he said, still chuckling.

"Oh by the way . . ." I added, remembering I had another request for Jack. Despite the looming threat of war, by a weird twist in America's cultural fate, the Oscars would be awarded the coming weekend. Alice and Claire were going to LA for all the parties. Claire's PR company was sponsoring one of the events, and at the last minute she had suddenly been given a spare plane ticket and had asked me if I wanted to go too. I'd never been to LA—let alone on an exciting, all-expenses-paid Oscars jaunt.

"Claire said there's space in her hotel room in LA for me. They're staying at the Four Seasons in Beverly Hills. Do you reckon I could take Friday off work and go?"

Okay, so I knew it was a *tad* late notice, but I didn't expect Jack's reaction. He dropped my hand and swung around, his eyes blazing at me as if I had just told him I had murdered the editor-in-chief.

"Are you out of your mind? Have you forgotten that you're supposed to be a news reporter? They're going into Iraq this weekend. We need everyone in the office."

I recoiled. His reaction hit my deepest insecurity. "Supposed" to be a news reporter? What did that mean? Now embarrassed that I'd asked and feeling defensive, I went for the easiest option: fury.

"Oh, come on. You can survive without me there one weekend. I've never been to LA, and it's not like the war is going to be over in three days," I replied.

"Don't you get it? I can't give anyone time off. Least of all you."

We were at his apartment now and he slammed the door behind us, stomped into the kitchen, and poured himself a whiskey. I'd never seen him so angry, but I couldn't leave him alone.

It pissed me off that Jack was so geared up by the war. It reminded me how much he loved his job. More than he loved me?

"Just because you're getting such a hard-on about the war, don't expect everyone else to be rubbing their hands together in glee about it."

He threw back his drink and poured himself another one, holding onto the counter as if to steady himself.

"Go on then. Go to the fucking Oscars. Do whatever you want to do, Bridge. You always do," he shouted.

"So is that cool with you then?" I said cautiously.

"No, it is not cool with me."

"But I don't want to go without your approval."

"Well, I'm sorry but you don't have it."

"God, you're so bloody unreasonable."

That was it, he seemed to snap. He turned to me as if I had suddenly developed learning disabilities.

"Unreasonable? Me? Bridge, every week I have to read something about myself in the paper—your friends come from the UK and you wish you were still single, I get too drunk in the evenings, you're hot for your sailing instructor in Turkey, you don't want to celebrate Valentine's Day with me because you think it's cheesy, you're still flirting on e-mail with that horse guy in Argentina. People laugh at me every week behind my back, and now you're asking me, as your editor, for time off during a fucking war?"

God, had I written all those things? Hmm, so it might be time to back off.

"Okay, I won't go to L.A. But don't expect me to be good-natured about it."

"Oh joy," said Jack sarcastically. "No, I guess that would be too much to ask."

The U.S. began bombing Baghdad that Thursday, March 20. Alice and Claire left for LA the day after, reminding me the Oscars were on every year. Would I listen to them? Hell, no.

On Saturday I stomped into the office, which was full of reporters who'd offered to come in and work extra shifts—making me feel even more guilty. So I sat at my desk and sulked. By now "Operation Iraqi Freedom" was in full swing.

The war coverage was divided into three—land, sea, and air. The movement of the U.S. and British forces was updated each minute on the international wires and beamed out across the office from the TV news stations. I was assigned land, which required frantic writing and constant reading, all the while listening to fast-moving coverage as dozens of journalists embedded with military units filed their reports from tanks, aircraft carriers, and air-force bases. Jonathan Foreman, our former movie critic, was now rushing across the desert in a tank with the U.S. Army's 3rd Infantry Division, and our Albany reporter, Vince Morris, was with the Marines. Up at the editors' section, they were compiling extravagant graphics, maps, photo montages—all to ensure that our coverage of the war was brighter and better than that of any other paper in the city.

I watched Jack rushing around at the other end of the office, intently keeping track of every new story, picture, and report, and I truly felt proud. Here we were, both working away on a huge, historic story. But when he came down to my desk to give me instructions, my pettiness won out and I stared straight ahead at my screen.

At the end of the day when first deadline had passed and I'd filed my story, he appeared at my desk again. By now his eyes were bloodshot. He looked drained.

"Thank you for staying this weekend. You did a great job," he said.

"No problem."

"Wanna hang out later?" he said quietly. "I'm shattered. I'd love to just go home and chill with you."

"I'm busy," I snapped. What? Why was I saying that? All I wanted was for him to hug me—but it was hardly his fault he couldn't do so at my terminal. I glanced at him desperately, hoping he'd know.

His face had turned red. He stood at a loss.

"Okay then," he said. "Enjoy the rest of your weekend."

He walked away.

I headed to the elevators a few minutes later. He was back at his desk concentrating on a page layout. When I got downstairs I stood by his pillar on the concourse, smoking cigarettes and hoping he might come out. But he didn't. So in the end I walked to Times Square and caught a taxi home. Then I sat for the rest of the night in front of CNN, cursing the war, America, and President Bush . . . but mostly myself.

It was at 4:30 P.M. the following Friday when we finally made contact again.

"Are you around tonight? Think we need to talk," said his e-mail.

We had hardly spoken all week. He had been frantic with the war coverage. I had been frantically getting drunk in Langan's—the natural thing to when life in the office got shitty. Occasionally it occurred to me that I was now drinking and smoking more than I ever had in my life. But then I was a Brit in a city where bars never closed, and not only was the country at war, but I was at war with my boyfriend. What the hell did anyone expect? When Jack and I made up, I'd quit all vodka and tonics and Marlboro Lights.

He got to Langan's at 8:05 P.M. I was waiting at the bar and gave him a hello kiss.

"What do you want to drink, babe?" I asked chirpily. Perhaps with a massive stroke of luck, I could turn this into a nice, ordinary evening in the bar.

"I don't really want to get a drink here." Okay, so maybe not.

"Well, the girls are still in LA. Want to come to my place?"

"Sure," he said.

We sat in the cab going downtown and made tense small talk about the paper's coverage of the war. But out of the cab window, from the corner of my eye I watched the street numbers decreasing to 14th Street with rising anxiety. Shit, why hadn't I apologized earlier in the week? Jack hadn't been *that* busy.

At my building I walked up ahead, thinking of the night he'd touched my calf after that first magical, drunken kiss in Rhone. Tonight he was silent, his hands firmly in his pockets.

The apartment was cold when we walked in. I went to pull the blinds at the end of the long, wood-floored room. Jack lingered by the door.

"Hey, sit down," I said. "D'you want a drink? Whiskey, a beer, cup of tea."

Jack took off his coat, folded it over the arm of chair, and sat down on the sofa.

"I'll have a glass of water," he said.

This was a bad sign. Water meant "I want to stay sober, I want this over with quickly. I'm not sticking around."

I filled the kettle anyway and put it on the stove. I was having tea. I opened the cupboard above the sink and took out a box of Yorkshire Tea bags. Making it calmed me.

And now it was prolonging the moment before our Talk.

I looked down the room at Jack dipping his head to light a cigarette. He had taken out the page proofs of tomorrow's paper and was leafing through them. I wondered if he was really concentrating on their contents tonight. Knowing him, probably. But suddenly that didn't annoy me anymore.

The kettle boiled. I filled my cup with hot water, spooned the tea bag out, and poured in the milk I'd got out of the fridge. Then I walked down to his end, put my tea and his glass of water down on the table, and sat down at the other end of the sofa to face him.

He put the proofs back into his bag and stubbed out his half-smoked cigarette. He glanced at the window as if to draw courage from somewhere. Then he turned back to me.

"Bridge, I can't do this anymore."

There they were. Six little words, enough to change my whole world.

He looked at me. His eyes were unbearably sad but also resolute.

"I know." I couldn't get anything else out of my mouth.

I wanted to tell him I had been a total idiot for taking out my insecurities on him, that I loved him, desperately. But his tone of voice told me that old chestnut wasn't an option tonight. So instead my mind went numb.

We sat in silence.

Then he began struggling to say everything he'd come to say.

"Bridge, you know I love you. I've loved you with my heart and soul, with every ounce of my being. There's nothing I've wanted more in the world than to make you happy." He wiped a tear from his eye. "But whatever I do, you are never fucking happy. And I'm exhausted."

I stared miserably at my lap.

"I mean, do you believe being in love should be this hard?" he said.

Funny, that's exactly what my mate Kathryn says, I wanted to crack. But then my heart heaved. It *was* hard loving Jack, but I couldn't even imagine being in love with someone else who it might be "easier" to love. I only wanted to love him.

"Look, I mean, it hasn't all been that bad," I managed.

"No, no, of course it hasn't." He looked enormously sad again. "It's been amazing. You've been the love of my life—so far. But we have tried and argued and tried and argued and . . ." he paused. "I guess my heart isn't in it any more."

The words hit me so hard I thought I might throw up. I put my hand up to my face to catch my tears. His heart that had been so hard to win. We'd always relied on the fact that no matter what happened at the office, we were mad about each other. And now that wasn't the case.

I hailed the gods of self-preservation as the others were failing me. I reminded myself that I hated my argumentative, unreasonable behavior towards Jack. After all, I was perfectly nice to my friends. I had never been a psycho towards Angus. There was something about Jack, his contained manner, his closed nature, that brought out the worst in me. Perhaps breaking up would make sense—maybe it was for the best.

"Well, maybe too many things weren't right," I said, still not sure if I really meant it.

He seemed relieved that I'd finally agreed with him. He picked up his cigarettes and put them in his pocket. He wanted to leave now. Suddenly were we hurtling towards the last moment that we would still be "us"?

The loft phone rang. We both jumped. I picked it up to stop it ringing.

"Hey, Bridget, I'm here! Just landed at JFK and I'm getting a cab now. I'm with Joseph, can't wait for you to meet him!"

Jesus. I'd totally forgotten. My old university friend Stephen was coming to stay tonight. He had flown to New York en route home from a trip to New Zealand. Worse, he was with his nine-month-old kid.

"Um, great. It's West 14th Street. Ring the buzzer . . . "

I put the phone down. "My mate Stephen. I forgot he's coming to stay with his baby . . ." Another time we would have found this hilarious.

"I'd better get going," he said. He got up, then stopped in his tracks. "I just remembered—your parents. Are they still coming too?"

My parents. Oh God, my parents. The dinner.

"Yes, they're arriving late tonight."

"Are they still expecting to go out—tomorrow?"

"Yes." Now I was fighting tears.

"Do you want me to still come with you?"

"No. I don't think there would be much point."

He got up and moved towards the door. I followed him. He opened it himself and I held it for him.

"Will you be okay, Bridge?" he said.

"Yup," I replied.

He turned and disappeared down the stairs.

I closed the door and returned to the sofa and sat on the spot he had been sitting in. I stared into the middle distance with tears now cascading down my cheeks. It was impossible to comprehend that he wasn't mine anymore.

I was still sitting in the same spot when the door buzzed forty minutes later. I got up, pasted on a smile, and opened it again. A perfect blonde, blue-eyed baby was jiggling at me from a sling attached to my friend Stephen's chest. Just what I needed to see.

Meet the parents? Not this time

My parents had booked into the Chelsea Savoy, a pleasant little tourist hotel next to the more famous Chelsea Hotel. I stood in its mirrored elevator heading up to their sixth-floor room in a trance. They had called me from the airport the previous night shortly after Stephen had arrived, but I hadn't been able to cope with breaking the news over the phone.

My mother opened the door to their hotel room, smiling with excitement. She looked very youthful, in a pretty green paisley top and skirt. She was wearing dangly gold earrings and a matching necklace. I could see she had made an effort. Bugger, if Jack had been with me, he could have seen that I at least might grow old gracefully too.

"Hi, you look nice," I said, kissing her.

"I bought this in Express today. What an amazing shop—everything is so cheap." Her eyes flicked over my shoulder.

"That shop's for teenagers, Mummy," I said.

I went to kiss my father, who was sitting at the hotel room desk, peering over his glasses and filing some credit card receipts in his wallet. He smiled too. Now I felt sad that not only would they not meet Jack, but Jack wouldn't meet them. For all my adolescent behavior towards them, my parents were pretty cool.

"So, we've booked a lovely little French bistro we spotted on Seventh Avenue. Do you think Jack will approve?" said my mum, still looking towards the door.

"Are we waiting for him here?"

I picked up a tourist pamphlet from the desk where my father was sitting and flicked through it nonchalantly.

"Um, actually, I don't think Jack's going to make it."

My mother looked confused. My father looked up from his receipts.

I had a split-second left to work out what I was going to say. Suddenly I wanted to pretend he'd had to go away for some work emergency. But that would have been too tragic.

"The thing is . . ." I willed my voice not to crack. "We're kinda not seeing each other anymore."

"Oh." My mother looked at me, concerned and disappointed. "When did that happen then?"

"Oh, you know, it's hard to say."

"Last night" *was* just too hard to say.

"We just thought it might be better to take a bit of a break." Understatement of the century. "But anyhow, the French place sounds cool. What's it called? I'm starving."

"Le Singe Vert," said my mum. She tried to sound cheery, but I could tell she was putting it on. They had been looking forward to the meeting with Jack as much as I had.

"Is that 'green' something?"

"Monkey," she said.

My parents picked up their coats, and we headed back down to the corridor in silence. As we all stood in the confined space of the elevator, they seemed hesitant to keep prying. I realized they could probably tell I was struggling to hold it together. Parents always know you better than you think.

To reassure them, I began to babble about how busy we'd been in the office covering all the action in Iraq. As we walked the six blocks down Seventh Avenue to the restaurant, I kept on this safe subject—considerably safer, I supposed, now that Jack wasn't here to make it an awkward choice.

"How is everyone at home taking news of the war?"

"Oh, horrified," said my mother. "I mean, it's ridiculous. No one's supporting it except Tony Blair, and he's lost all his credibility. Most people think that George Bush is a complete moron."

Well, at least Jack wasn't here to have to listen to that.

Le Singe Vert was indeed a cozy-looking bistro, with rows of square tables with white cloths on them. Not too formal, but intimate. And it was ideal for a meet-the-boyfriend dinner.

"Hello there, it's Harrison. We rang up earlier to book a table," said my father politely to a maitre d'.

"Yes! Harrison. Table for four."

"It's three, actually," I said.

The waiter showed us to our table for four anyway. We all sat down and watched in silence as he took away the extra place setting. I wondered if I could order a huge vodka and tonic straight away without giving my parents the impression that I was an alcoholic. Oh, what the hell, I ordered it anyway. We picked up our menus.

"Fancy sharing the hangar steak for two persons?" chirped my dad. "I bet it's huge."

"Mmm, yummy, that sounds great," I said, closing the menu. The thought of food was beyond me.

The conversation died—as it often does when a big, fat, unmentionable topic is sitting in the middle of a table and everyone is pretending it isn't.

I tried to divert them again.

"So Stephen's staying with his baby. He's on his way back from New Zealand."

"Stephen? Your friend from university, he's had a baby too?" said my mother. She almost sounded hurt. They had always seen Stephen as a bit of a lost cause.

"Yeah, I've never seen anyone so changed by fatherhood. He's so mellow, it's incredible. It was a bit of an accident with his girlfriend, but they decided to keep it. She had to get back to London to work, but you should see how proud Stephen is that he's taking care of a nine-month-old alone. There are already nappies and baby shit strewn all over the apartment."

"And I hear Nancy's had another one," said my mum, referring to another university friend. "And Natasha's getting married in June."

It was like the moment at Christmas when she handed me the annual family newsletters from their old friends, updates that were always full of smug tales of weddings and photos of grandchildren. Why couldn't my parents letter simply say: "Well, it was a great year for our dysfunctional kids. Our oldest son, Andrew, thirty-six, is still an unattached doctor. Our youngest, Jacqui, at thirty-one, is living alone with her dog on a canal boat, And our darling middle daughter, Bridget, who is about to be thirty-three, is still living in America, writing embarrassing stories about her sex life and seems to have broken up with yet another boyfriend."

"Yup, there's not many of us single ones left," I said just for the hell of it. "Even Kathryn has just met a bloke she thinks she's going to marry. And Tilly came with her twins at Christmas. They were divine. Jack and I even did some baby-sitting . . ." The conversation died at the sound of his name.

Oh God. That lovely night. But now was not the time to remember the night we had sat by the Christmas tree, pretending that we were young parents. Or, come to think of it now, had that fantasy just been mine?

Four diners were being shown to the table next to us. I glanced at them as they got settled and noticed two were nudging each other and nodding in my direction. What the fuck were they looking at?

The waiter brought our drinks and as he put them down, one of the foursome—a guy—leaned across to our table.

"Hey, I'm really sorry to interrupt, but you're Bridget Harrison, right? The *Post* columnist."

I blushed, nodding. Wow, I had been recognized in front of my parents! That was a small consolation in this dire evening.

"Yes, I'm just having a quiet dinner with my mum and dad from England." I said with a smile, gesturing at them across the table.

The guy said "hi" to them, and they smiled back. Then he suddenly became even more excited.

"Oh, my God. Are you on that dinner you wrote about in your column last week? The one when your parents get to meet Aaron?" Then he noticed there was no Aaron. He glanced at the bathrooms as if he expected him suddenly to appear.

"Actually, he's not with us tonight," I said gaily. "Anyway, enjoy your evening." I grasped for my vodka and tonic.

"So that was nice that they knew who you were," said my mum, eyeing the vigor with which I was now sucking on my straw.

"It happens all the time," I lied.

The food came. I put a piece of steak in my mouth and tried to chew. It felt like a door wedge.

"Any plans for the summer?" said my mum.

"Not really," I said. More like "not now."

I got home two hours later, feeling like I'd just stepped out of a tumble dryer. Stephen was on the sofa, contentedly watching *Will & Grace* with baby Joseph flopped on his chest.

"Shouldn't that kid be in bed by now?" I said, plonking myself down next to them.

"He's got jet lag," said Stephen dreamily. The baby stirred, opened his eyes for a second, and pulled out an infuriatingly sweet yawn. Stephen looked besotted.

"Bridge, I know you don't want to hear this right now, just when you've broken up with yet another boyfriend. But having children, I can't tell you, it just changes everything. Suddenly there is this thing in your life that's more important than anything."

Yeah, tell me something I didn't know. I ran my hand gently over the baby's little blonde wisps.

"The thing is, Stephen, it's not that I don't want children. In fact, even I, of all people, finally do feel ready to have a baby. But I don't want to have one with the wrong person—and, well, I can't seem to find someone that's right. I thought Jack was right, but he obviously doesn't think so. But then maybe it's just me who isn't right. I don't even seem to know that."

"Just don't put it off forever," said Stephen. Through clenched teeth, I reminded myself he was trying to be nice.

That night I lay in bed, pinned to the mattress with such a distinctly physical pain in my chest that I wondered what the biological explanation for heartache was.

The next morning I woke up feeling fine for a second before remembering what had happened, and then the ache hit again. Sunday passed in a daze. I took my parents to the Met, and then fortunately they decamped to see old friends in Brooklyn.

That evening, I ate takeout pasta with Stephen and Joseph and drank most of the bottle of wine I produced from our cupboard. Every time I tried to think of Jack on his sofa in his apartment, I thought my heart might actually stop, it hurt so much. I hoped he might call, but he didn't. So I did.

"Hallo?" he snapped when he picked up.

"Er, hi, it's me."

"Oh, hey." He sounded a bit strangled himself.

"Just though we should talk—before work tomorrow . . . "

He paused. It was as if there were nothing to talk about.

"How was dinner with your parents?"

"Fine. Really jolly, actually."

"Good, well, I guess I'll see you tomorrow then," he said and hung up.

He had sounded like he'd rather see the Grim Reaper doing a jig at the end of his bed.

I walked into work the next day like a zombie and headed straight down the office, staring at the floor. I stayed there all day, crouched behind my terminal, writing about the war.

Jack did not move from the safety of the editors' arena. I saw the back of his head moving around twice and forced myself to look away. Only now did I remember the stupid phrase: Never fish off the company pier. Yes, in case you fell off it and drowned.

That evening my parents asked me to join them for dinner in Carroll Gardens at the home of their friends Anne and David. I couldn't turn them down. My father and Anne had been at Oxford together. Both couples had been married for over thirty-five years.

Anne and David had moved to the States after they got married. Now, over grilled shrimp which David had cooked in their cozy brownstone kitchen, I suddenly thought how easy it would have been to be married and stay in New York. Flights to see grandchildren were only seven hours long. Jack and I could have moved to Brooklyn, and one day he might have been grilling shrimp . . . well, perhaps ordering shrimp delivery.

In fact, why had I even worried about the future? Jack had always said if we were in love, we could work the rest out. Why had I constantly obsessed over where we were going rather than enjoying what we had? Oh yes, those glorious pearls of hindsight.

I made it through the dinner on autopilot until the clock on the kitchen wall had finally dragged itself to four minutes past eleven. Then I lied and said I had a dreadfully early start.

"So, anyway, before you go, we hear you've split up with your boyfriend," said Anne. "So what happened?"

I jolted against the back of my chair like she had stuck me with a javelin. I felt like saying "Well, shall we just chat about your sex life first?" but obviously I couldn't. My mother looked sheepishly into her coffee cup. I felt like sticking *her* with a javelin as she had clearly put her friend up to it.

Again I willed my voice not to crack.

"Oh, you know, it just wasn't working out. We worked together, and I guess it was too much pressure."

Four pairs of eyes looked at me, waiting for me to elaborate.

"You know, my column and stuff," I said, knowing that hadn't been the reason at all. I looked so uncomfortable, I think they decided to take pity on me.

"Well, there you go," joked Anne. "It's just that all mothers our age really want to know is when they're going to get some grandchildren!"

"I think that might be some time yet," I croaked.

He made the lunge,
I took the plunge

······································

"New York. It's a pig pen. It's a choice festival! You gotta love it," said the balding man standing next to me at the bar ordering three martinis. "There are so many people to date. Even if one falls through, there's a whole new lottery to choose from!"

He scanned the room triumphantly to prove his point. In front of us, a mob of New York's elite were knocking back free drinks and shouting in each other's ears. Perfectly groomed women were flicking their freshly blown-out hair over gym-worked bodies clad in Matthew Williamson, Marc Jacobs, and Stella McCartney. Guys in trendy shirt-and-jeans combos were not so subtly eyeing them up.

"I mean, with women like this to choose from, why get stuck with just one?" said the man.

"Oh, I dunno. Small things like companionship. Love. Kids," I offered, gulping down my vodka and tonic. Why was I even having this conversation with a random punter at the bar? More to the point, why was I at this chic party wearing a tight T-shirt that said "Pillow Talk Is Extra" emblazoned across my boobs?

For this was the much-anticipated grand opening of Soho House New York. The UK–based members club—which in London was popular with media and advertising types who wanted to get a drink after pub closing hours—had now renovated the top four floors of a warehouse in the Meatpacking District, conveniently right across the street from our loft. New Yorkers had been fussing for months over its arrival, claiming a members-only bar would never work in Manhattan, where bars stayed open until 4 A.M. anyway. But of course everyone wanted to join.

Alice's sister Lucy and Lucy's suave, sociable husband, Euan, were on the club committee and had snagged Alice, Claire, and me entrance. But as usual here I was among the great and good of the city's social scene looking like I had taken a wrong turn from a hen night in the Hog Pit. Ironic T-shirts at glamorous parties in New York never worked.

Meanwhile, my new friend the dating expert was still philosophizing in my ear.

"Companionship? Who's got time for it? I mean, even if you break up with someone in New York, you're too busy to worry about it."

And right on cue I spotted Jack standing on the other side of the bar.

He was ordering drinks, squeezed next to the perfect, brown shoulders of a tall woman in a yellow, sequined halter. Oh God, was she with him? I watched him put down a wad of dollars on the counter, then turn and say something to her as the barman poured out two whiskeys. No! No! No! Then he glanced up, straight into the range of my horrified stare.

Our eyes met. He gave me a short, little smile. I gripped my glass so hard I was lucky it didn't implode.

He picked up the drinks and turned away. Phew. The sequined impostor stayed at the counter. Then I saw that he was with his friend Mark, and they were making their way through the party towards me.

It was now six weeks since Jack and I had broken up, and the physical pain of missing him had not lessened for one second. The back of his head was still the first sight to greet me each morning when I walked through the office door. He still had to walk past my desk to talk to the reporters in the business section and Page Six, making me grab my phone and pretend to be on an important call. Sometimes we'd had to talk to each other about the news assignments I was working on. But already it was back to the old Jack. Guard up, emotion buried.

"Hey there! Hey, great to see you, Mark!" I said, as chirpy as the Easter Bunny, when they arrived at my side.

I noticed Jack notice my T-shirt as he leaned in to give me a kiss hello. Shit.

"I didn't expect to see you here," I said before he could come out with a crushing comment.

"Actually, we're not staying long." His voice was strangled. "We just thought we'd check the place out before going for dinner. You?"

"I'm here with the girls. The drinks are free, so I'm sure we'll be here all night."

Mark, realizing he had become invisible, pretended to have spotted a friend and excused himself.

We were left standing and staring at each other. It was amazing how someone whose presence had once triggered my nonstop talk button now had me on mute.

"Amazing bar," I finally said, looking across the packed, noisy room. It was divided by glass doors separating the bar area from the lounge, which was filled with sofas on which people were sprawled, watching the party go by.

"Yeah, they've done a great job on the renovation," he replied.

We pretended to admire the new tin ceiling.

"So how have you been?" I tried in a more intimate tone, wishing I could cry "Babe, do you miss me? Because I desperately miss you!"

"Good, actually. I'm thinking of getting a new apartment."

Good? He was *good*? He was making small talk about apartments?

"Looking anywhere particular?"

"Not sure. I think I'll stick on the West Side."

Mark came back to join us. Jack looked at the time on his cell phone.

"Bridge, we've got reservations, so we've got to take off." He turned to Mark. "Shall we?"

"Bye-ee then," I said.

They moved off towards the club elevators. I turned back towards the bar. There was now only one of two ways this party could go— absolute misery or Absolut Vodka.

I ordered another two free drinks, then was relieved to spot Alice and Claire huddled together in a drunk heap on a sofa in the lounge room, celebrity-spotting. There was Alan Cumming, Ethan Hawke,

Salman Rushdie. I walked over and plonked myself down between them

"Uh-oh, Jack attack," said Alice, seeing the look on my face. She had already spent hours of diligent girl time on our own sofa comforting me. And she always had the same sage advice that she'd got from her mum, who'd been through a bad divorce. Once you've reached the black pit of despair, there's only one way out and that's up. You can either waste time wallowing, or you can pick yourself up and deal.

Tonight I was definitely up for the wallowing option. Then I heard my name being called across the room.

"Bridge, Bridge? Hey, I thought that was you."

I looked up to see an old friend of Sacha's, who had once come over for dinner in our loft. I remembered he'd decamped to LA to try to make it as a screenwriter.

"Milo!" I said, suddenly one percent more cheerful.

Claire nudged me. "*Milo?* Who the hell is called Milo?" she exclaimed in an overloud whisper.

"Dunno, but he looks cute to me," said Alice in an equally loud whisper as he approached.

"Out of my way, girls," I slurred.

I stood up swaying.

"Hey, Bridge. Great T-shirt," he said, staring at my breasts. It was as if the God of the Brokenhearted had sent me salvation.

Milo *was* cute—he'd always reminded me of the actor Vince Vaughn. I'd even confessed once to Sacha that I'd quite fancied him, although she'd warned me he was a major womanizer. But, hey, a major womanizer was just what I needed tonight.

Milo quickly spotted the fact that the three of us were drunk, bordering on incoherent, and ordered us more drinks. After half an hour, he was holding court on our sofa with his arm around me, telling us stories about the women in LA. Anything not to think about Jack.

"You think New York's bad. In LA, if you're not going to help someone get a part in a movie, then forget about it," he said.

"So it works that you're a screenwriter then, I presume?" I quipped.

"Oh, Bridge, never lost for words," he said. "I always had such a crush on you back at those dinners in your loft."

"*Really?*" Alice and Claire chirped in unison, now wildly nudging each other.

An hour later, I was inspecting the minibar in Milo's hotel room.

He was staying at 60 Thompson, a chic little boutique hotel in SoHo—where I'd posed naked for my photographer friend Circe the previous year. I'd agreed to go back there for a nightcap, nothing more. But like most nightcaps in nice hotels, it wasn't long before we were rolling around on his nice hotel bed.

"You know," I said between slightly mal-coordinated kisses. "I once did a very glamorous naked photo shoot in this hotel."

"Yeah?" Milo looked suitably lecherous and intrigued.

"A friend of mine's a photographer, and I wanted to write about what it was like to be photographed naked."

"Go on then. Show us a pose," he said. I stood up, peeled off my T-shirt and bra in one go, and then stepped out of my jeans and knickers. No more black pit of despair for me! Then I stumbled back into the room's sheer curtains with my arms in the air.

"Okay, so one was like this," I said, twirling myself in the scratchy, cream-colored fabric like a ballerina with a balance problem.

"It's working for me," said Milo.

"And another was like this." I extracted myself from the curtain and tumbled onto the floor. Then I got on my knees with my bum in the air and grabbed the metal legs of the bedside table as if I were clinging on for dear life in the cabin of a keeling ship. The way my head was spinning, I might as well have been.

Milo lay back on the pillows, sniggering. I clambered onto his still-clothed body.

I undid the buttons of his shirt and then yanked it off his body. He flicked it onto the floor in a well-practiced move. I flopped my spinning head onto his shoulder.

As I nestled into him, a chill went through me. There was no scent of cigarettes and clean laundry, just the reek of unidentifiable aftershave. His chest was different too. More hairy and buff. I was naked, clamped to a stranger. Misery engulfed me. He wasn't Jack.

Undeterred, Milo lunged at me while I tried to see straight. I reminded myself I was in a fabulous room with a hot guy—who had always fancied me, he'd said. And I was now a single woman in New York again, this was what I was supposed to be doing. I gave myself over to the helicopter head-spins and decided not to think too much about it at all.

We woke up the next morning on different sides of the bed. My head pounded so much, I thought I would be sick if I moved. Squinting, I spotted my clothes strewn across the floor. Oh God, I *had* done naked posing. And then I'd had sex that I could barely remember. And now I was going to die of alcohol poisoning.

I closed my eyes and thought of Jack. Oh, how I had taken for granted waking up in the lovely, familiar safety of his bed. Damn him, I hated him. How could he have cast me back out into the shark pool of New York single life? How could he have said he loved me and then reduced me to this? Okay, so I was probably still drunk—and forgetting my somewhat key role in our breakup.

The clock radio on the bedside table to which I had clung the night before said 11:07 A.M. It was Sunday. On the new schedule, I had to be at work at 1 P.M. With a bagel and an IV coffee drip, perhaps I'd be okay. Michelle was in charge today, thank Christ.

I threw one leg out from under the covers and searched for the floor with my foot. I sent the other one to join it and cautiously stood up. Then I staggered, step by step, into the bathroom. Without making the mistake of looking at myself in the mirror, I reached into the marble shower cubicle, turned the dial onto "cool," and stepped under the spray. The cold water cascaded onto the crown of my head, bringing instant relief. I washed my hair, stepped out to reach for a hotel toothbrush, and cleaned my teeth. Okay. I was feeling a bit better now.

I had all my clothes on again when Milo woke up. He sat up, rubbing his eyes, staring at me like he was trying to remember who I was.

"Hey, so are you off?" he asked.

"I've got to go to work," I replied, moving towards the door.

"Work?"

"Yeah, lame, right? Anyway thanks for a great night. See you next time," I said.

"Yeah, next time." He crashed back down on the bed again.

I closed the door behind and staggered down the dimly lit hotel corridor in shame. How could I have been so intimate with someone one minute and the next be throwing them such a perfunctory good-bye? Would I ever get used to one-night stands?

I stood waiting for the elevator, full of self-hatred.

"Bridget, come back here for two minutes." He was more awake now, standing in the corridor with a towel around his waist, scratching his head.

I turned back, hesitant.

"What time do you have to be at work?" he asked.

"One."

"Then you're not going anywhere yet." He pulled me back into the room towards the bed. I protested as he began to pull up my T-shirt.

"Hey, I've got to get going," I said.

"Bridge." He leaned on one arm to look at me. "I can't remember anything about last night apart from you spinning around in the curtains, which wasn't a pretty sight. But I would like to be able to remember this morning."

Okay, so what if Milo was a womanizer and he wasn't Jack? He still fancied me. And I would have to get past Jack sooner or later. And maybe having a guy's—any guy's—arms around me, making me feel wanted, was just what I needed after all.

Two hours later I got out of a taxi at 1211 Avenue of the Americas with my T-shirt now on inside-out. I was ten minutes late for my shift already, but I had time to nip to the diner on 47th Street to get a bagel and coffee. As I rounded the corner, I felt the most light-hearted I'd felt for six weeks. So sex with strangers in hotels wasn't so bad. Then I looked up and saw Jack. He was walking back from the same diner towards me, holding a brown bag containing a coffee.

"What are you doing here?" I blurted, going crimson

"I'm covering for Michelle." He eyed my T-shirt for the second time in less than twenty-four hours and went crimson too.

"Stay out late?" he asked. I felt my heart wrenching again. Again I longed to throw myself at him, to tell him how the pain of being away from him was physical, raw, and agonizing.

"Quite late. Is it busy up there?"

"Not really."

He pushed past me.

"Jack." He stopped and looked back at me with sad eyes.

"Do you want to go for a drink next week?"

"Sure." He looked like he'd rather pull his own teeth.

I sat at my computer three days later. I wanted to write about Milo. After all, surely I wasn't the only person to have struggled through the multi-emotioned sensation of sleeping with someone else for the first time after a breakup. But then Jack would read it—and so would the rest of the office, along with my parents of course. Was six weeks too short a time to be jumping into bed with someone else? Had *he*? Oh God, had *he*?

Oh, fuck it. I had already lost Jack partly due to my column. What was the point of worrying about it now?

Sex for the single girl, as I have said before, is more complicated than we'd all like to believe. Having sex for the first time after you've become single is trickier still.

It's like getting back on skis after you've had a wipe-out. Running into a freezing ocean on the first day of your vacation. Eating oysters after getting food poisoning, various friends have said.

Because it's tough to go from regularly falling into bed with someone so familiar that you know every twist and turn of their body to taking the plunge and doing the same act with someone new.

But even as I wrote, I knew I didn't want to run into any new oceans or eat oysters after food poisoning. A morning of anonymous sex in a hotel room may have cured my hangover—but it hadn't touched my heartache. All the handsome men in the world wouldn't get me over my beloved Jack. And surely when he read the column he would know that. Wouldn't he?

A week later on Sunday, I walked down Washington Street through the back of the Meatpacking District wearing a brand-new, pink, flowery Diane von Furstenberg dress and talking on my cell phone. It was a warm, early summer evening.

"I know, I know . . . I just have to do it," I said.

"Okay, but just remember, if there were reasons why you broke up, it's likely those reasons won't go away."

I was talking to Becky, an English girl who'd moved to the city at the same time I had—under slightly different circumstances. She had married a New Yorker after spending just twenty-one days with him and now had a blissfully happy marriage. Not surprisingly, I often turned to her for advice.

"But I love him," I said.

"Okay, well, come 'round and see us later if it doesn't work out. Josh'll have the basketball on. I'm making dinner."

Oh, how had I ever scorned settled, predictable married life?

Jack had suggested we meet for our drink at the Other Room on Perry Street, a quiet little neighborhood bar equidistant between our homes. Just the idea of being alone with him again made me feel ridiculously happy.

I thought back to the look in his eye when I'd bumped into him the Sunday before. He had to be finding this as hard as me. Surely he would consider trying one more time. Hopefully life would work out—just like it had that night in Rhone.

He was waiting for me outside the bar on the sidewalk, smoking a cigarette. I kissed him and went to fetch two pints. Then we sat on a bench in the sunshine.

"So, I read your column today. The one about food poisoning," he said quietly.

Shit, the darn column. Did he have to bring that up now?

"Yeah, well, you know, gotta fill those column inches somehow . . ." I trailed off. Suddenly I had a bad feeling this was about to go horribly wrong.

But I took a deep breath and got ready to say the speech I had been practicing in my head every night since we had broken up.

"Look, Jack," I glanced at him, "I know I fucked up. I took out all my insecurities about being over thirty and living in a different country and worrying about my job on you . . . and I know I wrote dumb and tactless stuff in my column."

Uh-oh, had he just gone really tense? I didn't dare look.

"I know I was nasty to you for no reason and picked fights with you to get attention. But I love you, and being apart from you has been, frankly, unbearable. And we were unbelievably happy a lot of the time. I just think that it would be mad to throw away what we had . . . "

Now I wished I hadn't put on the dress. Rejection was going to be so much more embarrassing for both of us with me in a bright pink, low-cut Diane von Furstenberg. And before I'd finished and could look at Jack, I could tell what he was going to say.

He looked suitably sad, but resolute. Already there was a distance about him.

"You know, all my friends have told me how great we were together. When they ask why we split up, I can't even explain it. Sometimes I wonder why we did myself."

Hope? Was there hope?

He dipped his head. "Bridge, I loved you more than anything."

Fuck. He was using the past tense.

"But I'm sorry, I don't think I can put myself through being with you all over again. That weekend when we were covering the start of the war in the office, I've never felt more hurt in my life. I just don't think I can go back."

And that was it. Jack had made up his mind.

"So anyway, have you been back to Soho House?" he said. "That roof deck where you can smoke, it's rapidly becoming my favorite spot in New York."

I clutched my pint glass hard to stop myself throwing it at him in despair. Only Jack could so infuriatingly step behind his barriers and then blithely carry on.

"I don't think there's much point in getting another drink," he said the moment our glasses were empty enough. Then we got up off our bench, hugged awkwardly, and he walked away down Perry Street.

As I watched him walk away from me, he ducked his head to light a cigarette, and the smoke wafted out behind him. Suddenly I remembered the first time I had watched him heading up Broadway with his friend Mike while Angus had been in the Leica Gallery.

Tears fell down my face. So there it was. I had yearned for Jack, finally won him, and then lost him again. And now no matter how much I fought it and regretted it, he, like Angus, was gone for good.

Ten dates until Christmas

··

Find a Husband After 35: Using What I Learned at Harvard Business School

Men Are Like a Pair of Shoes: A Single Woman's Guide to Finding the Right Pair

Mr. Right Now: When Dating Is Better Than Saying "I Do"

Meet Me, Don't Delete Me! Internet Dating: I've Made All the Mistakes So You Don't Have To

Self-help dating books. They all landed on my desk. As the *Post*'s unlucky-in-love dating columnist, I was a magnet for them. And they all advised the same thing. You had to get out there. Staying at home watching reruns of *Sex and the City* was never going to get you a new man.

But there was one thing I wanted to know as I flicked through them at my desk. Would forcing yourself out on dates—most of which inevitably would turn out to be raving nightmares—really increase your chances of finding the right person? Or would it only make you feel more disheartened and depressed than before?

It was now six months since Jack and I had broken up, and I had got through them in a numb daze. But recently I'd noticed him sitting in his office with the door closed, laughing on his telephone. And sometimes I saw him rushing out of the office suspiciously early. Not that I was stalking him or anything.

I'd banned Paula, Jeane, and Michelle from telling me if he had a new love interest, because I knew it would be better not to know. Meanwhile, I told myself the best way to cope was to set about finding someone new.

Paula, who by now had also broken up with Paul—they were too different in the end, she said—reminded me daily that the best way to get over someone was to distract yourself with someone else.

"Honey, I'm telling you, it may not be pleasant, but one day you just have to close the door and walk on," she said, puffing at a cigarette on the concourse. "Sometimes I want to kill myself—or more often Paul—when I see him in the office. But it's not like either of us is getting another job."

And neither were Jack and I. So I concocted a plan. Being a dating columnist did have its uses.

"Girls, I've come up with a mission," I announced to Alice and Claire one October evening as Claire put her signature dish of sausage-and-pea pasta with vodka sauce on our kitchen table. "I'm going to conduct an experiment for my column and go on one date every single week until Christmas to see if I can find a new boyfriend!"

Claire and Alice looked at me as if I'd just announced I planned to ski solo to the north pole in a bikini.

"Oh God, but, Bridge, blind dates are the worst," said Alice. "Do you remember all those hideous ones I went on last winter?"

After one unfortunate episode, Alice had been horrified to find her entire chin rubbed raw because her blind date had scraped his prickly goatee so much on her as she had kissed him. She had acquired a goatee of her very own. The following night she'd had to go to a swanky fashion dinner full of models and designers—and had resorted to covering her face with a can of the spray-on foundation that news anchors wear to mask the damage.

But Alice had now got together with a thirty-five-year-old English photographer who she had met through her brother and was suddenly madly in love. But I pointed out, just because she had miraculously been fished from the shark pool, I didn't have much choice.

Of course there was one other option—moving back to London. And sometimes I felt so desperate to get away from seeing Jack at work every day that I got as far as picking up my phone to book a one-way flight. But I couldn't bear the idea of knowing I had left New York brokenhearted.

And I had to admit it, the longer I was away from London, the less enticing it became. What was I going to do? Rattle around in my empty Shepherd's Bush house, calling married friends for movie dates just to be told they couldn't get a baby-sitter? At least in New York half the city was single. What had that guy in Soho House called it? "A pig pen"? No, "a choice festival!" Well, actually both. It was time I made the most of it.

"Stepping up to play the field," I titled my column.

It may seem like my love life has been hexed by a spell worse that the Curse of the Bambino—but baseball season has inspired me to change all that.

In the name of the great game, I've decided to personally test the theory that the more times you go out to bat, the more likely you are to hit a home run.

As instructed by my pile of self-help books, I found dates through dating websites, friends who knew guys who were happy to be fixed up, and any other means possible. I also began to trawl through the dozens of offers of dates I had from readers. And most sounded just like me.

Dear Bridget, Hi, my name is Mike. I'm a twenty-nine-year-old musician from Jersey. I have been reading your column for a while and can really relate to how tough it is out there. I haven't had much luck due to my work schedule, and I find the women I meet are too picky to want to commit. It would be wonderful if you would like to get together with me for drinks and commiserate, if nothing else.

Dear Bridget, I am twenty-six, Asian-American, 5' 6, slim, and muscular. I'm an attorney and swing dancer. I love jazz, baking, and singing. I would love to meet you for a coffee/drink at least just once.

Dear Bridget, I am a fifty-eight-year-old widower whose wife died about two years ago after a twenty-year marriage. I'm six feet tall and weigh 170 pounds, and I can still see my feet when I shower. I'd be happy to meet you for a drink sometime and, hey, if there's some chemistry . . .

Dear Bridget, I suppose it is too much to ask for a glimmer of depth in the vast black hole of vapidness that is your personality. But I'll probably be going to The Mercury Lounge on Wednesday. Care to join me?

My first date was not with a reader but with a guy called Nathan, a twenty-nine-year-old documentary filmmaker who I'd met briefly at a party over the summer. He'd asked me out on a date back then, but at the time the idea of having a romantic dinner with anyone but Jack made me want to run home and put my head in the oven.

We met in Bar 6, a cozy French-style bar on Sixth Avenue, and thanks to his interesting job, I was confident that we wouldn't run out of conversation. And I was right. I asked him what he'd been up to, and he didn't draw breath for thirty minutes.

He told me about the indie film festival he'd attended in Germany, and then how he'd been to LA to meet his agent, who he was worried wasn't working hard enough for him. I interjected with the words "oh" and "right," and threw in a few pertinent questions. My great dating rule number one: Listen and take interest.

Then he told me he wanted to make a film about China.

"Oh that's interesting. I've been thinking of booking a trip to Tibet."

"Cool," he replied, before speaking for another twenty minutes about his film. "So anyway, I'm starving. D'you wanna get some dinner?"

Paula's great dating rule number one: Don't go for dinner if you didn't get a word in edgeways over drinks. Even if he is cute.

I made an excuse about having to make it to a friend's birthday party, but as we left the bar he suddenly pulled me into a doorway. I thought I might get a snog.

"Look, sit down for a moment," he said. We squatted on a concrete step, and I wondered what had been wrong with the bar stools we had left two seconds earlier.

He looked at me earnestly.

"I'm also making a film about being in Jerusalem. I was near a bar where a suicide bomb went off."

And why exactly are you telling me this? I wanted to shout. Instead I scrambled for an appropriate reply.

"I was there with my girlfriend," he continued before I could speak anyway. "We were totally in love for three years. Neither of us was hurt, but we haven't been the same since. I'm making a film about all my emotions and hers and how I feel about her and how she feels about me since this all happened."

"I think maybe you should talk to her about that. Take it from me, dragging people you love into your own creative endeavors can backfire horribly."

"You think?

"No, I know."

I hailed him a cab, and he got in it thanking me profusely for my words of wisdom. I walked the five avenues back to my loft, smiling to myself. At least I wasn't the only saddo in this city to be hung up on an ex.

Which I found out again on my next date with a guy called Greg. He was thirty-five, a bartender and old school friend of Becky's husband, Josh. They had bumped into each other walking their dogs, and he had asked Josh if he knew any hot women. We met at Temple, a dimly lit, slinky bar on Lafayette that served killer martinis and bowls of the most delicious popcorn in the city. Eternally fascinated by anything to do with alcohol—because at least you knew where you stood with a killer martini—I munched away and grilled him on the bar business, and I began to think things were going quite well. Then suddenly from nowhere he began banging his hand against his forehead. Alarmed, I asked him if he was okay.

"Look, I wasn't going to tell you this, but we've being having such a great conversation I gotta."

Did he have genital herpes? Was he on the lam?

"I broke up with my on-again-off-again girlfriend a month ago. . . . "

Ah, that old beauty. Guys thought that expression got them off the hook for everything.

"Yeah?" I said, throwing a piece of popcorn into my mouth.

"Well, she's pregnant with my kid."

The popcorn reappeared and nose-dived into my martini.

"Fuck. Well, have you talked to her about it?" I was back in therapist mode.

"Yes, but she thinks I'm the most useless guy on the planet. Which I am. I just don't know if I'm ready to commit to one woman, let alone deal with being a dad."

I wondered if I should put him on the phone for a man-to-man chat with my friend Stephen about the joys of parenthood while I escaped to the ladies' room—and climbed out of a window.

Two more dates passed. Including one with a forty-two-year-old Wall Streeter who said he'd never let a woman sit with her back to the wall in a restaurant, because in the olden times it was the guy's job to watch the door. When I suggested that women liked to watch what was going on in restaurant, he looked horrified.

"No woman should be looking at other guys when she's having dinner with me."

I knew we would never last.

Next I set out to meet Michael, a blonde-haired German photographer who was recommended to me by a sane-sounding reader who sent me a snap of him. Michael asked me to meet him in Café Noir in SoHo, and I got to the bar a well-planned four minutes after the designated time. I immediately spotted a cute man with long, blonde hair standing at the bar next to a group of guys. I strode over, pleased.

"Hey, Michael?"

The guy looked around. "No."

"I'll be Michael if you want," said the guy next to him. His mates all burst out laughing.

"Hah, hah!" I gaily laughed back. One of the worst things about going on blind dates was other people being able to tell that you're on one. Now I was about to be that girl at the bar who is all dressed up waiting for a stranger and trying not to glance at the door.

I squeezed up next to the guys and ordered a Corona. On the other side of me a couple sharing a bottle of wine looked over at me with pity. I glared at them, then got out my phone and tried to look busy by sending some text messages.

Half an hour later, I was still there.

"Another drink?" offered the barman.

"Hey, honey, if he doesn't show soon, you can join us," said another of the guys next to me.

Yes, there was only one thing worse than people knowing you were on a blind date—people knowing you'd been stood up on one.

Then something occurred to me. Didn't Cafe Noir have windows along one side of it? Oh, holy shit, was I sitting in the wrong bar? I couldn't face asking the barman in front of everyone, so I ran to the loo and called 411—to be told me that Café Noir was in fact a few blocks away and I was in an almost identical-looking bar called 203 Lounge—which was so trendy it didn't need to have its name on the door.

I found the right Michael ten minutes later, and he was amazingly good-humored about it. He told me he'd been on a lunch blind date two weeks ago, and the girl hadn't turned up at all. Then he told me he didn't want to get into "anything heavy" with anyone—which meant he didn't want to get into "anything heavy" with me.

My next date I found on Nerve.com, the artsy Internet site which specialized in erotic photography, whose personals had become a staple for New York singles looking to hook up. Matteus's profile said he was thirty-nine, of Dutch origin, and in his photo he looked a dead ringer for Owen Wilson. He wrote that he liked his river view of the Hudson, 400-thread-count sheets, and Monty Python—so I knew he would be tempted by a Brit.

We met on a freezing November night at Malatesta, a low-key Italian restaurant one convenient block from his house. And for once the picture had not lied. The moment he walked in the restaurant, I noticed a couple of women clock him—which was always a bonus. I smugly sat through our date picturing myself getting wild between his 400-thread-count sheets.

Even so, when he suggested I "come up and check out his place," I assumed we might at least chat at little more before we actually got down to the wildness. But the moment we got into his elevator, he began kissing me. Then he gave me an intense "are you ready?" look—which was so unnerving I closed my eyes.

As we walked into his apartment, I realized I should have got a lot more drunk before I could get up the courage to leap into bed with another stranger and still-fragile heart. But it was okay, I reassured myself. I just needed a little time to get geared up. Matteus had different ideas.

He marched me towards his bedroom, mouth clamped to my neck. Then in one swift movement he ripped off my dainty, black Ghost shirt, sending all the buttons flying.

"Hey, steady on," I said, wildly scrabbling around on the floor.

"Come here," he commanded, leaping onto his bed like an over-sexed chimp.

This wasn't the sort of foreplay I'd been hoping for. The moment I joined him on the bed, he unceremoniously heaved off my jeans, took off my socks, and threw them all across the room. I dutifully unbuttoned his shirt while he rubbed himself up and down on his bare chest and belly—a small detail I tried to ignore.

Then he sprawled back on to the bed.

"Take off my pants!" he commanded.

Hmm, this was a tad pushy, but, hey o-kay.

I reached down to undo his flies, struggled with his belt, then inched down his jeans. His unfamiliar erection bulged at me alarmingly from behind a pair of black briefs. I grinned at it with fake enthusiasm. I didn't want him to think I was being selfish.

"Now take off my underpants too," he said, kicking off the last leg of his jeans. That was the last straw.

"Stop being so bloody bossy," I snapped.

"Bossy? I'm just trying to get things going." He snapped back.

"Well, give us a chance," I mumbled.

He turned over in a huff like he was stuck with the worst lover in the world. I sat next to him in my knickers feeling at a bit of a loss. I was rapidly going off the idea of doing anything. The idea of unleashing the erection now had absolutely no appeal.

"Look, I'm not sticking around if you're going to make me feel uncomfortable," I said.

"Don't then."

"Okay then, I won't."

He ignored me as I searched around for my clothes. He ignored me when I had to get on the floor and look for a stray sock. It was below freezing outside, but after searching in vain I decided to sacrifice it to the night, along with the shirt buttons.

When I was dressed, he stomped to the door in his briefs to see me out.

"Well, thanks for a lovely dinner anyway," I said.

"You know, at my age I just can't be bothered with women who have issues," he replied.

As I walked up Greenwich Street back to my apartment, I remembered my earliest theory about why everyone remained single in the Manhattan: You could easily hook up with someone and then escape because home was never far away. Okay, so I had escaped before I'd even managed to hook up, but at least I was only a ten-minute walk from the safe haven of 14th Street. Wearing just one sock in the freezing night and a buttonless shirt under my coat, I had never been more glad of anything in my life.

In all, I managed eight dates in the weeks running up to Christmas, and the last one was my most successful—with a writer called David. Two days later—on a Friday night—we went for dinner in Odeon, followed by a gig at the Knitting Factory. We were still together on Sunday when I had to leave for work. But I began to have doubts about David when I realized that he seemed more excited about reading about himself in my column than dating me. And although I had enjoyed his company, I was pretty sure I wasn't going to fall in love with him.

And this was what made dating in your thirties so much harder. No one wanted to take a risk and waste time getting things wrong. But my dating mission had taught me something, at least. Each time I had walked out of the loft to go and meet someone, I'd had a new spring in my step wondering "what if?"

And even though I knew most of the dates would probably be failures, there was still that tiny chance that one would work out. Yes, somewhere along with my column experiment, I had rediscovered hope. And every time I came home again, I had a new story to tell.

> Dear Bridget, The reason I buy the Sunday *Post* is to read about your latest dating exploits. It's like watching auto racing on TV— you don't watch to see who wins but for the inevitable crashes. Having been on a few blind dates myself, I can understand the anxiety.

> Dear Bridget, Today I'm going on my twentieth date. Yup, twenty men and practically none dateable. Just like yours, some made it perfectly clear that all they want is to have fun, others were trying desperately to get over some ex. Many were sleazy, some just boring. But here's to the next twenty. Getting out there is what it's all about.

> Dear Bridget, Thanks for your tales, we've all been there. You make this single life in the city a bit more bearable.

> Dear Bridget, Would you be offended if I asked you your height and shape? I'm forty, professionally employed in the music industry, and somewhat attractive myself.

I returned to Ealing for Christmas—and felt the annual pangs of guilt. The grandchildren's tree was still growing happily at the bottom of the garden. I knew my parents now hoped I would move back home soon—especially as it had become clear Jack had not made a last-minute reappearance in my life.

My mother drove me back to Heathrow on Boxing Day, and as we pulled up to Terminal Three for yet another good-bye, she finally couldn't restrain herself.

"Bridgie, we're so proud of what you've done in New York, but you're not getting any younger. And nor are we."

"I know," I said glumly. It already seemed like a lifetime since they had first dropped me off at the airport that gray February morning and I'd had the photo of Angus and me in my bag.

"You know, we've never wanted to put pressure on you, but do you think you are ever going to find the man of your dreams in New York?"

As I sat on the plane crossing the Atlantic once more, I already knew the answer. As long as New York remained a honey pot for intelligent, successful women, and as long as those women still outnumbered the available men, New York guys would always behave like kids in candy store. Mr. Right might be among them, but single we would all stay.

But as my taxi from JFK sped once more towards the great view of Manhattan sparkling in the winter night, my heart instinctively lifted and I smiled at the thought of what was waiting for me there—a job on a New York tabloid; a multitude of restaurants and bars where it *was* possible to go on one date every week until Christmas—and twenty more if I wanted; a loft full of designer clothes and exclusive party invites (even if they were secondhand). There was nothing that could beat the thrill of really living in New York. The city was a candy store for us all.

Stepping down the well-trod path

Exactly a year after Jack and I broke up, I found myself walking back down Washington Street on the well-trodden route to his apartment. We'd arranged to "hang out" for a Saturday afternoon, and I guessed he was now reasonably confident that I would refrain from turning up in an electric pink DVF dress, begging him to reconsider.

Jack had bought his new apartment—a swanky loft in a newly renovated West Village building—and while packing up his old place, he had found a couple of coats that I had left in his closet. He could have brought them in to work, but we vetoed the idea of his plonking a big bag full of my stuff at my desk—the office had already had enough entertainment on us. Instead he suggested I meet him at his old apartment, and then, if I liked, he would love to show me his new digs.

It was a sunny spring day, and by now the Meatpacking District was barely recognizable from the old days. Most of the companies that had actually packed meat had been priced out for hip, loft-style offices, hair salons, and designer shops. An ugly, metal-clad, towering hotel called The Gansevoort was about to be completed smack in the middle of the old warehouses. The Hog Pit, which once had been a beacon in the dark neighborhood, was now surrounded by bright, new, trendy bars. New York was ever-changing. And we were too.

At Jack's building the doorman no longer recognized me and the elevator had been renovated. The apartment where we had giggled, drunk whiskey, filled ashtrays, and made love was about to disappear. Jack—much to his unbelievably irritating smugness—didn't even smoke anymore.

But I stayed breezy while I got my stuff together and gave the apartment one last glance. Already the books, CDs, and pictures had been packed up. Then we headed back out into the sunshine, walking downtown towards his new place, acting like we were just good old friends out for an afternoon stroll.

"And so how are the girls?" he said as we headed south.

"Well, Claire has finally broken up with her Chris and has decided to move back to England," I said. "And Alice is pregnant."

Jack spun around, shocked. Truth be told, Alice had been as shocked herself when she'd found out the news three months before.

"Alice is pregnant?" he stammered. "I didn't even know she had a boyfriend."

"Well, you haven't really been around for a year. She met a photographer, also called Chris, last summer, not long after you and I broke up, and that was it. The baby wasn't exactly planned, but they knew they wanted to be together, so it made sense to keep it."

Jack scratched his head.

"It seems like everyone is having children these days," he said. "All I seem to do is hang out in kiddie playgrounds with my friends."

"Hope people don't think you're a pedophile," I cracked.

Jack ignored my comment.

"How do people know so quickly?" he said.

"Dunno, I think some do and some don't. Some people want to move to the next stage, so they take their chances when they find themselves in a relationship that looks like it might work out. Others, like Alice, give themselves up to fate. And the hopelessly idealistic among us try to stick it out, waiting for the thunderbolt. What I'm now realizing is there isn't a right or a wrong to it. It's just people are different, and they settle down in different ways."

He stopped in the street and looked at me.

"I still believe in waiting for that one who rocks your world, the one who leaves you in no doubt," he said.

"Me too." We smiled at each other. Guess we still have some things in common, I didn't say.

Jack's new apartment had an open-plan living and kitchen area with vast windows that looked out onto an amazing view of the

Village. It was still empty and plastic sheets protected an attractive, dark hardwood floor.

"Hope that didn't come from the Amazon rain forest," I said, sticking my toe under the wrapping.

"Oh, here we go, Miss Geography," smiled Jack, already absorbed in a pile of bills. It was just like old times.

I began nosing around, checking out his balcony, his closet space and bathrooms, and the room he said he wanted to make into his study. Last I demanded to see his bedroom, and he showed me to an empty room at the back of the apartment that had a small window overlooking a narrow street. We stood together in the doorway as I took it in.

"Hmm, it's nice and dark in here. Good for hungover mornings."

"I'm thinking of putting the bed there, what do you think?" he said, holding out his arms to show where it would extend from the wall.

I pondered the possibilities of where his big, comfy bed would work best in the space—and as I did so, a strange sensation hit me. Here I was, looking into Jack's future, knowing I would not be in it. The bed in which I had once slept was already slept in by other girls—not that I wanted to know who they were. No doubt one would soon be waking up with him in this room. It occurred to me that I now accepted this.

We walked back to the main area of the apartment, and I thought again how the space in which Jack and I had shared our moments of passion and love was about to be dismantled—and instead all his hopes, dreams, and excitements would take place here in this new place. And I wouldn't be around for any of them.

It was then that I knew I had reached the last part of my breakup with Jack—I had faced his future without me in it. I had let him go.

The next day at my computer I wrote about "Aaron" for the last time.

The path to disentangling yourself from a big past love is a precarious one, and one I have traipsed down more than once.

Guys tend to run down it without looking back. Girls often plod along it with misgivings, especially when they're surrounded by friends who are getting married and pregnant.

Part of the path is dealing with the nasty wrench that comes when you are suddenly reminded of a moment, good or bad, that you shared with someone.

Part of it is dealing with seeing an ex when the dynamic between you has changed. Part of it is getting used to enjoying new dates. But the real aspect of moving on is dealing with the future—not just yours, but theirs. . . .

. . . What I'm trying to say is this: When you split up with someone who you've really loved and imagined a future with, the hardest part is not the breakup dramas, the jealousies, or even the painful memories. It's accepting that eventually you will let them go.

Part Three

....

Life's a Beach

Farewell to kiss-and-tell

"Hello, hello, is this the *New York Post*? This is Mrs. Livingston. You just called me and left a message about a blob?"

"Mrs. Livingston. Thanks so much for calling back. Yes, I'm a reporter at the *New York Post*, and I'm writing a story about a blob in the lagoon behind your home. I guess it must be pretty distressing, right?"

This was the eleventh time—I had actually counted—that I had spoken to a complete stranger and said, "Hello, I am writing about the blob in your lagoon."

I was beginning to wonder if I'd finally had enough of my illustrious career in tabloid news reporting.

It was a month since my epiphany in Jack's apartment. A local hack in a place called Little Egg Harbor, New Jersey, had run a story on the AP wire about a strange jelly-like growth that had been found in the their local Timberton Creek.

A resident had happened to called it "The Blob" in passing—and, hey, presto, a managing editor at the *Post* had spotted it and got excited.

Now he wanted to run a *Post*-style version of the tale, heavy with sci-fi references and a big photo of terrified locals staring at the blob—plus a picture of the original film poster. I had been assigned the task.

That morning I'd Mapquested Timberton Creek, noted down all the streets that ran up to the water's edge, and had asked a researcher in our office library to print the phone numbers of every person who lived there for me to cold-call.

But as was often the case with these kinds of stories, most of the residents of Little Egg Harbor had had no idea what blob I was talking about, if they picked up the phone at all.

Now the afternoon was flying towards deadline, and the managing editor was getting impatient for the story. I needed this old lady's "witness quote"—and I needed the quote to fit the story.

"So Mrs. Livingston, describe this strange thing. It's huge and mysterious and brightly colored, am I right?"

"Well, my husband took a boat out yesterday morning and tried to break it up with an oar. We've been told it's some kind of dead algae, you see."

Sorry, not good enough.

"So would you say it's really like something out of a science-fiction movie? Like say *The Blob,* or, or *The Thing*?"

"Well . . . I'm not sure about that."

Time to rephrase the question.

"Well, would you say it's more 'sci-fi' than anything you might normally see in your very nice lagoon out there?"

"Oh, definitely. I've never seen anything like it before in my life, and nor has my husband, and he's been a seaman for fifty years. Yes, I suppose it is quite scary—like something out of a sci-fi movie."

Bingo! I thanked Mrs. Livingston and slammed down the phone.

I switched back to my file containing the blob interview I'd managed to squeeze out of the local environmental company. I had enough material—just about. Now I tried to think of my intro.

"Residents in a quiet New Jersey township have been terrorized by a Blob-like creature inhabiting their lagoon . . . "

Hmm, perhaps this was a bit over the top, even for the *Post.* Especially as most of the residents hadn't even heard of it . . .

I looked up from my terminal and across the grungy office for inspiration, watching as the rows of reporters tapped away at their computers or took notes on the phone.

At the desk next to me, Todd, a chubby, thirty-three-year-old reporter with a goatee, was getting irate with a copy kid who had been sent out to the scene of a traffic accident in Queens.

"Stop, stop. Let's go back to the beginning. Can you tell me exactly how many people were in the car and how many were standing at the bus stop?" he huffed down the phone. "Right, five in the car, one dead, eight at the scene, three in Jamaica Hospital? Now this guy with the bleeding foot, what was going through his mind when he saw the van was heading for him?

"But there was a huge, great bus coming towards him. He must have seen something . . ." Todd rolled his eyes at me from his desk and I giggled.

Then suddenly it hit me. I had been in this garbage can of a newspaper floor for four years, I was 3,000 miles from home, I was laughing about a gory traffic accident and writing about fungus in some old lady's lagoon.

I tried to concentrate on my blob intro again, but instead I now thought about what Pom had said two years ago when she had left me standing on 14th Street waving good-bye. "There never seems to be a good time to leave New York, but when you do, you know you've done the right thing."

I had debated going back to London for long enough. My mother was right: I would never find the man of my dreams in New York. Tomorrow I would call my parents and tell them I was coming home.

"Hey, Bridge." My head jerked up instinctively at the sound of Jack's voice. He was standing at my desk. "When you've filed that blob, can you come down to my office?"

Shit, had I screwed up any stories recently?

Half an hour later, I was sitting in a chair opposite him.

"So I've got an offer for you," Jack said.

"Oh, yeah?"

"We need two reporters to move to the Hamptons for the summer to write gossip for a daily 'Hamptons Diary.' We've rented a small house in Sag Harbor which would be your base and office for three months. Is that something you might be interested in?"

"Gossip? Shit, I don't know if I'll be any good at that."

Jack looked at me like I was the biggest loser on the planet.

I continued. "I mean, I just have never really been to the Hamptons before . . . "

"Bridge, I wouldn't be asking you to do it if I didn't think you'd be great at it."

Okay, so maybe I wasn't going to call my parents after all.

Three weeks later a fellow reporter, Dan Kadison, a photographer called Thomas Hinton, and I arrived at a small cottage in a leafy street in Sag Harbor, a former whaling village on the bay side of Long Island's illustrious South Fork.

From this cottage it would be our job to cover every spat, piece of scandal, and tidbit of gossip that happened in the thirty-mile stretch of Long Island that included the quaint former settler towns of Southampton, Bridgehampton, East Hampton, and Montauk—and all the fancy oceanfront mansions, farms, and hamlets that lay in between them. This was where New York's wealthiest spent their summers, along with the likes of Steven Spielberg, Sarah Jessica Parker and Matthew Broderick, Gwyneth Paltrow and Chris Martin, Richard Gere, Kim Catrall, John Bon Jovi, Jerry Seinfeld, Martha Stewart, Paris Hilton, and Sean Combs, among many others.

The Hamptons diary was to take up two columns in the paper every day from Memorial Day to Labor Day, and *Post* readers were ready to devour it just like they did Page Six.

That first evening in our new home, Dan and Thomas slaved in the kitchen setting up phone and Internet lines, hooking up a fax machine, and installing a printer—gradually turning the small, sunny room in it into our office. As they worked, I took my laptop out into the garden.

I took a deep breath, then wrote my Sunday column for the last time. Other people might think I was crazy to give it up. But I knew this summer I would have no time for romance and dating. My new assignment was to write about other people, not myself. I had pandered to my vanity for too long. And the next time I fell in love—if I ever managed it—I didn't want anything to get in the way.

FAREWELL TO KISS-AND-TELL

He was a green-eyed banker who summered in Martha's Vineyard and promised to be a "great date." I was a New York novice fresh off the boat from London. We met in the Whiskey Bar, and I thought I was about to get my first American boyfriend. How little I knew about dating in the city back then.

It seems a lifetime ago since that first date, and back then I had no idea I'd spend the next three and a half years sharing every twist and turn of my love life with the city. . . .

But as I stumbled through an excruciating meal in Rue 57 in which the banker glanced at the door every minute, hoping Cindy Adams might walk in (he'd heard she ate there), and I glanced at his Bud Light, wishing I could order a bottle of wine just for myself, I wondered, "Does this happen to everyone else?" I soon found out that it did.

New York life is nothing but a roller coaster. There have been plenty of nights when I have slumped in the back of a taxi on my way back to 14th Street despairing that I'll be lonely for the rest of my life. Times I've felt like the biggest loser for supposedly being the smart and savvy dating columnist, but still not playing my cards right or managing to be special to anyone.

But there have been as many days when I have gone running down the West Side Highway, or found myself on a rooftop bar or in the park with my friends and thought that I could explode with the buzz of being free and single here.

In misery or elation, there have been two things I've learned from writing this column: that everything has a funny side and that someone else has been there too.

Now without readers sharing their stories with me, I would just have to remember that on my own.

High life in the Hamptons

"Yo, we're on P. Diddy's private guest list. There's just three of us. You gotta sort this shit out."

"I'm with Nick Carter from the Back Street boys, we're V–I–Peee."

"Paris is at the bottom of the driveway in her limo, and she ain't standing in this line."

"I don't care if Madonna is sitting down there in a limo. *Nobody* ain't standing in this line."

It was a familiar scrum-like scene of anger and frustration in the Hamptons as Dan and I walked up the driveway to a $6 million mansion on Middle Line Highway to Sean "P. Diddy" Combs's annual "White Party" on the Fourth of July.

Three hundred of New York's most connected in fashion and music were crammed against each other like cattle, dressed in a multitude of variations in white. Behind us, the narrow Bridgehampton lane was jammed with honking Hummers, Mercedes, Porsches, and stretch limos.

"Last year they were turning people away who didn't have white laces in their shoes," said Dan.

"Fuck." I eyed my tatty blue denim bag that contained my notepad, press tags, disposable camera, pen, and phone as we cut to the top of the line, where the crowd's demands had reached hysteria point. An army of beefcakes stood glaring at them impassively while a blonde girl clutching a clipboard and a walkie-talkie looked so stressed she might have a heart attack at any second.

"Stacy!" called Dan. She looked over. At 6-foot-5 with messy black hair and dark-rimmed glasses, Dan was easy to spot. She extracted herself from the mayhem to greet us.

"Guys, give me five, will you? This is *insane!* P. Diddy's security guards think they're policing a day trip out from Rikers Island. Diddy's choppering in with a copy of the Declaration of Independence any second now, and half the party's still in the friggin' driveway." She whipped two silver wristbands out of her pocket, handed them to us, and shoved her walkie-talkie to her lip-glossed mouth.

"Red carpet, I got Hamptons Diary down here. I need a ride-up, pronto. Over."

Three minutes later a golf cart sped down the driveway, and Dan and I made a dash to it while a bouncer ran at us with his arms flapping open like he was trying to catch a couple of chickens.

"Hey, you, I said *nobody's* going up there right now!" he shouted.

"The tall guy and the girl, they're good! They're Hamptons Diary," retorted Stacy.

Finally after four years in New York, I had access to all areas.

I'd been in the Hamptons a month now and had already learned that Manhattan's summer playground wasn't a corner of the world you would necessarily call relaxed. Fighting to get into parties and clubs, just like battling through traffic to get to the beach or hustling to snag a table in the best restaurants, was all part of the great weekend getaway.

The melee began on Friday mornings, when traffic jammed the Long Island Expressway out of the city, making the sixty-mile journey to the Hamptons an arduous six hours unless you had a private jet or helicopter, of course. Then the small country roads were crammed all weekend with fleets of SUVs, 40-percent inflation on everything from parking to pints of blueberries, and a summer population made up of the kind of New Yorkers who thought that if they could afford to be in the Hamptons, they had a divine right not be frustrated by other people—meaning everyone was.

On July Fourth—the big three-day holiday weekend—the crowds were worse than ever, and in typical attention-seeking style, Sean "P. Diddy" Combs had decided to throw the biggest bash of the holiday to launch a campaign to encourage voting in the upcoming hotly contested November presidential election.

Few people cared about the voting bit. All they knew was that at P. Diddy's White Party last year, Bruce Willis and Leonardo di Caprio had choppered in at 3 A.M., and a hoard of beautiful women had taken off their clothes and frolicked in the pool.

Dan and I jumped off the golf buggy onto the red carpet, next to which a gated-in group of photographers was waiting for celebrities as impatiently as the guests in the driveway were waiting to get in. "Hey, man, what's happening?" "Who's coming next?" "When you gonna give us a heads-up about Paris Hilton?" "When's P. Diddy getting here?" I already knew most of them. We all trawled the party circuit together.

Matt Heine, a New York PR guy who was helping run the party, rushed over to greet us. "Guys, this is going to be insane, *insane!* Beyonce and Jay-Z are here already. So is Reverend Al Sharpton, Aretha Franklin, and LL Cool J. Paris and Nick should be arriving any minute. Anything happens, you know I'm all eyes for you guys."

Ever chipper and perma-tanned, Matt was one of a flock of press and event organizers who flooded to the Hamptons for the summer to promote clubs, parties, and fundraisers. And there was no mocking the seriousness of their jobs. The Hamptons' party scene had a herd mentality that would put sheep to shame. The buzz around a club or nightclub could make or break it for a summer. And thanks to the power of the *New York Post,* the Hamptons Diary could help create that buzz.

Tonight the action was in a huge, domed tent where hundreds of white-clad party guests were already milling around six bars that were serving free champagne and a sushi station that was churning out platters of spicy tuna rolls. The whole place was strewn with white leather cushions, and Aretha Franklin was reclining like Cleopatra on a sofa.

Dan hurried off to the mansion—a modern cookie-cutter job with tacky pillars and a pink-lit swimming pool, where Beyonce was apparently holding court. I stayed by the red carpet to catch others arriving. The mission was to get quotes from the celebrities, spot disasters and dramas, and check who was hanging out with whom.

But the task of getting *any* celebrity to talk to you at a party is not as easy as it sounds. I soon spotted dreadlocked boxer Lennox Lewis wandering past me with a drink in his hand. I whipped out my notepad and I hurried up behind his towering frame.

"Hi, sir, Mr. Lewis, I'm from the *New York Post*. So what do you think of the party?"

Mr. Lewis carried on walking as if he were deaf.

"Hey, Lennox, do you have a minute?" Now I skipped next to him, breaking into a trot to keep up.

"Lennox, what do you think of the party?"

He glanced at me as if a fly had caught his vision for a second—then looked away again as if, no, he'd been mistaken.

"Mr. Lewis, got any plans to fight again?"

He kept going.

"I guess that would be no, then," I said to his back.

Two minutes later, His Diddiness arrived with so much fanfare you'd be forgiven for thinking he was the second coming of the Messiah. Dressed in a white fedora, a white linen suit, and dripping in diamonds, he paraded around the party trailed by TV crews, bodyguards, and hangers-on, who all rushed behind him like adoring disciples. He beamed like he was on the biggest ego trip of his life—while I shouted questions which he also ignored. Meanwhile I had already begun to overhear snippets of the most common conversational topic at all Hamptons parties—discussion of where to go next.

Dan reappeared. "I'm giving this ten minutes. Southampton Town code enforcers are here."

And now you could see grumpy-looking local cops weaving their way through the glitzy party guests. I rushed back to find Matt in the driveway, who was by now pleading with the local officials not to close the party down. Sorry, they said, they had never, ever given permission for this kind of party. The music was too loud, nearby residents were jamming the phone lines in a rage because they couldn't sleep, and there was a bumper-to-bumper backup for fifteen miles.

This no-expense-spared party, like many in the Hamptons, had become a victim of its own hype. So much for everyone getting naked in the pool.

But the night was by no means over. Dan and I cut through the bushes, ran back down the driveway, and jogged a quarter of a mile down the country lane to where we had left our car. (Not a Porsche or Hummer, but a sensible, burgundy-colored Pontiac given to us by budget-conscious Anne Aquilina.) Because after any big party, there was always an after-party to cover too.

Diddy's was to be held at the Star Room, a club on the main road between East Hampton and Bridgehampton, which had become the hottest place of the summer because its owners had hired every pro-moter in the Hamptons to give it spin. The fact that it cost $20 to park there, $20 to get in, and $400 for a bottle of booze if you wanted a table didn't deter hundreds of people every weekend from clamoring to get through its doors.

When we got there, the scene was as chaotic as it had been outside the first party as hundreds of people surged towards the door. We cut the line with a nod from the bouncer and steeled ourselves to enter a better-dressed version of the Black Hole of Calcutta.

A doorman pointed out Paris Hilton making out with her Back Street Boys boyfriend, Nick Carter. P. Diddy—who'd somehow beat us there—was in a corner surrounded by his posse, who were dancing on the tables. Lennox Lewis was with him, but I doubted he'd warmed up. But by now the fact that the party had been closed down by Southampton Town was a better story than any bland celebrity quotes. We had three other nightclubs and parties to visit, so after half an hour we battled back to the car. Five minutes later, we got a call from the Star Room's doorman, who told us Paris Hilton and Nick Carter's makeout session had now turned into a screaming match in the parking lot, be-cause he thought she was flirting with another guy. We spun the car around.

Three days later I was sitting on the sand in my wet bikini, watching the sun inch towards Noyack Bay, experiencing a significantly more mel-low Hamptons. A warm wind blew off the gold-tinted water and above me the sky was awash with pinks. This evening, like usual, people sat quietly in deckchairs dotting the wide sweep of the beach to enjoy the sunset. Near me, two middle-aged women had stoked up a portable barbecue and opened a bottle of wine. A guy was doing yoga a little way up the shoreline. Out in the water, someone was still swimming, their dark head bobbing in the sparkling waves.

This was the peaceful bit after deadline when our diary had been sent for the day and, if we had no events to cover, I could cycle off for a sunset swim at Three Mile Beach, a strip of bay shoreline not far from our house. And here, alone by the water each evening, I understood why an acre-plot of land in the Hamptons sold for over a million dollars and why you couldn't get near a beach house unless you had $10–$50 million in your pocket. Despite the aggravation and attitude, this slip of Long Island where the pale light could turn the rainiest afternoon into a kaleidoscope of silvers, was the most beautiful place I had ever lived.

A young couple walked down the beach towards me with two small children in tow. The kids stopped at the water's edge to make splashes with sticks they were carrying. The father stood keeping an eye on them while the mother looked back and laughed.

But so what if most people my age had families by now? That was someone else's criteria for success. I was running around the Hamptons like a maniac for the *New York Post*. I had moved to New York for adventures, and that's exactly what I had got.

Now, sitting on the sand happily enjoying my own personal sunset, I realized for the first time in my life that there was absolutely nothing tragic about being alone.

Show me the Lear Jet

Money. In the Hamptons it grew on trees. It was sewn into the perfectly mown lawns that lay in front of every white, wood-framed, ten-bedroom summer house. You could see it in the cashmere draped over tennis-coached shoulders strolling down Main Street in East Hampton and in the sparkling rocks jammed on women's fingers in the posh restaurant Nick and Tony's. It glinted in the windshields of the Maseratis and Aston Martins parked up at the beaches and in the polished portholes of the gargantuan five-story motor yachts docked in Sag Harbor's marina.

Because in the Hamptons there was no shame about having money—shit, loads of it. Likewise there was no shame in being a single woman on the prowl for a wealthy guy.

When I'd first arrived from London—where no one discussed money, even though we all knew who had it—I had been amazed by how honest women in New York were about admitting that they wanted a man with means. After all, posh dinners, hair appointments in swanky salons, nanny bills, kids' educations, and summer houses all added up. In the Hamptons that mentality was more cutthroat still. If you were a rich guy, you had the pick of the crop. If you were a pauper, you might as well go get a tan in Coney Island.

The dynamic was easy to spot in hangouts like Jean Luc East in East Hampton—a restaurant that turned into an after-hours disco where Manhattan's summering singles went to have dinner and then hit the bar.

316

Women sat in twos and threes sipping cocktails in designer dresses that clung to their perfect physiques. Approaching guys would then have the first minute of conversation to prove their worth.

"Hey there, great to meet you girls, I'm John. I came in last night on my buddy's Lear Jet . . . "

"So what do you do? I work in private equity. Boy, we've had a great year. I've snagged a great little beach house in Sagaponac for the summer. On Thursdays it's only a two-hour drive in the Ferrari from my penthouse in Tribeca. . . . "

"So girls, if you want a ride home tonight, I've got my driver on all night."

Women were constantly on show, displaying tanned, gym-toned bodies and manicured nails. In the Hamptons, every guy wanted a beautiful woman on his arm, and if they had the money they'd get one. Indeed the sight of towering, modelesque young women with pudgy, self-satisfied aging men was as common as Porches in the parking lots. Maybe I was cynical, but I wondered if half the couples in the Hamptons would be together if Botox and a seven-figure bank balance weren't involved.

And there were different strata of wealth, of course. At the top of the tree were the über-rich and über-private, the hedge fund guys, CEOs, and Hollywood royalty who sat in their $45 million ocean-view mansions—the houses you'd see along the beach and have fantasies about. Theirs was a mellow summer of jetting in by private plane, hiring caterers for discreet home dinner parties, and sipping quiet cocktails served by staff on the deck. No need to get involved in the traffic and shit-fights for tables in restaurants when you could pay for everything to come to you.

Next on the ladder was the social set—the celebrities and Hamptons scene regulars who were addicted to a weekly round of charity benefits, functions, and fancy parties. Among them were morning-show TV presenters Kelly Ripa and Star Jones, Martha Stewart, Billy Joel's ex Christie Brinkley, Alec Baldwin, Russell Simmons, and Jason Binn, the boyish publisher of the super-successful *Hamptons Magazine* which was monthly filled with snaps of everyone who'd been out and about. Then there were the wealthy kids set—Paris and Nicky Hilton, Alex von Furstenberg (son of designer Diane and stepson of media magnate Barry Diller), magazine heiress Amanda Hearst, Johnson and Johnson heiress Casey Johnson, and all their hanger-on pals who amassed in VIP rooms to dance on tables, knock back tequila shots, and act as if they believed hedonism was their birthright.

On Saturday afternoons in July, the social scene was centered on the big, white VIP tent at the Mercedes-Benz Polo Challenge in Bridge-hampton, where the glammed-up hoards checked out each other's outfits, noted who was in the even-more-exclusive VIP enclosure next to the VIP tent, and found out where everyone was going that night. Later the herd would embark on the night's treadmill of parties, constantly discussing where they had just come from, who they had seen, and where everyone was going next. It was topic numero uno in the Hamptons social scene.

Further down on the strata were the house sharers. The twentysomething generation of New York—young bankers, Jewish princesses, and lesser trust-fund kids, who forked out $3,000 for a place in a summer house which didn't even guarantee you a bed when you got home. They were the regulars who amassed outside the clubs like Star Room, Resort, Jet East, and Cabana, still willing to plunk down $400 for a bottle of vodka if it secured entrance for them and their friends.

And then there was the army of entrepreneurs who spent their summers beefing up their bank balances—PR people and promoters slaving to get their clubs and themselves noticed; bartenders who pulled in $800 a night in tips; landscapers who charged $55,000 per house for a season of mowing, weeding, and trimming; the tennis pros, personal trainers, and house-calling massage therapists all raking in $150 an hour, plus tips. Midweek the local bars in Sag Harbor would get rowdy with the motor yacht crews—tanned, macho young guys from Australia, New Zealand, South Africa, and Florida—who got paralytic every night and sneaked different girls back to the decks of their $50 million yachts. The boys partied nonstop until Friday, when the boat owners arrived and the crews would be transformed from roguish playboys to uniformed deck boys until Sunday night.

Whoever said a class system didn't exist in America was wrong. And Dan, Thomas, and I were keeping tabs on it all.

The mid-July sunshine was pounding down, and I stood watching the crowd milling under the VIP tent at the Mercedes-Benz Bridgehampton Polo Challenge. To my right, eight six-figure thoroughbreds thundered back and forth across a pristine green field, ridden by young Argentine polo champions hired by wealthy American team captains for the summer to raise the talent level of their teams.

To my left, on a stretch of grass behind the tent, Paris Hilton was holed up in an SUV with black-tinted windows and which was surrounded by security guards. A pack of photographers was waiting for her in the confines of the VIP area, champing like greyhounds in their traps. Paris had apparently had another bust-up with her boyfriend Nick Carter and had a black eye. Everyone wanted the shot.

My phone rang. I pulled it out squinting at the SUV. Paris now appeared from the passenger door, wearing a canary yellow sundress and tossing her white blonde hair as the photographers charged towards her. Privately I wondered if she made up half the dramas in her life just to get the attention.

"Hey, Bridge, it's Heather. What time are you done with that Hamptons Diary tonight?" Heather, a feisty, blonde Australian, had taken Alice's room in our loft two months ago after Alice had moved in with Chris before the baby arrived.

"We've got about a hundred events, why?"

"I'm down for the weekend with these crazy girls who have a house-share. They're going to a costume party thrown by some private equity guy on Shelter Island. It sounds like it might be a crack."

"Will there be any bold-faced names there?" I was ever in work mode.

"I doubt it, doll. I just thought you could come let your hair down at the end of the night."

I scanned through our plan for the evening ahead. A benefit at East Hampton's art gallery at The Guild Hall, a *Hamptons Magazine* party for cover girls Lauren Bush and Amanda Hearst at the Bridgehampton Tennis and Surf Club. Calvin Klein was having a housewarming at his

$29 million pad on Meadow Lane in Southampton. Former Clinton fundraiser Denise Rich had organized a benefit at her $600,000-a-season-to-rent Southampton mansion in memory of her daughter who'd died of leukemia.

"Heather, I'll try."

Dan appeared. "Okay, so I got Jessica Alba. Paris's mom, Kathy, is over there spouting about her new reality TV show. Paris and Nicky are going to give out the winner's cup at the end of the polo match."

"Cool," I said. "I got that the fight between Paris and Nick at the Star Room two weeks ago was what started their breakup. Meanwhile, my mate who works at Corcoran real estate just called to say Howard Stern just lost out on a $20 million oceanfront pad on Further Lane in East Hampton. Apparently a local developer outbid him when he thought he had the contract in his hand."

Thomas, our photographer, joined us, wiping his brow with a hanky as he lugged his long-lens cameras over his shoulders.

"This is crazy, I'm so over Paris Hilton. You can't even see this supposed black eye. I just got a call. Chris Martin is surfing at Georgica Beach outside Steven Spielberg's house, and Gwyneth was on East Hampton Main Street with the baby buggy, buying a smoothie in Babettes. I'm gonna run down there, see if I can get a shot."

"Yeah, let's get going too," said Dan. "We got what we need here. The Guildhall fundraiser is starting in fifteen minutes."

We returned to the car and Dan drove while I leaned over into the back seat and pulled out a flowery dress I had brought to wear for the smarter evening functions. I yanked off my T-shirt and wriggled into the dress, kicked off my flip-flops and slipped on my Hollywould tan heels. There was never time to go home and change.

In the following three hours we hit all the events on our list. At Denise Rich's home, 400 guests were hobnobbing around a swimming pool next to a house built to look like a Spanish villa. Apple martinis and watermelon Cosmos were being served through ice statues. Tables—sold off for $25,000 each—had been adorned with white and pink roses for a three-course dinner. Michael Bolton was due to perform. All the regulars were there, discussing at which point they should move to Calvin's party. At one point, I nipped to a fancy portaloo, where a pretty girl wearing a $400 backless sundress that I'd coveted in Scoop in East Hampton was staring at herself in despair in the mirror. She was as slim as a tennis player, had smooth, blown-out, blonde hair, perfectly plucked eyebrows, and snowy white teeth.

"I wish I could take a 'not ugly' pill," she wailed.

Sometimes I still found the Hamptons to be as alien as the moon.

We arrived at Calvin Klein's party in a traffic jam of Mercedes, BMWs, and Jags as an army of attendants rushed to valet-park cars for the guests. The house was a faux Gothic mansion with a vast hallway crammed with people, which opened into a sitting room filled with white furniture and fur that backed onto the beach. I spotted Barbara Walters, Martha Stewart, Christie Brinkley, and photographer Bruce Webber standing around a table feeding on two vats of caviar. Dozens of buff, bare-chested male models were serving drinks. Out on the beach, a sea of orange Chinese lanterns bobbed in the breeze, and more white cushions where strewn across the sand. The vast buffet was also manned by nearly bare models serving lobster and steak. Around a fire, Barry Diller, Diane von Furstenberg, and Lauren Bush and her mother Sharon, who was recently divorced from the President's brother, were lying on cushions, their faces illuminated by the flames. Waves crashed down on the sand in the darkness ten feet away.

I stood with my back to the ocean, looking back up at the enormous turreted house with every window lit. Strains of salsa music echoed down from a terrace. An Outkast song thudded in a marquee next to the house. Already I had become accustomed to so much wealth. But I knew that once the summer was over, I'd never witness parties like this again.

Euan, Alice's well-connected, ever-social brother-in-law who'd got me a membership to Soho House the year before, rushed over, breaking into my thoughts.

"Hey, here's one for the Diary. I was just talking to Calvin, and guess what? After this party's over, he's going to pull the whole house down and start again! He says the place is haunted and it doesn't work."

Dan finally dropped me back at our cottage just before midnight. We had decided that I should now go on to the Shelter Island costume party with Heather, just in case anyone turned up there, while he took on the Saturday night round of the clubs.

I ran upstairs to my little attic room, threw off my flowery "function dress," threw on sweatpants and a T-shirt with an electric-pink palm tree on it, and then tied my hair into bunches. My special rendition of "surfer girl" would have to do.

Heather and her house-share friend, Sara, picked me up in their SUV ten minutes later. They were dressed as mermaids with elaborate blonde wigs and sequined tops. I didn't care. I'd already dressed as a mermaid for one *Post* photo shoot the previous Christmas, which was quite enough for me. And besides, this party was only work.

Shelter Island was situated in the middle of the bay between the north and south forks of Long Island. A small ferry took cars across from the backside of Sag Harbor, and we sped down the country lanes to catch it. Once on the ferry, rumbling across the dark water to the other side, the girls cranked up the stereo in excitement.

"Hey, I wonder what this guy will be like. I wonder if he'll have any rich friends," said Sara. "Apparently the ferry normally stops running at 1 A.M., but he chartered the whole service so people could get back from his party as late as they like."

"Sounds like a wanker to me," I said.

Heather and Sara smirked.

"You're not getting bitter, are you, Bridge?" said Heather, never one to keep her opinions to herself. "You've got the best gig of the summer, you live in paradise, you've just been to *Calvin Klein's* housewarming. I do believe you are getting money envy!"

"I bloody am not," I said. "These rich guys are all the same. All they want is a trophy wife to go with their trophy sports cars, boats, and beach houses. And when you get too old, like with their other possessions, they simply exchange you for a younger model. Believe me, I've witnessed it all summer long."

We arrived at the private equity guy's address to find a long driveway lined with candles and dozens of golden lanterns dangling from the trees. The driveway led up to a classic Hamptons colonial house with an elegant, pillared porch, built on a grassy headland that sloped straight down the huge expanse of the bay.

"Nice pad," whispered Heather. I had to admit, it was the prettiest place I'd seen all night.

The party was in full swing on the headland. A DJ was playing old disco songs, wait staff served champagne cocktails and a potent punch. A host of pretty girls wore hula outfits and fairy wings. I spotted several gladiators and superheroes. But compared to the over-the-top scenes I had just left, this party seemed positively cozy. I scanned it anyway, looking for anything or anyone that might make an item for the Hamptons Diary.

The others headed for the bar, and when I was sure that there was no one famous around, I went to join them. Heather was already chatting to a guy who was wearing a leopard-skin jacket over a horrendous silver, spangly, flared pantsuit, and with a huge medallion dangling from his chest.

I could hear her saying "*New York Post.*" And she was pointing at me.

"Yeah, that's Bridget Harrison there," she said. "Bridge, come here, someone wants to meet you."

Shit. I'd told her on the ferry not to mention that I'd come from the Hamptons Diary. I fixed a fake smile on my face, cursing her under my breath.

"Bridge, this is Evan. It's his party. He's a big fan of your column."

"Oh, right!" Now I faked modesty. "I hope you don't mind us crashing."

He was over six foot, with sandy sunbleached hair and deep brown eyes. He looked endearingly ridiculous in his costume. I put out my hand to shake his.

"It's extremely cool to meet you in person," he said, taking my hand. "I have to admit, I don't buy the *Post,* but I used to read your column online. That one you wrote about New York guys being like kids in a candy store, it was so true. I actually e-mailed it to all my friends."

"Well, I hope I didn't sound too bitter." I smiled coyly at him. What, was I flirting? Was I flirting with the private equity guy? No, no, I was just being friendly towards my host.

"I think I even wrote you an e-mail about it myself, which is something I've never done before, but you didn't reply. Then I guess you get a ton of mail."

"Oh, no, not really. I mean, sometimes I do." I had my fake modest voice back on again. "People did seem to like that column. I guess we've all had similar experiences in New York. Too much choice, not enough time, everyone jumpy about what's around the corner."

"Tell me about it. It's the story of my life."

Heather rolled her eyes and wandered off.

"What are you dressed as, by the way?" I said playfully, yanking his medallion. He eyed my pigtails.

"Elvis Presley. Who are you, Pippi Longstocking?"

We smirked at each other, and his eyes creased into appealing crow's feet. He looked like he spent a lot of time outdoors.

Suddenly I thought how sweet he was to have put all the candles in the driveway and lanterns in the trees—then I reminded myself he probably hadn't done it himself.

"Really, this party looks brilliant. Thanks again for having us," I said. "I guess I should go find my friends."

Some time and several glasses of white wine later, Heather and I were jumping around on the headland to the music. I had kicked off my flip-flops and was enjoying feeling the cool grass under my feet and the breeze from the bay on my face. This was the first party in the Hamptons at which I'd actually been able to relax.

Then Evan appeared next to me.

"Hey, dance with me," I said, shimmying up to him, full of wine and enthusiasm.

"I never dance. I'm terrible at it," he said.

"Bollocks." I grabbed his leopard-skin coat and pulled his hips to mine. We fell in synch, moving back and forth. I couldn't remember the last time I'd slow danced, and it was fun.

"You know, I'm actually having a really good time," he said before excusing himself to say good-bye to some guests who were leaving.

Later, tired from dancing, I nipped back to the drinks table. An attractive guy in a pale-blue cotton shirt and khaki shorts appeared next to me, holding out a glass.

"It was white, wasn't it?" he said.

For a second I didn't recognize him. Then I realized it was Evan. Minus the Elvis outfit, he suddenly looked incredibly sexy. His well-cut, pale-blue shirt, just thrown on, was clearly expensive and accentuated his deep tan. He was relaxed yet confident, and his obvious ease made him even more attractive.

"You're the only person I really want to talk to at this party," he said. "Will you come and sit by the bay with me?"

"Anything to please the host," I said. Now I knew that I was flirting.

We walked down to the edge of the headland, out to a small wooden jetty to which a sailing dinghy was tied. We sat down and let our feet dangle in the cool, black water. Out across the bay you could see the lights of the north fork.

He asked me what it was like to write the Hamptons Diary, explaining that he rarely left the island over the weekend and couldn't stand the social scene of East Hampton.

I liked him even more. Then we returned to the subject of my column.

"So, Miss Ex-Dating Columnist, do you think that it's actually possible to have a normal relationship in New York?"

"I don't know. Everyone here is so guarded. They've all been burned so many times. No one wants to let go and take a chance. Everyone has these 'just casual enough' relationships where you hang out, date, but no one dares mention anything about the future or make plans, just in case they show too much of themselves.

"And then if you do have a relationship, there's that obsession with things being perfect." I thought of the mistakes I'd made with Jack. "People should have the confidence to appreciate what they have, rather than constantly worry about what they don't. I think that's the one thing I've actually learned while living in this city."

"Bridget, there you are," Heather's voice came, calling down towards us. "I've been looking for you everywhere. Sara's, leaving, we have to go."

I grabbed my flip-flops. Evan leaped up and pulled me up with his hand.

"So how would you feel if I got in touch with you again?" he asked.

"You've got my e-mail address already, right?" I gave him a kiss on the cheek, flashed him my best smile, then ran off to join the girls in the car.

"Oh my God, Bridge, did you snog him? Did you snog the million-dollar private equity guy?"

"Don't be ridiculous," I said.

"He's not that good-looking, but he seemed like quite a decent bloke," said Heather.

"I heard he flies in by sea plane from Manhattan every Friday," said Sara. "And apparently he often flies in chicks too, but he never likes them because they're all gold diggers. He's looking for a real, down-to-earth girl—*The One.*"

I stared out of the window and I made a silent vow. If I ever heard from Evan again, I would never, ever accept a ride on his sea plane or be impressed by his wealth.

That said, the cottage, the headland, the bay . . . I had to admit it—it was all pretty darn nice.

Intrepid Brit girl
on Fantasy Island

....

"Uh-oh."

Dan looked over his glasses at me from across the kitchen table. I was grinning inanely at my computer like it had just told me I'd won the New York State lottery.

"So what's he written then?" Dan put down his pile of Southampton and East Hampton police reports on top of the shambles of paper already strewn all around us.

"He says he's sitting in the BA flight lounge heading to London on business, and all he can think about is meeting me at his party . . . And . . . wait for it! Would I like to come over to Shelter Island for dinner—sans masses and notebook some time?

"*Yes!*" I mock-punched the air.

"Are you sure some banker dude is really your type?"

"Oh, I don't care about his money," I said grandly. "He was so down-to-earth and thoughtful. He even remembered what I was drinking at the party."

"Well, seeing as you have a drink in your hand most of the time, that wouldn't be too difficult."

"Shut it," I said.

We turned back to the police incident reports that I had collected from the police stations in Southampton and East Hampton that morning. It was Monday, and after a star-studded weekend filled with parties, clubbing, and scandal, we now had to develop new stories for the week.

The "cop sheets," as we called them, logged the names of everyone who had been arrested in the Hamptons over the past seven days, as well as all the burglaries, domestic disputes, assaults, drunken driving incidents, and other mishaps that had taken place.

Crime in the area was pretty low—a bunch of rich people on vacation naturally had better things to do than rob each other—but we searched meticulously for any incidents involving the names or addresses of famous people.

"59 Middle Lane," read the third sheet I picked up. "Property caretaker Kaye Mayne reports tampering with electronic gates on several occasions, possible attempt at a break-in." I immediately recognized the address. This was the house in which Wall Street financier Ted Ammon had been bludgeoned to death three years before. Instantly I was reminded of the nightmare assignment to Guildford to find his widow. I shivered. Since that trip, Generosa had died of cancer, and her second husband, Danny Pelosi, had been arrested for the murder. Kaye Mayne was the nanny who now cared for the pair's long-suffering twins. A lot could happen in three years.

"What about this one? It happened last night," said Dan, interrupting my thoughts. "Harper Simon. Pulled over on Montauk Highway at safety stop in 1998 Chrysler. When subject rolled down window, officer smelt strong aroma of burnt marijuana. Officer then spotted marijuana cigarette in plain view near to the stick shift of vehicle."

"Harper. I bet that's Paul Simon's son!" I said. "I know he's called Harper, what's the date of birth?"

The age fit. Paul Simon owned a secluded estate ten miles north of East Hampton in Montauk.

"Last night Paul Simon played at a charity benefit at the TalkHouse. I bet he was sneaking in a quick joint on the way to see his dad."

Dan picked up his phone to call the East Hampton police chief. We already had two juicy new items underway.

I went back to daydreaming about Evan. And I had to admit, I couldn't help feeling a little bit smug. Here I was surrounded by all this power, wealth, and glamour, and someone with shedloads of it had passed over all the beautiful butterflies, fairies, mermaids, and hula girls at his party—for sweatpant-dressed me!

And even though our meeting had been brief, I noticed thoughts of Evan had swiftly extinguished the occasional pangs I had for Jack—just like Jack had for Angus. Maybe I would be third-time lucky? Okay, so I was being a little bit premature, but I wasn't going to blow it this time. And after three years of being a dating columnist, I had to know something about guys by now.

I thought back to all the advice I had got from readers over the years.

Dear Bridget, To be attractive to guys, girls should be true to themselves, not their desire to have a relationship.

That was me all right. Two days ago I hadn't even wanted a boyfriend. But then a girl can change her mind.

Dear Bridget, Guys love to date a girl who has a lot going on so they can gradually get to know her without feeling like they'll suddenly be cornered into being the center of her world.

With the Hamptons Diary to run, there was no danger of anyone being at the center of my world apart from Paris Hilton.

Dear Bridget, A girl who enjoys her own life and doesn't begrudge a guy enjoying his will always get the call.

On that note, I waited until the following day to accept Evan's invitation, just to seem frightfully busy. Two weeks later I was back on the Shelter Island ferry, wearing a brand-new, lace-trimmed T-shirt, Joe Jeans, and pink Havaiana flip-flops. Hidden away were my new La Perla bra and knickers, dainty white, almost see-through. Purely for a little confidence boost, of course.

I'd spent the morning on the beach topping up my tan and freckles, and all afternoon rushing around the stores in East Hampton, searching for an outfit that would appear just thrown on.

I had taken our car with the agreement that if Dan needed me, I could be back on the job within half an hour—as I wasn't sure if the editor-in-chief, or Jack, would approve of my sneaking off on dates. But the good thing about driving was that it meant that I couldn't get pissed—a key advantage for this play-hard-to-get first date. Word slurring, drunk lunging, or bed jumping were all a no-no tonight.

I decided to get to Evan's house seventeen minutes late (fifteen minutes was too keen, twenty minutes too late), but I was early off the ferry, so I sat in the lane a few meters from the end of his driveway, taking deep breaths and hoping he wouldn't suddenly appear walking a dog. Someone like Evan probably had a dog.

At 7:46 P.M. exactly, I turned in through his gateway. But my hand was shaking so much on the steeling wheel that I swerved, mounted the curb, and careered into a flowering shrub.

"*Shit, shit.*" I swerved back onto the drive again and stopped the car, my heart pounding. I checked in the direction of the house 100 yards away to see if he had seen or heard me, then I got out of my seat and scuttled, bent double, to inspect the damage.

The shrub was broken at its base with half its flowers now on the ground. I propped it up, stamped the soil around it with my foot, scooped up the evidence, then darted back into the car.

Two minutes later I parked our horrible Pontiac next to Evan's massive Mercedes SUV. I was still frantically shoving greenery into the glove compartment when he emerged from the house, barefoot, in another exquisite shirt and surfer shorts.

"Bridget," he said, opening my door for me. "It's good to see you again."

"Hey, hi," I stammered, deciding not to mention the small fact that I'd just careered off the drive headlong into his landscaping.

He led me through his front door into a huge room which was painted sea grass green and had a high white painted ceiling which made the room feel enormous. There were low bookshelves around all the walls and three leather sofas, each with a chocolate-colored cashmere blanket thrown over the arm, in front of a large brick fireplace. A Bose stereo system was fitted into one shelf, and beautiful, framed line drawings of sailing ships hung on the walls. The far side of the room opened to a wide, screened deck which looked directly out onto the blue expanse of the bay. The setting sun was throwing a golden light back through the cottage.

DO NOT gush about the pad, I told myself, already fantasizing about cuddling up under the cashmere blankets in front of a roaring fire.

"Nice of you to lay on the sunset," I said, walking out onto the deck to position myself in the flattering light.

"I made a couple of calls," said Evan. "Drink?"

"Oh, just any old bottle of beer for me."

"I opened a bottle of Puligny Montrachet, if you'd prefer."

"Oh, well, okay then. If it's open."

I followed Evan into the kitchen which was next to the main room. Here his dinner preparations included a salad of mozzarella and vine tomatoes, strewn with basil.

"I baked you some olive bread," he said, handing me a glass of wine.

"You baked me bread?" I was stunned.

He smiled. "It's really yummy. And I hope you like rack of lamb. It's organic. I brought everything down from the city in the plane this afternoon."

"Gosh, that's so sweet of you to do all that shopping. I haven't had a home-cooked dinner for years."

"I didn't actually do the shopping. My secretary had it delivered," he said.

We went back out onto the deck and he brought with him a plate of olives and sliced chorizo for us to nibble at.

"Did your secretary slice the chorizo too?" I cracked. He looked offended for a second, then laughed.

We sat on the deck, watching a blaze of color changing across the sky. A motorboat scudded by on the water, leaving a frothy white wake in its trail. It had been my dream to own a house overlooking the sea. I didn't tell him that, just in case he thought I had my eye on his.

He told me he'd bought the place almost derelict and had had the whole place renovated in three months. He'd bought the land on either side of it to make into a nature reserve.

"Oh my God, that's so great you're into conservation. I did geography for my degree."

"Actually, it was to stop anyone from building next to me," he said.

Then he pointed to the spot where his sea plane landed every Friday afternoon after a forty-five-minute flight from Midtown. No six-hour traffic for him.

DO NOT be impressed by the plane, I reminded myself.

"Convenient," I said.

We had dinner in candlelight on the deck and soon returned to what seemed to be Evan's favorite subject—the difficulties of dating in New York.

"So many guys, especially those who work in finance, spend their twenties and early thirties aggressively devoted to making money. They have no time for anything else. It's only about getting to the top of the ladder."

"And does that apply to you?" I asked.

"It did. Now I'm thirty-four, I'm realizing that there are more important things in life. Money is great, but it will never make you happy."

"No, no, no, I agree," I said, sipping another glass of fine wine, gazing at a millionaire in his Hamptons mansion.

"So why do wealthy, smart guys who clearly need to be stimulated end up serial-dating women just for their looks?" I asked. It was a question that had always bugged me.

"I don't know. Maybe because money guys have such high stress in the office that when they get home at the end of the day, they just want someone easy on the eye with whom they can relax."

"Shit, none of my boyfriends have ever described coming home to me as relaxing," I said.

"Well, who wants relaxing? My dream is to find someone who is spirited and independent and doesn't take any shit. I want a soul mate," he said.

I told him that my parents had been married for forty years, and on the anniversary of their engagement in Paris—where my mum was working at the time—they had gone back to find the bench by the River Seine where my father had proposed. I had asked them how they had known they were soul mates—and had written a column about it.

"So what did they say?" he asked, leaning across the table.

"My mum liked my dad because he was organized, she respected his judgment, and he didn't get on her nerves. My dad liked my mum because she was great with other people and devoted to her family and could sew."

"*Sew*?" blurted Evan incredulously.

Damn, that didn't sound as romantic as I'd planned.

"I mean, what they said was that they agreed on the things that were important. They respected each other's independence, and they got excited about the same stuff—like traveling. And they both had a similar attitude to money."

Money, shit. Perhaps best not to mention that again either.

"My mum said the secret of a happy marriage is being able to talk about everything and also accept that you have made a life-long commitment that you're not going to chuck it in the moment you don't agree on stuff. She said when you first get married, you have no idea just how much you will have to compromise."

"Compromise, ech, that sounds scary," laughed Evan.

"Yup, we selfish, single New Yorkers are all far too set in our ways for that."

"Unless you meet someone who makes you want to compromise," he said quietly. "I think a lot of people in New York get together simply because they see what they can get from each other. In that way, people set themselves up for all the soulless shit that follows."

Now he looked serious and his brown eyes seemed to glitter against his tanned complexion.

"In your heart, you have to know the difference between a perfectly pleasant evening with someone who you think looks good on paper . . . and genuinely sparking off someone's company," he said.

We knew which category *this* dinner fell into.

A full moon had risen over the bay by the time we had finished eating, and he suggested we walk down to the waterfront for the best view. We padded barefoot over the damp grass of the headland, back to the little wooden jetty. Water was lapping against the side of the tethered sailboat, and I noticed Evan's fleet also now boasted a large speedboat, tied up at the end of the dock.

Hmm . . . a speedboat . . . me in a Prada bikini, my hair blowing in the wind, zooming back for cocktails . . .

I felt his hands on my shoulders. I leaned back against his tall, strong body, and he rested his chin on the top of my head.

Okay, so surely it was okay to rewrite the rules a little for our first date. Kissing was fine. I was still going home at the end of the night. Then suddenly I didn't have time to think about it anymore. He turned me around and bent down to kiss my lips, his arms encircling my shoulders. A warm, sweet, salty breeze whipped off the water and ruffled our hair. I wondered if I had ever made out with anyone somewhere so perfect.

"You know, I would never have seen you again if you were still writing your column," he said as I stood in his arms.

"And this is exactly why I gave my column up," I said.

The following morning, back in Sag Harbor, I woke up early with excited butterflies in my tummy. When I sat down at the kitchen table and opened my laptop, there was already was an e-mail waiting from him.

"Here we go. You've just left, and I'm sure I'm breaking all the rules in the book. I know I should be very cool but I won't. I enjoyed your company, I loved your mischievous smile and laugh and your British honesty. I hope very much I can see you again."

I was so excited I had to go and pace our little garden and replay the whole wonderful evening in my mind. Evan had Jack's intelligence and wit, along with Angus's easy self-confidence. Perhaps fate had even caused me to lose Angus and Jack so I could now have a perfect combination of them both!

Evan returned to Manhattan for the week, but text messages and e-mails from him began to pop up every day.

I forced myself to return each one with restraint, sticking to my plan that however keen Evan seemed, I wouldn't risk scaring him off.

One night a text message came at midnight telling me I was the last thing on his mind before he went to sleep—for the third night in a row he wished me "Sweet dreams, Bridget."

"You need to get out more," was my witty reply.

Next day he sent all his numbers—his place in Tribeca, Shelter Island, his cell phone, even his British cell phone—begging me to call so he could hear my voice.

"Sorry, no time, have world-changing Hamptons Diary to write," went back my text.

And I did. One morning he caught me early when I'd rushed to Bridgehampton on a tip from our local photographer, Doug Kuntz, that a Mexican laborer working on a multimillion dollar home had fallen through a roof and been killed. The street address was the same as Richard Gere's palatial oceanview retreat, which would have made the story extra juicy—but when I jumped out of the car to talk to the cops investigating, it turned out to be a different house.

"Did I wake you up?" Evan said, not bothering to announce himself when I grabbed my phone in the mansion's driveway.

"Actually, I'm in the middle of a conversation with a chief detective of East Hampton Police Department," I retorted importantly.

But this time I couldn't resist redialing him the moment I got back into my car.

A week and several increasingly lovey-dovey phone chats later, I was standing surrounded by a new fleet of Bentley cars, again on the phone to Evan. He'd called while I was at a champagne reception for the $100,000 luxury motors, where Hamptonites had gathered to order custom-made ones of their own.

"It's already been seven days, and I can't wait much longer to see you again. When can you spare me a day?" he said.

I was now desperate to see him too, but I'd had to book a last-minute four-day trip to England. The tenants were moving out of my house in Shepherd's Bush, and the whole place needed to be cleaned before it was repainted.

"Can't you hire people to do that?" he said, incredulous.

"No, the whole place needs sorting out," I said.

"Well, when are you back?"

"Sunday night. It's an Air Miles flight, so I can't change it."

"What if I buy you a new ticket for an earlier flight on Sunday? Then you could see me in the city, and I'll fly you down to Sag Harbor on Monday in the plane."

The plane! No, *not* the plane. Buy me a new flight? Would it be business-class? No, what was I thinking? No, no, no.

"Really, I don't need that fuss. I'd love to see you Sunday night, but it might be a bit late. I don't land until 9:30 P.M."

"Okay, so I'll pick you up at the airport and then take you for a late dinner."

"It's JFK, it's miles from the city."

"Yes, I do know where it is."

"Well then, only if you're sure."

"Of course I'm sure."

Wow. I hadn't been met off a plane at JFK in all my four years of living in New York. We said good-bye and I turned back to the Bentleys, catching sight of my reflection in the window of the million-dollar mansion where the event was being held. I was grinning with excitement.

No taxi, thanks

....

I sat on Primrose Hill, relishing the novelty of being home in London again. All around me groups of people lounged on the grass enjoying the glorious English summer. Down the hill, behind the eclectic jumble of London Zoo's animal enclosures, the panorama of the city spread out in all its glory.

Angus walked towards me with a packet of crisps clenched between his teeth, his hands full with two pints. I lay back on the grass, watching him approach. I had been scrubbing my kitchen in Shepherd's Bush, reminiscing about the old days with Tilly and Kathryn when he had called to say he'd heard I was back in town and did I want to meet for a drink. Our paths had barely crossed since Milly and Luke's wedding, but this time when we'd spotted each other on the hill, I'd run freely into his arms. Now his familiar smell was comforting—happy memories, not ex-boyfriend angst. Fuck, it was just really nice to see him again.

When we'd been going out with each other, we'd often come to Primrose Hill on summer evenings because it was near his flat. And now as I watched him returning from the pub with his familiar quick step, in his faded, pink Fred Perry shirt and jeans, it was almost like we had gone back in time. Except we were four years on instead. He was now cautiously optimistic about spending the rest of his life with India; Tilly's twins were now exuberant little girls, full of curiosity and whys; Kathryn was organizing a huge December wedding to the actor she had seen "standing under a beam of light" at a party. And I was fantasizing about tomorrow night when I would finally be reunited with Evan at JFK.

As Angus sat down again, I thought of the heartbreaking afternoon at the *Post* when he'd called me to tell me about India, and how I had feared I would never recover—until Jack had come along. And now there was Evan.

"It's funny how when you break up with a boyfriend, you think you'll never find anyone ever again—and then you do," I mused, staring up at the blue, cloudless English sky.

"So who is this guy? I've never seen you with such a shit-eating grin on your face," Angus said.

I smugly sipped my cold pint.

"Evan is like the perfect combination of you and Jack."

"He must be a fucking rock star," Angus replied.

The seat belt sign pinged on at 8:45 P.M. and my stomach turned with excitement. Below me, the dark expanse of America was becoming increasingly scattered with lights as we inched down the East Coast.

I got up, squeezed past the man sitting next to me who had flown all they way from Dehli to visit cousins in Queens, pulled my duffel bag from the overhead locker, and took out my "Arrival Preparation Kit."

I headed down the aisle to the bathroom, locked the door, wiped down the sink with paper towels, and laid out my wares. One Airport Outfit—washing machine–fresh gray cotton pants that looked good on my bum, faded blue American Apparel tank to show off freckles on shoulders, the pink Havaiana flip-flops now set off with newly pedicured pink toes, the La Perla underwear. One Wash Bag—containing Ecco Bella lemon verbena body lotion for au natural aura of citrus, honey hair wax to enhance tousled surfer-girl hair, MAC mascara for "barely there" application, Visine, E 45 Cream, toothbrush, floss, extra strong mints. It had now been over two weeks since I had seen Evan. I wanted our reunion to be perfect.

The plane changed gear and dropped a little. I expected we were now heading along the top of Long Island. Far below, Evan would be sitting in the back of his limo, heading for JFK. I thought again about his last e-mail to me: "I can't wait to see your smiling face as you walk through Arrivals." For a ruthless New York Wall Streeter, he loved those cheesy messages.

I looked at myself in the mirror. My eyes were bleary from the ration of one Temazepan sleep tablet my mother had given me, intended for my overnight flight back to London come Christmas, which I had swallowed to make the journey go faster. My skin was dull and sagging with airplane air. But thanks to four days of kitchen scrubbing and a starvation diet, I was at least fairly skinny.

I applied the Visine, followed by a good slapping of the cheeks and a splashing of cold water. Then I stripped off my Juicy Couture jogging pants, holey Father Christmas knickers, and graying bra. I gave myself a standing-up washdown with the aid of paper towels and slathered on the Ecco Bella and E45 cream. Then on went the outfit, the honey wax, the mascara. Then I brushed my teeth and moisturized my feet.

I looked back in the mirror. Evan was about to meet a tanned and freckly, blonde thirty-three-year-old who—with a generous stretch of the imagination—might pass for a hip twentysomething, springing from a seven-hour flight with natural sexiness and style.

Yeah, right.

I returned to my seat, suddenly self-conscious of my obvious "being met" overhaul. But then, I told myself, why should I care? All those times I'd flown the Atlantic—for Christmases, weddings, and never once had someone been waiting for me when I got back to JKF—not even Jack. Now it was my turn.

As the plane bumped over the Rockaways in its final approach to the airport and I began to envision my long kiss with Evan on the dock—the bay white with moonlight, the smell of the sea on the breeze. I smirked out of the airplane window into the darkness.

We landed fifteen minutes early, but then got stuck on the taxi runway, waiting for an Air Canada jumbo to vacate our allotted loading dock. The man from Delhi perked up and asked me how long I'd lived in New York. I answered him on autopilot, trying to decide whether I should wear my baby-blue Juicy Couture cashmere jumper tied around my waist or if a flash of brown belly would work better for the crucial "first sight" moment. Would Evan pass the airport test I had tried on Angus four years ago? I didn't care. I had learned a lot since then. These days I knew to stay focused on the small things. I was being met, and that was enough.

Once off the plane I moved fast, overtaking fellow passengers walking towards the immigration hall to get to the front of the visa lines. The vast room, crisscrossed by nylon tapes, where non–US citizens always had to queue up for an eternity, was mercifully empty for a change. And this time I beamed at my stoney-faced immigration inspector when he took my fingerprint and photo and asked me what I did at the *Post*.

I had done this ritual so many times, and now at last life was actually working out. I had found someone again who made me sleepless with excitement, and who—no less—had found me thanks to my column! Now he was just a few steps away, with a waiting limo—not that I cared about the limo, of course.

Just before I walked through Customs, I picked up and dropped my duffel bag and handbag several times. Should I hold one in each hand so my arm muscles would look taut and worked out, or sling the duffel bag over my shoulder like I normally did? I wrapped the cashmere jumper around my waist and opted for the arm muscle–enhancing look. Then I tousled my hair and headed through the Exit towards him.

Terminal Four Arrivals was packed—the usual wall of waiting relatives, friends, shady-looking cab drivers, and chauffeurs holding signs. I walked towards them, doing my best to appear cool and relaxed. Evan would probably see me before I spotted him, although in among this lot, I reckoned, his tall, frame would be fairly easy to spot. I scanned the faces, trying not to look eager.

Not locating him initially, I got past the crowd and put down my bags, looking around.

"You wan taxi? You wan taxi?" said a Chinese cabbie, with several others hot on his heels heading towards me.

"No, thanks, I'm being met," I said.

I still couldn't see Evan and wondered if he'd nipped away for a coffee. I also decided to go check out the chauffeurs' signs in case he'd sent his driver to get me while he waited in the car. None had my name on them, so I weaved back and forth twice more through the waiting crowd, wondering how else he might have missed me.

As I stood by my bags, perplexed, the stream of passengers from my plane gradually dwindled, as did the waiting mêlée. It was now easier to see everyone in the terminal. Evan was still nowhere in sight.

I checked my phone for messages. There were none, so I called his Blackberry. It rang, then switched to his message box.

"Hey, it's Bridge, I'm at the airport. I'm worried I might have missed you. I'm, um, I'm standing by the Hudson newsstand, Terminal Four . . . that's if you are here."

Of course he would be here. But suddenly I felt self-conscious—as if he were hiding somewhere watching me, playing a practical joke. But I didn't imagine Evan was that big on practical jokes. Which was lucky, because nor was I.

I stood at the Hudson newsstand, and out of habit I looked at the *Post*'s front page: OSAMA: NEW EVIL PLOT. But tonight I didn't feel like picking it up. Then the newsstand shut up for the night, and I told myself I should now leave and make my way home. But then perhaps he had been delayed. It would be a disaster if he got all the way there and I'd left too quickly.

I went to an Internet station in a line of phone booths and remotely logged onto my e-mail on the off-chance that he may have tried to contact me, but there were no new messages from him. So I walked the length of the Arrivals hall again, just in case. By now it was close to 11 P.M. and my arms were getting tired from carrying my bags.

Finally I took out my phone again and texted him.

"Hope I didn't miss you, leaving now, sorry." Then I walked out to the taxi line with a sinking feeling. Evan was never far from his phone.

On the journey back to Manhattan, I stared out blankly at the passing ends of streets lined with the familiar suburban houses of Queens. Of course, I was happy doing this journey alone—I'd done it a million times before. So what if I had been stood up at the airport by some banker I hardly knew? Fuck him, he didn't deserve another thought. But had I been stood up? I couldn't quite believe it.

My mind went back to our last phone and e-mail exchanges before I had left for the UK four days ago.

"So are you going to give me your flight details or not?" Evan had demanded.

"Feel free to call and cancel if you need to," I'd replied one more time before handing them over.

"STOP. You are becoming a NY woman. Please give me an inch of trust. Be happy, I can't wait to see your smiling face as you walk out of the arrivals gate," had been his reply.

That was Tuesday. I'd left for the UK the following day, calling him on the way to the airport to leave a message saying I was looking forward to seeing him Sunday. I hadn't called while I was away, as I'd reckoned it was more romantic and less needy to leave our arrangement as it stood.

The taxi climbed the LIE flyover towards the Queenstown Tunnel, and I instinctively watched as the Manhattan skyline sprung up ahead. Tonight was unusually clear for late summer, and the familiar panorama seemed to sparkle more than ever. The great wall of Gotham was welcoming me back home. My spirits lifted for a second. But it just didn't make sense.

This time I had not fucked up. Despite Evan's enthusiasm, I had remained cool. I had been independent, not too in his face, interesting, interested, a little bit of a challenge. Everything my column and New York life had taught me to be. *So where the fuck was he?*

I went straight to bed when I got back home to the Meatpacking District, but I barely slept. I worried there may have been an accident. But despite being used to covering all manner of tragedies at the *Post,* I knew there rarely were accidents in these cases.

The following day, I booked the late Jitney bus back to Sag Harbor just on the futile off-chance we could still meet for lunch. But the longer my phone stayed silent, the more my disappointment and anger merged into insane curiosity. He must have got my messages at least.

I considered calling his office, but decided against it in case I was humiliatingly blown off by his secretary. I decided to call his Tribeca apartment early that evening when I might catch him at home.

At 7:30 P.M. exactly, I sat on my bed and with a shaking hand I dialed his number. He picked up the phone on the second ring. *Huh? He picked up?*

"Oh, so you're not dead then," I said.

"No." He sounded flustered.

"So what the fuck happened to meeting me at the airport?"

The was a pause. Whatever, this was going to be good.

"Sweetie, why the hell would I make the trek all the way to pick you up from JFK when I didn't hear from you for four days?"

My jaw dropped.

"*What*? You're fucking joking, right?"

"No, I'm not. I won't be taken for granted. Sorry, I'm in the middle of something right now," he said. The phone clicked dead.

I sat on my bed in a daze. "Sweetie" rang in my ears. No way. How could this be? Of all the times I had screwed up with guys for calling them too many times or too soon, I had now been blown off for not calling someone *enough*?

I stayed sitting still for a whole minute, shaking my head, waiting for him to come to his senses and call back. He didn't. Then I walked to the window and looked down on 14th Street.

A group of Mexican workers was painting a new sign across the street in a boutique which had taken the space of the little Belgian breakfast place, Petite Abeille, that had been Pom's favorite. A scrawny model in a miniskirt and Ugg boots lugged her look-book towards trendy Milk Studios on the end of the block. Outside a chic glass office that had been built on the roof opposite our loft, a bloke came out to smoke a cigarette. The guys of Ladder Co. 12 pulled up their fire truck outside Western Beef for a grocery run. The truck had "We will never forget," a memorial to September 11, emblazoned on the side.

I'd lived so much in this never-stopping, ever-evolving metropolis. And it felt like I had got absolutely nowhere at all.

No pride, and a fall

Pride is not a virtue—but peacemaking and forgiveness are, I told myself as I sat at my laptop in a quandary. The late August sunshine was casting peachy evening light across our chaotic office-kitchen in Sag Harbor. It was now a month since the airport debacle with Evan and barely two weeks until Labor Day, when our Diary packed up and went back to the city. Surely, I told myself, it would be a shame to leave Long Island with animosity towards anyone.

After the grim phone call with Evan, I had curtly e-mailed to tell him that he had seriously hurt my feelings, adding—in a rather pleasing creative flurry—that "bad manners and cowardice were a winning combination." He had replied with silence.

Since, Dan and I had been working around the clock, and the *Post* had been selling like hotcakes in local stores as Hamptonites salivated over the scandals of the season in our Diary and Page Six. But I knew my summer would always be blighted if I didn't make peace with Evan—total humiliation at JFK or not.

So finally I opened a blank e-mail and took a deep breath.

"Hey, hope you're well. It's the end of the summer. If I overreacted about the airport, I'm sorry. Hope there are no bad feelings," I wrote. Then I quickly pressed SEND before Dan could stop me—and remind me that pride had its virtues, too. When I confessed to him, he lit a cigarette, exhaled slowly, and shook his head in despair.

It took two hours for Evan to respond—in a far more pleasing way.

"No bad feelings," came his e-mail. He suggested dinner to make up for any "misunderstanding."

My heart leapt as I read it. So he did want to see me again! And maybe it *had* all been a misunderstanding—even though I still wasn't entirely sure how.

"See! See! All it takes is having the humility to let bygones be by-gones," I shouted cheerfully to Dan, who by now was quietly reading the *East Hampton Star* and chomping on a pastrami-laden hero. "Why be enemies with anyone?"

"I'm just not sure if this guy is worth being friends with," he said, offering me a carton of coleslaw. "The fact is he still did a shitty thing to you and he hasn't actually called to say sorry, yet."

Okay, so Evan didn't actually call, but he sent a fresh barrage of texts suggesting Thursday for us to meet. He'd fly down from Manhattan and take me for a sunset sail—with wine, followed by dinner. Who needed sorry?

On the delicate subject of the airport, he simply repeated that he hated to be taken for granted. His explanation was that if he liked someone, he wanted to hear from them and did not consider "Sorry I'm busy" to be the three sexiest words in the English language.

"What are the three sexiest words in the English language then?" I fired back.

"Bridget, Dinner, Thursday," came his reply.

So the following Thursday I found myself nervously waiting for Evan again—this time at the ferry terminal on Shelter Island. I was dressed in my same airport outfit—plus a bikini in preparation for a bit of swimming during the sunset sail. After all, it seemed a pity not to take him up on such an exciting offer now.

It took ten minutes for his SUV to growl up next to me. I leaped up, my heart in my mouth, pulled open the passenger door, and faux-nonchalantly hopped into a leather-clad seat. We looked at each other cautiously. In the same pressed-shirt, surf-shorts, deep-tan combo, he was as attractive as ever. Then he took my hand and gently kissed my cheek.

"Hello, stranger," he said.

"Hey there," I replied, my face breaking into a massive grin. Thank God I had swallowed my pride.

Back at the headland house once more, he poured us wine on his deck, and I sensed he didn't want to bring up the airport again. Which was fine. I was more interested in our sunset sail.

"Are we going out in the boat? I've worn my bikini especially," I ventured.

"There's no time," he replied. "I'll take you to dinner instead."

"Fine, fine, absolutely no prob," I replied, hiding my disappointment.

Instead of heading off into the sunset, we headed to the Vine Street Café, a tiny restaurant in the middle of the island that was crammed with elderly, wealthy couples. It was known, Evan said, for its excellent chef. We sat down. He smiled at me sweetly.

"I'm really glad you e-mailed. I have been thinking about you a lot."

Now I couldn't contain myself. "But you do feel a bit bad, right? For standing me up at JKF. You haven't actually apologized."

His brown eyes bored into mine.

"I won't apologize for not coming to pick you up because I was justified in not doing so. But I am sorry if I hurt your feelings. Now can we talk about something else?"

So in the spirit of letting bygones be bygones, I bit my tongue and told him about the Diary's latest escapades instead. I described how the previous evening I had noticed police standing outside the Stephen TalkHouse in Amagansett, a popular club where reggae star Jimmy Cliff had been playing, and had gone to investigate.

"Turns out that when the band was on its way to the show, the saxophonist stabbed the backing singer with a knife in an argument over the tour bus TV remote control!"

"No way. You're kidding me!" said Evan, visibly cheering up.

"Not at all. The singer had to be rushed to Southampton Hospital to be patched up right before the gig. Then they all went on to perform as if nothing had happened!"

Evan began to giggle, and I did too. The tension between us evaporated. We were interrupted by the diners on the next table, two couples in their sixties.

"We just wanted to say how nice it is to see a young couple having such a wonderful evening. It reminded us of all those exciting dates you have when you're first falling in love," they said.

We looked at each other, taken aback. If only they knew the half of it. And we hardly qualified as young. Evan reached his golden-brown arm over the table and put his hand over mine.

"I know the summer's nearly over, but now we're reconciled, I hope you're not thinking of moving back to England anytime soon," he said.

I smiled demurely and thought: "You might be a bit unpredictable . . . but, hey, leaving you for England full of boring married couples all smug with their toddlers? No Way."

Back at the cottage again, we lay on the sofa on his deck, and I tried to work out if I could hear the water lapping in the bay.

"You can in the winter," said Evan. "Sometimes I come down here for a week alone, just to listen to the wind and the waves and read books and chill out."

Hmmm, I was back to my fantasy about snuggling under cashmere blankets. After all, Evan didn't have to leave *his* house after Labor Day . . . Suddenly I noticed the time on his silver Tag Heuer watch. It was almost 1 A.M.

"Shit, shit, I can't miss the ferry," I said. Even if I had trashed my pride, I was going to keep my dignity.

Evan sprang up and we hauled ourselves out to his SUV. While he drove he used his Blackberry to call for a taxi to collect me when the ferry reached the mainland. But when we got to the dock, a ferry had just left. The lights of the next one were still several minutes away. Evan pulled the car over to the side of the road. Then he leaned over and took my face in his hands. As the lights of the oncoming ferry got nearer, I slid across the walnut gear console and snaked my hands under his shirt to feel the strong muscles down the side of his shoulder blades. He ran his palm across the delicate material of my bikini under my tank top. The ferry docked, two cars behind us rumbled over its gangplank.

"Don't get the ferry. Stay with me tonight," he whispered into my hair. "I want you there in my arms tomorrow when I wake up."

"Oh, all right. If you absolutely insist," I replied.

I awoke next day to watery sunlight bouncing off the bay and through the windows of Evan's large, luxurious bedroom. He was lying next to me, on the telephone, getting the lowdown on the financial markets. Not a life I had ever before pictured for myself, but, hey, why complain if the guy had a high-powered job? His bed was the most comfortable I had ever slept in—and he had spent half the night kissing me as I stretched out on his silky Pratesi sheets.

Then my own phone rang—it was Dan. He sounded tense. An elderly couple had been killed crossing the road after leaving a restaurant in East Hampton the previous night. It was my day off, but I immediately told him I would come back. If any other news broke, he and Thomas would need someone at the house.

After checking his e-mails, Evan offered to give me a lift to Sag Harbor's marina in his speedboat—and as we burned across the bay, I gleefully lived out my hair-blowing, bikini fantasy (except it wasn't Prada). Evan waved me off, promising to call later. I leaped onto the jetty feeling like Grace Kelly arriving in Monte Carlo.

As soon as Evan got back to Shelter Island, he began texting and e-mailing. He could still smell my hair. Next time he would light candles, smear oil over my gorgeous body. He would be thinking about me all weekend. When could we meet again?

I excitedly replied with flirtatious flourishes—until abruptly the messages stopped. I assumed he was probably busy with houseguests for the weekend, and got on with our busy Diary schedule. Two days later I was still jumping every time my phone rang or beeped—and every time it wasn't him. I grew increasingly anxious and called. I was in no hurry for any more misunderstandings—especially as he'd said he detested busyness as an excuse not to be in touch with someone. But maybe he was extra busy, because he didn't pick up.

Two days after that, there was still silence. Frantic, I rang again, begging him to call, just to let me know everything was okay. Still silence. Our final Hamptons events came and went. I watched my phone constantly, paced the garden, and swore.

On our last night in the Hamptons, Dan and I sat on the porch of our cottage smoking cigarettes, our office packed up, our suitcases by the door. In the morning we would be heading back to the city. The most extraordinary summer of my life was now over.

"So he never called you, huh?" said Dan kindly as we watched another full moon rise over our quiet street lined with quaint, white-painted New England houses, most now packed up for the winter.

"Nope. Looks like I got myself blown off twice by the bloody same guy." I shook my head ruefully, feeling sick to my stomach and stumped again by New York dating life.

"If someone treats you badly, you're better off without them," Dan said, grinding his cigarette butt into our flowerpot ashtray.

"Guess you're right." So why was something so obvious always easier said than done?

Strangely, two weeks later, a text appeared from Evan out of the blue. He wrote that he had just arrived in London and would call me in the morning—as if nothing odd had happened at all. But this time I didn't wait for the phone to ring. It never did.

Thirty-four isn't too old, right?

Sometimes you just want to lie down, give up, and ask: Where the fuck did I go wrong?

Like when your old single roommate who used to get so drunk she made you feel like a teetotaler gives you a lecture on the special joys of motherhood (while you *still* can't make it to the third date). Or like when you sit in a bar listening to your ex gushing about his new love, then find yourself pretending you have a boyfriend—when you don't. Like when you find out that the only guy you've wanted to date in a year not only stood you up at the airport and then unceremoniously blew you off *again* after you went crawling back to him—also happened to use all his same lines on another girl.

It was fall once more. Paris Hilton and P. Diddy had moved their partying to Miami. I was back in New York, having "one of those days" again—in fact, one of those seasons.

My sunny summer optimism had evaporated into black angst about the future. I was back to square one—no boyfriend, just an encyclopedia of failed dates behind me and barely a year now before I had to think about freezing my eggs. And now I couldn't even blame my bad luck on my dating column.

Oh, come on, thirty-four isn't too old at all, I said to myself. In the summer you didn't even want a boyfriend. So what if you got messed around by a guy? You won't be the first—or the last.

But then, what was that saying about men? They were like rush-hour versus off-peak subway cars. In your twenties they came every minute, in your thirties you could be waiting for one all night. So you were really fucked if you kept getting on the wrong one.

350

My glumness had really set in after I had been to a cocktail party one evening and found myself chatting about dating to an old acquaintance I ran into there. I had just started to relay my Evan debacle to her—not that I was obsessed or anything—when she'd stopped me midsentence.

"Wait, I know that guy, *I know him!* My friend Angela dated him in the spring. She thought they were getting serious, then one day he got pissed with her and she never heard from him again."

"No! Are you sure?"

"His name was Evan, definitely."

Of course, I had decided never to give Evan another passing thought. But when she suggested a drink with Angela so we could compare notes, I agreed like a shot.

Angela was a pretty, witty, dark-haired art dealer. We met at Bar 6 for a bottle of pinot noir. We wasted barely five minutes on small talk before we got down to business—and we didn't pause for breath.

"He seemed so down-to-earth, like he really detested the whole dating game," said Angela. "I wasn't even that taken with him at first. I mean, it wasn't like he was even that good-looking, he was a bit gawky and shy. But we went for a drink, and afterwards he sent me such a sweet text saying 'I'm probably breaking every rule in the book, but I don't want to play cool. I enjoyed your company, I'd love to see you again.'"

I nearly dropped my wine glass.

"Hey, I got that too. The first time we had dinner. Was it waiting for you on your e-mail when you got home?"

"I got it on my Blackberry in the cab *on the way* home."

I put my forehead on the bar. No.

"On my first date, he invited me over for his home cooking," I said.

"We flew to Shelter Island in the sea plane with all the deliveries a couple of times. He baked this amazing bread," she replied.

"He baked you bread? He baked *me* bread!"

"Yup, olive bread."

"Shut up! Don't tell me you snogged on the dock too?"

"Snogged? Is that making out? We did that. It was this gorgeous moonlit evening, and we sat for hours kissing, dangling our feet in the water."

Oh my God. Had Evan even picked the date for our dinner to coincide with the full moon? No, now I was being paranoid.

"He had a nice boat tied up down there too," said Angela. "Did you ever go out on the speedboat?"

"Yes, he gave me a lift back to the mainland in it, promised to call and that was the last time I saw him."

Angela said that even though Evan had told her he didn't want to play things cool, she had been reserved about getting into a relationship. But gradually she had come around after he texted and e-mailed her every day to say how happy he was to have met her.

"He sent me messages about how I was the last name floating across his mind when he went to sleep at night."

"You're joking!" I said again. "I can't believe it. Actually, your texts were a bit more poetic than mine. Same gist though. How about the limo?"

"Now the limo was good," said Angela. "He had a driver, and often sent him to pick me up from work—but mainly when he couldn't be bothered to leave his apartment."

"And what about the shagging?" It wasn't like I wasn't going to ask.

She smirked. "Yeah, that was pretty good. He was really into the candles. He had them all over his bedroom in Tribeca."

I groaned. "Massage oil?"

"He got that out at the beginning . . . and sometime he sent texts in the day talking about what he was going to do too."

"Oh God, I don't think I want to know any more." I had my head back on the bar.

"So how did it end?" I asked eventually.

Angela looked angry for a moment.

"There was a week when I had made some of my own arrangements, and he told me he was too tired to join me because he'd had a tough time in the office. All the time he kept expecting me to rush over and be there for him, but when I told him I couldn't break the arrangement with my friends, he got mad. He told me he wouldn't be taken for granted and I had no understanding of his needs. That was it, he never returned my calls after that."

"Well, cheers, darling," I said, raising my glass to Angela's. "Guess we both got dropped by the same guy."

We clinked.

"You've gotta laugh, I guess," said Angela. "But I don't mind admitting I was upset about it for months. Here was a guy who seemed to be so down-to-earth and an amazing catch. And just when it seemed like we were getting serious, puff! The whole thing blew up in my face. Guess that's New York for you."

That night I lay in bed cursing myself. There I had been smugly thinking I was so different—the know-it-all dating columnist, the savvy, low-key British chick. And I'd fallen for every line Evan had come out with, too.

And I had to hand it to him. He had a winning formula. All the money and sophistication to make a girl's knees go weak—while he pretended to be just a regular, shy guy, wearing his fragile heart on his sleeve. As long as it suited him, that was.

And that was the irony about New York. Ruthless dating rules made the city's singles so guarded—and yet underneath everyone was desperate to meet someone who was prepared to say they didn't want to play things cool.

But the problem was that the city would always breed wealthy egomaniacs who thought nothing of hurting other people's feelings, because there would always be a conveyer belt of new women who couldn't resist their charms. In Evan's eyes, he probably hadn't even done anything wrong. He'd taken a girl out a couple of times, fired off some flirtatious texts, and then got distracted by something—or someone—else. In this city, canning a date by not calling was as acceptable as canning them the moment a better option appeared.

No wonder it was so hard to find love in New York.

But then some people had managed it. Two weeks after my drink with Angela, my old roommate Alice gave birth to a 5-pound, 6-ounce baby girl. In typical chaotic fashion, her waters had broken in a pizza restaurant in Roxbury, a little village in the middle of nowhere upstate, just as she and Chris were trying to have one last romantic weekend a deux. Alice, who had neglected to check whether there were maternity facilities nearby, had to be rushed ninety miles across the Catskill Mountains in an ambulance.

When they got back to the city three days later with new baby Scarlet, I dutifully went to Alice's apartment for a visitation. I cradled the tiny, pink-faced infant while she stared blindly up at me with milky blue eyes. I ran my finger over her mini-toenails in amazement at how perfect they were. She was so warm and vulnerable, I wanted to hold her forever. I reminded myself that the way my luck was going, I might have to accept that I might never be a mother.

"I tell you, Bridge, having a baby, it's the scariest thing. Suddenly there's this other being here that is totally and utterly dependent on you," said Alice. "I mean, I don't even have a clue. When my waters broke, I thought I'd peed myself."

We began to giggle, and I felt less inadequate at the thought of hopeless Alice grappling with motherhood.

"But it's weird," she said, dreamily stroking Scarlet's silky wisps of blond hair as she now snoozed in my arms. "When you have a baby, suddenly all your maternal instincts kick in and you realize why you've been put on this earth."

Oh, great, there went another one.

"Okay, Al, enough of the Earth Mother act," I snapped, handing Scarlet back.

I walked home miserable. It seemed like only yesterday that Alice had woken me up when she showed up on our loft doorstep clinging to a pizza delivery guy. She'd got so drunk on a blind date on Thompson Street that she'd lost her wallet. Her date had run away when her her back was turned, and the pizza guy was the only person who was prepared to take pity on her and show her the way home. And now she was lecturing me about maternity. Where the fuck was my happily ever after?

A text message two weeks later from my old friend Fi back in the UK did nothing to improve my mood.

"Call me. I've got some news," it said.

Which meant only one thing. I dialed her number.

"Bridge, you may not like this very much . . . I got engaged, and I'm pregnant!"

"Congratulations, Fi. But tell me, why does everyone think I would not be happy for other people's bloody engagements and pregnancies?" I huffed.

Well, that was probably why.

A few bleak weeks later, shortly before I was due to fly back for Kathryn's big December wedding in the UK, Jack and I met for a catch-up drink in the Hog Pit.

Since I'd returned to the *New York Post* office from the Hamptons, it was as if we had never dated. My summer away had obliterated any vibes that had still lingered between us. Out of habit, I still watched to see if he went into his office to talk intimately on the phone, seemed overly interested in his e-mail inbox, or rushed out of the office early. But Michelle, Jeane, and Paula told me that Jack was as single and overworked as ever. At least someone hadn't changed.

He was waiting for me in the Hog Pit with the page proofs from the day's paper and a whiskey. Just like my meeting with Angus on Primrose Hill, it too was almost a carbon copy of old times. But this time I didn't feel like being philosophical about it.

I ordered a vodka and tonic and told him all about baby Scarlet—and that Fi was also now engaged and pregnant.

"*Fi?* Christ, it seems like two days ago she was dancing on tables in Felix in the tightest jeans known to man. It amazes me that that skinny body of hers is even capable of containing a child."

"Jack, she never danced on the tables, just around them, and you always refused to come there," I tutted, smiling for the first time in ages. "But, yes, now she's going to be a wife and mother too. Everyone has moved on, you know."

"Well, if you ask me, blissful family-making isn't all it's cracked up to be," said Jack. "My friends who have kids just spend the whole time complaining that they've become boring losers who never go out."

I wanted to hug him.

"And how about you, any romancing in your life?" I said, confident I knew what the answer would be.

"Well." He smiled into his drink. "Actually, I have been dating a girl for quite a few months now."

What? My stomach liquidized. A horrified grimace attacked my mouth.

"I'm keeping it totally quiet in the office this time, though," said Jack, oblivious to my horror. "Not after the fiasco you and I went through."

Fiasco? Oh, fucking cheers. I hid behind my glass.

"We met at a poker tournament. We spent every weekend together this summer, and we didn't argue at all. So, actually, it's going pretty well."

If I inhaled vodka and tonic really quickly, could I drown myself?

"In fact, I'm meeting her shortly. We're going to Voyage for dinner."

Voyage? Our restaurant? No, it would be easier to go to the bathroom with the glass and slash my wrists.

Jack turned to me, smiling kindly.

"So how about you, baby? Word in the office is that you got it together with some hotshot in the Hamptons over the summer and you're actually happy at last."

"Yup, I am, actually."

What? Did I just say that? I was back behind my glass again.

"So? Who is he?" Jack had adopted an annoying conspiratorial tone. And he seemed genuinely pleased for me, which was even more annoying.

"Well, I met him at a party on Shelter Island, and one thing led to another, I guess."

"That's great. So what does he do?"

"Oh, you know, something on Wall Street."

"And what's his name?"

"Er, Evan. You won't know him."

"So, come on, is it as serious as everyone's making out?"

"Um, I'm not really sure, actually. But it's good. I mean I am happy and everything."

No, in fact I was beyond tragic. And this was beyond any sad, pathetic, tragic thing I had ever done before.

I was also bright red. Jack looked confused for a second but let it go.

"Well, Bridge, I really am pleased for you."

"Me too, and for you," I squeaked.

We had one more drink and talked about other things before Jack announced he had to get to his date. He paid the check and we walked outside and lingered on the sidewalk.

"So are you seeing Evan tonight?"

"Um, yes." I felt myself going red again. "Just a quiet dinner in, um, Tribeca."

Then I looked into Jack's steady blue eyes and remembered that he was the one person to whom I had vowed I would never lie.

"Jack, actually, I'm not going to dinner with Evan."

He looked confused again.

"In fact, I'm not actually even dating him. Sorry, I just made all that up."

Now he looked *really* confused.

"I mean, I did date him, and I did meet him at a party in Shelter Island and everything . . . And he does do something on Wall Street, a hedge fund I think . . . But when I flew back from England in August, he stood me up at the airport. And then I met him again and he blew me off a second time. So that was the end of that, really."

Jack looked uncomfortably at the sidewalk. "I'm sorry," he said.

Sorry for what? Sorry I'd been screwed around *twice*? Sorry that I didn't have a boyfriend, or sorry that I was simply the saddest woman on the planet?

But then what had I expected? For Jack to vow revenge via pistols at dawn with Evan?

"Well, anyway, guess you'd better get to Voyage," I said.

"Er, will you be alright?" he replied.

"Yup, of course." I turned and skipped away from him across the cobbles of Ninth Avenue, now crammed with taxis and crowds heading out to dinner.

"Plenty more fish in the sea," I said out loud to myself. I just didn't believe it anymore.

The girl in the red dress

I stood in the women's changing room in Henri Bendel on Fifth Avenue, wearing a $300 cherry-red satin Miguelina dress. It had a halter that gave me a bit of cleavage and a floaty A-line skirt that came to the knee. Did it look sexy yet subtle, even Marilyn Monroesque, for a winter wedding? Or like the shiny Dorothy Perkins number the office desperado would wear to her work Christmas party?

When it came to these things, I would never know. But what did I care? I couldn't even face the idea of Kathryn's wedding—yet another evening of standing around trying to be philosophical about love, counting the rapidly declining number of single people left before opting for obliteration by cheap white wine. Not that the wine would be cheap at this wedding. Kathryn had called the day before to give me an update on her fairy-tale plans.

"So the whole church is going to be candlelit, with trails of ivy strewn from the ceiling and down the aisles. Then the reception is going to be in this incredible fourteenth-century tithe barn—it's the longest one in Europe. Pretty lucky, really, that it's in our village, right? And afterwards we're going to get a 1940s tractor from the church to the barn, and there'll be flares all along the lanes. . . . "

Lovely. What the hell was a tithe barn, anyway?

I went out onto the Bendel floor, which was heaving with Christmas shoppers, to ask a store assistant for a second opinion on the dress—not that they ever told the truth if a sale was in the offing. I found a full-length mirror in the underwear section, and I stood in front of it frowning, noticing the creases on my forehead. Hmm, perhaps I should just spend the $300 on Botox instead. Low-cut dress or a smooth forehead, which was the better investment?

"Hey, hey. It is you! I thought it was. The girl in the red dress!"

I spun round.

"Deklin? *Deklin?*"

He came towards me though the racks of frilly bras. He had the same dark eyes and fluttery, thick lashes, but he was thinner than before, more grown-up–looking. I hadn't seen him since the night four years ago in the Great Lakes. With his girlfriend.

"Shit, you bastard. What the hell are you doing skulking around Henri Bendel's lingerie section. Have you turned gay?"

He laughed, flashing that same gap between his white front teeth. "No, I'm Christmas shopping for my sisters-in-law. They give me lists."

We hugged. The Great Lakes was a lifetime ago. It felt pointless to be cross with him now.

"So make yourself useful. What do you think?" I twirled for him.

"Well, I kinda liked the last red dress you had on, but this one is pretty hot too. In my opinion, you should never not wear a red dress."

"What am I to you? A walking Chris de Burgh song?"

"No, you're the exciting mystery girl at the party who looks like she loves life so much every guy wants to talk to her."

I rolled my eyes.

"Leave it out with the corny lines, Dek. I'm not falling for them twice. And anyway those days are long gone. This is for my best friend's posh wedding in England, and I will not be there loving life."

"Why ever not? Sounds ideal."

"You try to love life when you're at a wedding as a single woman who's pushing thirty-four."

"What, are you kidding me? I cannot imagine anything more fun. Try being a guy with an unengaged girlfriend at a wedding at *any* age over twenty-five."

"Ah, Melissa. How is she? No ring on the finger yet?"

"We broke up last year." Oops.

"I'm sorry."

"No, actually, it was the right decision. She was so great, the sweetest girl. She would have made the best wife, mother. But I always felt there was something missing, and the pressure to propose to her just got too much. Why the hell does everyone have to get married either just before or just after they hit thirty?"

"Because time is running out!" I blurted out dramatically, and it was his turn to roll his eyes.

"Screw that. I'm not getting married with doubts only to end up divorced after a couple of years. I don't mind waiting until I'm sixty for the right girl to come along. So how about you, are you still the best catch in New York?"

"Well, I've certainly been caught and put back in the pond a few times since I saw you last."

"Okay, take that dress, even if it costs one thousand dollars. We're going for a catch-up drink."

Fifth Avenue was teeming with Christmas shoppers, and the traffic was at a honking standstill as people rushed in and out of the road, battling each other for yellow taxis. Tourists were all puffing along, laden with bags, but we weaved through them expertly, our breath whipping on the freezing air.

The stores' lavish window displays glittered, and the trees on the sidewalk dripped with Christmas lights. The scene was hectic, hellish, and strangely invigorating. It was vintage preholiday New York.

We ran up the steps of the Plaza Hotel on 59th Street where across the street more tourists were lining up to take horse carriages through the wintry wonderland of Central Park. We sped through the Plaza's bustling, marbled lobby to its famous wood-paneled bar, the Oak Room. There we snagged the last two seats at the bar and for good measure ordered two Manhattans.

Suddenly my mood lifted—just a little. All around us were people from all over the world who'd flocked to New York just for a taste of it. And I'd had nearly five whole years of this magical city.

When I'd met him at the party in Park Slope, Deklin had been a struggling illustrator. Now he had a top job in the art department at the *New York Times*. And I was a seasoned news reporter for the *New*

York Post—okay, so not *that* seasoned, but at least I could wield a notepad.

"Here's to fulfilled dreams," I said.

"And old friends," Deklin replied, clinking my glass.

"Old friend? You're no friend of mine. You very callously taught me my first lesson about dating in New York."

"Which was?"

"Nothing, when it comes to men—or women for that matter—is ever as it seems." Damn, why hadn't I remembered that when dating Evan?

"Look, I'm sorry about that night with Melissa. I felt as awkward as you, and Melissa and I had taken a kind of break the night of the party. But then I hardly put you off New York men."

"And how would you know?"

"Because I bought that filthy, right-wing rag you work for every Sunday just to keep up with your adventures," he giggled. "Remember that guy who would never kiss you, even though you were *sooo* angling for it, then dumped you with the e-mail that said 'best and talk with you soon'?"

"Thanks for reminding me of that."

"Then there was that crazy Dutch guy you tried have sex with, and he ordered you to take his pants off. What a jerk."

"Now *he* was a jerk."

"It kept us entertained, though." Deklin was chuckling again. "But seriously, Bridge, if you think about it, it wasn't just the dates. What about all those other New York stories you covered? I mean, you've got to love the *Post*. That guy in the restaurant who had his head cut off, remember him? There was the one you did in Brooklyn about a seventeen-year-old who got told she might never have kids, so she stole a baby from a maternity ward and went on some crazy three-day odyssey with it. And didn't you go to Nantucket to chase that Tyco creep, Dennis Koslowski, on his $30 million yacht? And there was that old man who had a hot dog on Christmas Day because his wife got run over. Actually, that one was really sad. My mom cried when she read that."

"Fuck, you have a good memory," I said. I thought back to Mr. Russo myself, sitting on his sofa with the singing reindeer. After that story I had vowed never to complain about life again. A vow I had definitely forgotten.

"Don't you feel lucky, Bridge? You got to have your adventures. Everyone else just reads about them."

I'd never looked at it quite like that before. Not that my adventures had been that exciting. But if there was one thing I should have learned from working as a reporter, it was that in one instant your life could be changed forever.

"Guess sometimes I don't take enough time to appreciate stuff," I said.

"Who does? You have a dream, you promise yourself that if you fulfill it, you'll never ask for anything again. Then when you do, you just take it for granted and start worrying about the next thing. Every so often you should stop and say, Hey, life today, now, actually isn't so bad."

"Deklin, have you started doing some weirdie new-age yoga or something? What's with the life coaching?" I said.

He threw his cocktail napkin at me.

"I mean it. Bridget, you were the girl in the red dress at that party who came to Brooklyn on her own in a hooker's outfit because she was willing to give anything a go. Don't ever change."

"Isn't that the night I also happened to jump into bed with you behind my boyfriend's back?" I said.

"Well, I never said you were perfect," he said.

We spent another hour in the bar and this time parted promising it would be sooner than four years until we hung out again.

My flight back to the UK was on a Wednesday, three days before Kathryn's mega wedding. The evening before I left, Paula summoned me to her place on Sullivan Street in SoHo for a last-minute party makeover. Gone were the days of her quiet apartment in Cobble Hill. She was back in the city, writing a book, presenting a TV segment for hot gossip show "The Insider," and now—as she had long dreamed—she owned a Dachsund called Karl, who she professed to be her only love.

"So I got this dress," I said as I pulled the red satin Miguelina out of its stripy Henri Bendel bag, still a little worried about it. "And I've got my green Nichole Farhi coat to go over the top."

"God, Bridge no, no!" she said, inspecting my purchase. "This dress—it's to die for, fabulous—but not that old coat you've been wearing since you moved here. I mean, green and red? What do you want to look like? The wedding Christmas tree?"

She went to her wardrobe and pulled out a velvet black Gucci coat with luscious silk lining, a pair of black-and-white Sarah Jessica Parker Christian Lacroix heels, and a brown fur stole.

"This is coyote, totally hot," she said. "Now listen to me. Get your hair blow out straight, and get those hideous, messy eyebrows taken care of for a change. Wear minimal silver jewelry and bare legs. Black stockings will kill that dress. Lose the coat at the earliest opportunity, but keep, I repeat *keep* the fur on all night. You're gonna look great."

I picked up my new goodies, thanked her, and hugged her at the door of her apartment. Then I turned back.

"Paulita, do you think I need Botox?" I said.

She rolled her eyes.

"Bridge, just make sure you wear invisible-line panties and don't take off the coyote, okay?"

The following day it began to snow heavily, promising a White Christmas in New York. I took my bags to work so I could rush straight to the airport to catch the Virgin Atlantic red-eye to London. I spent the day writing about the 2004 Christmas "must haves" for kids. At least I didn't have to schlep around fifty shopping centers in a blizzard looking for a VideoNow color, portable video player or a dumb Tamagochi electronic pet. I thought kids had killed those off years ago. Yes, there was one good thing about a family Christmas for five which never changed—it was low-maintenance.

I headed out of the office shortly after 8 P.M. and was standing waiting for an elevator when Jack suddenly swung out of the office door, head down, coat on, his leather satchel over one shoulder. He only looked up and noticed me as we both stepped into the elevator. The doors closed and we found ourselves alone, standing on either side of the car.

Once upon a time, I'd have killed for a moment like this, but after my humiliating Evan confession, I'd done a good job of avoiding Jack in the office and even now I really would have preferred not to face him at all. I tried to pretend to be busy by rummaging in my bag to check I had my passport.

"So, flying home tonight?" he said eventually.

"Yeah, it's my friend Kathryn's wedding on Saturday."

"In London?"

"No, in the country. In a tithe barn."

"Sounds like fun."

I wanted to ask him what a tithe barn was. He would know. Instead we both studied our feet.

The elevator sped to the ground floor, pinged, and the doors opened. He waited for me to step out.

"Well, happy holidays then," he said cheerily.

"Yeah, Merry Christmas," I replied, heaving my bag over my shoulder and striding on ahead of him. I walked past the tree in the lobby that was surrounded by a massive pile of toys that News Corp collected for underprivileged kids, then pushed through the revolving doors. Outside, the concourse was already covered in white. Up ahead the sidewalk was crammed with yet more Christmas shoppers battling through the chilly air. "Jingle Bells" echoed down the street from a charity sound system. Not that tune again.

I did up the top button of my coat and began to walk towards the subway on 47th Street.

"Bridge," he called. I stopped and turned.

He was standing by the pillar he used to smoke next to, his hands in his overcoat. The pillar was wrapped in a red ribbon for Christmas.

I walked back to him.

"What's up?"

He had a strange, pained look on his face.

"Bridge, I know that since we broke up I've been a bit distant towards you." He looked at his feet. "I just want you to know that that's because sometimes I still find it very hard to see you and be around you."

He raised his eyes to mine.

"I still care a great deal for you, more than any woman I've ever met," he said.

I stared at him in surprise, a flush racing across my cheeks. His eyes did that twinkle and I smiled. We stood looking at each other and the clamor on Sixth Avenue fell away. Then I stepped towards him and lay my cheek on his shoulder. He put his arms around me and held me tightly against his overcoat. I smelled his smell one more time.

"And I you, Jack," I said softly. "By the way, what the fuck is a tithe barn?"

There are only two words to describe flying to London the week before Christmas: "utter" and "hell." At JFK, as I stood in the Virgin Atlantic check-in line for an hour and a half, I tried and failed not to think about the last time I was there, waiting for Evan. Eventually a beaming, red-suited attendant handed me my boarding card.

"Row 69, seat E!" she said jovially as if she'd just upgraded me to first-class—when in fact she'd given me the worst seat on the plane—at the back, near the toilets and the stench of airline food from the galley.

"Crowded flight?" I asked through gritted teeth.

"It sure is! But hopefully we won't be delayed."

At the gate—which was so overrun with people you wondered how they'd all fit onto one narrow tin tube—I pulled out the four Tylenol PM capsules I brought for the journey. The moment they announced we were boarding, I knocked them back with a bottle of Poland Spring. Alice had assured me that even though they were mild sleeping aids, if you took four in one go, they were pretty effective and took no more than ten minutes to kick in.

Once in my crappy row, I fastened my seat belt, sat very still, and tried not to scream bloody murder. To my left, two supersized teenage brothers were fighting over a supersized packet of potato chips. One, who was already bulging under my arm rest, kept whacking me with his elbow. To my right, a guy with a gray-flecked goatee was glancing weirdly at me. And to think I once got on planes with the pathetic hope that the seat next to me might contain my future husband.

In no mood for passenger chat, I took out my blanket and put it over my head like a criminal who doesn't want to get snapped on a perp walk. I shut my eyes and prayed for oblivion by Tylenol.

Instead, my thoughts went straight back to my encounter with Jack. Five years on I knew I loved him just as much as I always had. But then I supposed in real life it was possible to really love someone and for a relationship still not to work. We were just too different, his reserved nature and my natural mania had combined to bring out the worst in us. We couldn't make each other happy, but at least we knew we loved each other—and maybe we always would. And screw that jerk Evan. What had I wanted from him? To be shagging in cheesy candlelight for the rest of my life and pandering to his whims and bank account? Pah, no thanks, not even for his lovely house . . . or boat. Mmm, a sailing boat. I wished I was in one now, but not with him . . . with someone else, someone new. Someone I would meet in the future.

It was light again. I could tell from under my blanket. I felt like I'd been whacked with a sledgehammer and a skunk had hibernated in my mouth. Someone was nudging me again. Jesus, not that beardy weirdo still.

"Er, excuse me, would you like some breakfast?"

"No," I growled at him from under my shroud and tried to fall back asleep.

"Ma'am, can you pack up that blanket now, please? We're landing." It was a stewardess this time. I ignored her.

"Ma'am." She tugged on the blanket. I grabbed it back.

"Get off!"

"Ma'am, please, you can't land with a blanket on your head."

Was there no peace? Livid, I came out of my little world, red-faced and rubbing my eyes. My hair was like a bird's nest. Beardy weirdo was glancing at me *again*. I pulled a flight magazine from the seat in front of me and began flipping through it to look occupied. Then he touched me on the arm.

"I'm really sorry to bother you. I wanted to ask you last night. You're Bridget Harrison, right? That columnist from the *Post*?"

Oh. The magazine flopped in my lap. Shit, was that why he'd been staring at me?

"Erm, yes." I shoved my unruly hair behind my ears and tried to smile. One of my eyes was still clogged up with sleep.

"I thought it was you. I saw you on that dating show on TV."

And now I looked like a homeless person.

"You must watch some bad telly," I managed.

He laughed shyly.

"Look, I just wanted to tell you it's so strange that you're sitting next to me. I got divorced a couple of years ago, and I was really depressed. Then I read your column about going out to dinner with your parents after you broke up with that guy Aaron, and it was the first thing that made me laugh again. I'd so been there."

I felt myself go red. I wiped my sticky eye. I wished I hadn't just had a tug-of-war with the stewardess.

"Oh, well, that's sweet of you to say that. Um, I'm glad to have helped."

"No, really. You always had this great attitude. That no matter how many dating disasters you had, you just got on out there again. You said you always remembered that everything has a funny side and that someone else has always been there too. And it's true."

"Yeah?" Had anyone else broken up with two guys they should have married, been on so many dates they'd lost count, been stood up at an airport by a serial dater, and lied about having a boyfriend when they didn't . . . ? Well, possibly. Quite probably, actually.

"Then you wrote that column about going to Aaron's new apartment and how you know you've healed again when you can look into a past love's future and accept that it won't be yours."

Wow. This guy was another *Post* fanatic.

"I met this great woman eight months ago. She's divorced too. We went to the same coffee shop near where I live in New Haven in Connecticut. After I read your column in the *Post*, it made me realize I could now face the thought of my ex-wife living without me. And that was the day I met my new girlfriend!"

"Nice coincidence," I said.

"The great thing about life is that it's not just about falling in love, but knowing you can fall in love again."

God, he made it sound so poetic. But he had a point. I reminded myself that once I had feared I would never get over Angus, and then I had fallen in love with Jack. And even though things had exploded in my face with Evan, at least I had been excited about him too. The bastard.

The plane made its final descent, and we thudded down onto the Heathrow tarmac. I put my hand up to the seat in front of me to break the surge forward.

"So you back to see your parents for the holidays?" he said.

"Actually, I'm back for one of my best friend's weddings."

"Man, that sounds great. If you're a single woman, there's not much more fun than that, right?"

Huh? That's what Deklin had said too. And to think that single girls did nothing but moan about going to weddings. But suddenly I did feel a flicker of excitement. After all, life wasn't *too* bad. So what if I would soon be thirty-four? I hadn't settled. I wasn't stuck with the wrong person. I wasn't in some grim, stale marriage where I argued about children and never had sex. I hadn't started divorce proceedings like a couple of people I now knew. I had a clean slate—still everything ahead of me. A future that would bring new loves and new adventures. And the wedding was bound to be a riot.

The plane jolted to a halt, and the rows of passengers leaped up in a frenzy of bag retrieval, desperate to escape and get on with their lives. I took a swig of water, rubbed my face, and put my hair into a ponytail. Now I was wide awake too. I smiled at the goatee guy. I couldn't believe I'd called him a weirdo. Back to my first New York lesson about first impressions . . .

"It was really great to meet you. I'm so sorry about the blanket," I said.

"Just never give up getting out there and getting excited about things," he said. "But then, you're Bridget Harrison! I know you won't."

As I picked up my bag and slipped into Paula's Gucci coat, I suddenly knew that he was right. I wouldn't stop getting excited about life, why would I? Because who knew what would happen tomorrow?

We edged along the aisle of the plane, and as I walked through its exit door towards London Arrivals, I felt a whole new spring in my step.

Right now I was going to be the single girl in a sexy red dress (and a hot pair of Christian Lacroix heels), fresh from New York at my best friend's wedding.

And what could be more exciting than that?

ACKNOWLEDGMENTS

I am indebted to countless people who have made this book possible, including all the friends, colleagues, dates, and strangers who helped me to survive in New York. I would also like to say a huge thank-you to my agents, Elisabeth Weed at Kneerim & Williams and Danny Baror at Baror International, my brilliant and ever-patient editors, Marnie Cochran at Da Capo Press and Gail Haslam at Transworld Publishers—and to everyone else both at Da Capo and Transworld who have worked so hard on this book. I'd like to thank my unofficial readers Michelle Gotthelf and Sacha Bonsor for their lifesaving encouragement and advice, Tom Folsom for his inspiration, and Circe Hamilton and Emma Lovell for my photos. I am also indebted to the entire amazing staff of the *New York Post*, including Editor-in-Chief, Col Allan; my column editors, Brad Hamilton and Maureen Callahan; Anne Aquilina who along with Sandra Parsons at the *Times* made my transfer to New York possible; Xana Antunes, Jonathan Auerbach, Faye Penn, and Lauren Ramsby, who all made my column possible; Paula Froelich for all her support (and cast-offs), Jeane MacIntosh, Dan Kadison, Heather Gilmore, Bruce Furman—and most of all Jesse Angelo. I'd like to thank Olly Keane and Pom Lampson for looking after me when I first arrived in New York, and everyone who has had to listen to me talking about myself since, especially Rebecca and Josh Veselka, Fiona Henderson, Alice Sykes, Claire Curran, Gavin Morris, Sophie Davis, Alexis Bloom, Daniel Kershaw, Tilly Blyth, Brian Rea, Stefano Hatfield, Keir Ashton, James, and Bun. I am also indebted to Otto Bathurst for his unwavering generosity of spirit. Finally, I'd like to say thank-you to my parents, Gillian and John Harrison, for letting me go to New York for three months and stay five years—and for teaching me that the most important thing in life isn't success but happiness.